THE LIFE OF A PERFECTLY AVERAGE HOMOSEXUAL

Jack Shaw

PUBLISHED BY BICTON DOUGLAS

ISBN-13: 978-0-9933226-0-0
ISBN-10: 0993322603

For all the Eleanor Rigby's of the world.

Contents

PREFACE

1. I PITY THE FOOL

2. I AIN'T SMELLING OF NO FISH

3. MICHAEL, ROW YOUR BOAT ASHORE

4. THERE WERE SIGNS…

5. THE INCIDENT WITH THE SHAVING FOAM

6. PENPALS

7. THE TENDER TOUCH OF A TEEN

8. A NEW DAWN?

9. NOTHING LIKE A DAME!

10. MY FIRST, ISH

11. PICKING UP SPEED

12. CITY LIFE!

13. ONE LAST SHOT AT WOMEN

14. COMING OUT… SORT OF…

15. GYM AND TONIC

16. TEN OUT OF TEN

17. STICK IT!

18. QUITE AN UNPLEASANT STORY

19. A SMALL PRICK

20. A BOMB GOES OFF

21. IT'S A SIN!

22. A NEW HOUSE

23. ONE TAP FOR YES

24. HITTING A BRIACK WALL

25. GROUND FLOOR…

26. BLIND DATES

27. A WEE DRAM TO KEEP OUT THE COLD

28. WHEN A MAN'S GOTTA GO

29. BAD GAY! NAUGHTY GAY!

30. BE MORE GAY!

31. DARKNESS DESCENDS

32. JUST ANOTHER DAY

33. SOME THOUGHTS

PREFACE

Hello.

My name is Jack and I am a perfectly average homosexual.

Well. When I say average…

I am nowhere near as 'fabulous' as you may expect and probably not as annoying as you'd fear. To that extent I am exceedingly average. A very average man who has decided to write a book about his life.

Peculiar…

Now, given that I'm not even remotely famous (assuming you discount accidentally standing next to a weather presenter and being made to nod at a thunder cloud), it does seem like a rather unusual thing to do. After all, why would you want to read a book about a complete stranger? A stranger who, quite evidently, is less than perfect. Is it bare-naked narcissism? Am I just full of myself? Am I one of those exceedingly annoying people who think they have 'a book in them' and resolve to write it one year and then proceed to bore the wits out of their friends and family telling them about their writer's block? Did we cover narcissism?

In truth, I've wanted to write this book for many years. This is probably my tenth attempt. Each and every time I get to the blank page, try and imagine what I am going to say – what I have to say – I shudder to a stop.

It's not because what I am about to write is bad (although it may very well be) I just stop to ask myself, 'is there any point in this book any more?' Isn't it a decade or two late? I was in no position to write this back then, but would it have been more meaningful when we lived with overt prejudice and intolerance? I mean, us gays can get married in most places in the Western World. In terms of following the equality Sat Nav, haven't we reached our destination?

Despite this, every time I discarded the idea, it continued to irritate me – like some especially zingy haemorrhoids. Still the idea persisted. Still the notion captivated me. The life of a perfectly average homosexual. Was there mileage? Would anyone want to read it? Does anyone care?

Surrounded by trashy celebrity shite most of the time, what chance would the humble story of a mundane man have? That's why I kept starting and stopping it. Am I just too mundane? (Almost probably yes…) Ah, but, there are more people who live a life like mine, whether they are gay or not. The world is full of the mundane. Yet still… Would people want to read about my miserable dribble across this planet or the salacious ghostwritten tittle-tattle from someone who once showed their camel toe on reality TV?

Let's see shall we?

So. Who am I?

I am a nobody. No one special. No one famous. The very anti-thesis of modern day celebrity culture. In a world of billions, on a continent of millions, I am but one person. Someone with spots and patches of dry skin. Don't worry, I have a cream now.

So why am I writing this? Why should you read on? What's this all about? Well, without wanting to make you miserable or bring you down, the real reason I wanted to write this is because of the Nazis. Oh yes. The Nazis.

I can't watch any World War II stuff. I suffer from a massive claustrophobia and occasional anxiety. Not quite a panic attack, but something close. Just mention concentration camps or gas chambers and I freak out. (Who wouldn't?) It has been suggested (by people who wear things made from hemp and who drink tea made from weeds) that this is all a past life memory. That I must have been in a concentration camp in a previous life. That's where the panic and claustrophobia come from. I was told that my dreams of being locked in a darkened room were past life memories leaking into my subconscious.

Maybe…

Unless you are a neo-Nazi (unlikely given the title of the book) I imagine you're as horrified by the holocaust as me. Not just because of the millions of Jews who perished but also the mentally ill, the 'gypsies' and of course – 'the gays'.

I am gay. If I was living in Europe 70 years ago, not only would my love have been illegal, I could have been gassed to death for it – depending upon where I lived. That's quite horrifying. Accordingly, we fought the bad guys and we won. Given that the baddies lost, freedom surely fell upon us like confetti at a wedding? Err, not quite.

There may have been the odd gay man who saw the Allied victory as a sign of liberation. How about the very man who helped bring a swift end to the Second World War – Alan Turing? A national hero – until a humble house burglary led to the revelation he was gay and in a relationship with another man. For this crime (it was illegal to be gay then) he was taken to court and charged with gross indecency. He pleaded guilty (on the advice of his brother). He was found guilty. All of his security clearances were rescinded, he wasn't allowed to travel to America and he was treated like a war criminal, not the hero he was. At the age of 39 he was forced to undergo chemical castration to reduce his libido and thus cure his 'gayness'. He did this for a year. A year later he killed himself having been shunned by the establishment. He poisoned himself, leaving a half eaten apple by his bed. No one knows if this iconic symbol was to administer the poison. Who cares… is that how we treat a hero? I don't think so. It was a tragedy, yet he was not alone. The people in charge of the good guys (who fought and defeated the bad guys) decided that the gays were a fair target. Never mind that many thousands of gays fought and died alongside their straight mates, gays were deemed to be a rather unpleasant entity. Like shit on the sole of the country's shoe.

It wasn't really that long ago that you'd be beaten up on the streets of the UK for being gay. I know, because I was. Gay bashing was a perfectly acceptable form of violence. People will say that it's almost a thing of the past now. So let's see. How many of us would kiss or hold hands in a shopping centre, in a bar or on a train platform? How many of us, having done that, would expect to get stares, tuts or gasps? Do you think two guys could kiss at a kid's birthday party or during leisure time at the local swimming pool? Have we really eradicated prejudice?

I look nervously at the resurgence in religious extremism clamouring for the eradication of all gay people. Once again we hear people calling for gays to be executed – the justification and reasoning for this is simple – us gays are simply a shared enemy of most religions. Haven't we been here before? Can this really all happen again? Are we on the brink of yet more oppression? Look at Russia. Look at Eastern Europe. Look at Africa. What's striking is some of these places (like Germany before the war) embraced gays. Then, usually after a financial depression, the right wing get in and start a trend that reverses liberation and gays become scapegoats, again.

For me, realising I was gay and 'being' gay was not about the person I slept with. It transcended that, (although that's one of the best bits!). Every life snuffed out, every soul burned, every hope extinguished, every smile suppressed, every love corrupted – simply because of a person's sexuality, all became linked together. Suffering transcends generations, race, sexuality, religion – it should draw us closer together. We are all in this together. We are all one.

Wherever you read this and whoever you are, think of this: On another day, in another age or in another country, you could be killed for being you. No matter what sexuality, race or religion you are. Maybe you still could. In this day and age, on this planet now, a woman can be killed for wanting an education or raped and murdered for saying 'no' to an advance. A foetus can legally be aborted because its parents think it'll be a girl whilst kids are strung up on cranes with ropes around their necks because someone suspected they might be gay. People are discriminated against because of their skin colour and killed for whom they love. This is happening now…

There are people on this planet today who know the horrific truth of this reality. There are around 85 countries where being gay is illegal. Of those, five believe that execution is an accepted redress for your 'choice' or 'condition'. The rest think imprisonment is sufficient. 85 out of 195. Forty three percent of the world cast it as illegal. How would that number look if we included those where it was legal on the statute book but not welcome on the streets?

If anyone reading this book thinks being gay is a choice, let me tell you once and for all, it's not. I was brought up in a tough working class area, which was saturated in sports, dirt and hard labour. When I was an infant I was still of a mind that a mother's hug was the warmest place on the planet and a dog's sloppy lick was everything that mattered in life. Yet, at about four years of age I knew that I was different. Naturally, I now know what those feelings meant, but back then I had no idea. Suffice to say; I was gay at four. Now, tragically, I know that there are right wing ideologists who suggest that at the tender age of four I somehow chose to be gay. Being gay was a concept that I didn't even understand when I was 18 let alone four years of age! I was born that way.

"Ah yes," they'll say, "but even if it wasn't a choice it still doesn't make it any less wrong, does it?"

What can I say? I did not elect to be gay. I was born gay. Anyone who assumes that this was a choice or that we are capable of selecting our sexualities are, of course, talking unbridled bullshit.

Yet they persist, still they exist. They think we should not be allowed to live or to love. That angers me greatly. I am normal. My feelings are normal. Being a man and loving a man doesn't make one of us a woman.

The constant subjugation of millions because of their sexuality, their race or their birth features is irrational, evil and dangerous. Does history not teach us that no one can tame the tornado? Why try and suppress nature yet celebrate the man who created it? Therefore, with the freedoms I have and the life I am able to lead, I am writing a book about myself. This book is about my journey from small nervous child in a bleak English village and my long and torturous path to personal acceptance. It is written to honour those no longer here. It is dedicated to those whose lives and loves perished before they were able to blossom.

It is for all those people, lost, trapped, afraid and scared.

This is not a handbook for life or survival. It is just my story. I am just me. I am you. I am one of the millions of who died and countless yet to suffer. We are all part of the same body of experience. We are all in this together.

I wanted to write this book not for me, but about me. I wanted to write a book about a perfectly average (sometimes drunk) homosexual and dedicate it to all the people who have never been able to experience life and love as perfectly average homosexuals.

My story is not exactly pretty, it's stupid, it's harsh and upsetting in places. Looking back, I realise that the reason I was so sad and upset was because I was simply afraid to be gay. I was unsure and scared to find out what being gay meant. Society shattered my emotions and it took me bloody ages to understand that and then piece them back together again. All of these pieces, clumsily stuck together, created many jagged edges with bits that could easily hurt. That emotional stich up could never be thought of as smooth – just like me. That is why this book is so important. That journey of discovery and acceptance should never be so distressing for anyone ever again.

It's written for all of those people who live in fear. For anyone who can't enjoy the kind of life I live. It's for the people who have never been able to look into someone's eyes and enjoy the warmth of pure, unadulterated, love.

This book is about a perfectly average human being, who is lucky to be just that, average. It's about someone quite unexceptional who, as a result, is able to be something quite remarkable. It's dedicated to people like you Alan and to the many people in Iran, Uganda, Russia and everywhere else that have died or suffered just because they were who they were.

Your names may never be known, but you will never be forgotten. This is our journey. These are my words. This is the story of my life and every word of it is true.

It's not every day you get offered a discount by a hooker. I dare say some men may be envious. 'A discount? I don't get a discount and I'm here every week. When's my loyalty card going to get stamped?'

Maybe some men (and women) who use the services of a 'lady of the night' may have good reason to feel aggrieved that they are forced into paying rack rates. Then again, for all I know, 'my' hooker may offer discounts to everyone. Maybe it was just happy hour? Maybe she was new in town and wanted everyone to benefit from her opening night promotion? Open with a bang? I didn't even have to haggle. (Not that I tried…)

Her: "It'll cost you 40."

Me: "Make it 20."

Her: "35."

Me: "25."

Her: "30, I can't go any lower."

Me: "Deal – and I'm hoping you can…"

It may have been all of those things – but it was far worse than that. It wasn't a sales pitch or sexual attraction, it wasn't a special offer, nor did she find me so attractive that she just had to have me there and then. It was pity.

She offered me a discount on a meaningless blowjob because she felt pity for me.

How do I know? Did I see the pity in her lifeless eyes? The

cold grey eyes of a woman who spent most of her working life with her forehead yo-yoing into a mound of stranger's pubes. Well, yes, I did. It wasn't that which tipped me off though. No, it was when she told me that she actually pitied me. That's when the penny dropped. I stood before this middle-aged woman in a city car park as she told me to my face that she felt sorry for me. You can imagine just how warm and fuzzy that can make one feel…

She didn't see me standing there cold and alone and feel maternal pangs of pity that drove her to offer her unique brand of compassion and caring: "If one of my sons was out here I'd want one of my colleagues to do the same for them…" Nope. It was cold, hard, loveless pity.

We stood in the bare grey car park, which was dotted by a handful of cars left there by revellers intent on having a good time. Where were they I wondered? Why wasn't I the type of person who left his car in a car park and went indoors to a nice civilised party? Or an uncivilised one come to that. Why was it that I was outside being offered cut-price oral sex by a woman who (for whatever reason) had only three visible teeth?

The orange sodium lights cast their insipid pall over the deep red brick buildings that hemmed the car park. The Satsuma glow from the lights accentuated the brick and gave a radioactive feel to the area, turning the occasional tree plumage from green to grey.

It was an insidious situation and yet the evening had started so brightly. It was rare indeed for me to get the opportunity to go out at night into the city. I was living with my parents and very firmly at the back of the closet, screaming at the light if the door ever nudged open. As such, I couldn't just give in to whimsy and stay out for the night. I had to call them and tell them I'd be late. When I did, they wanted to know why – given it was such a rare and odd occurrence. Frankly it was a bit suspicious given how unsocial my social life was.

On the even rarer occasions when I did manage to bag a shag and stayed out all night, I'd have to call my parents and explain why I was staying out. That was harder still. "Oh, I've bumped into friends," I'd say. "I'll crash at their house," I'd reassure. "I'll be fine. Don't worry." I'd add. That was always a lie. I am fairly sure they knew it. I certainly did, so I see no reason why they didn't.

Yet what else could I say? "I won't be back late as this bloke called *muffled sound* 'what's your name?' *muffled sound* I think he says he's called Terry or it could be Mary, has asked me back to his high rise in a shady part of town for some slap and tickle. So, anyhoo, don't wait up. Oh hold on, I think he said he's called Troy!"

My mother would have had a fit. Not so much that I was gay and going back with a man but that I was heading off to the dodgy part of town. She would have been into that city and would haul me back home by the scruff of my neck in seconds. To protect all concerned, and remain in said closet, I lied. The reality was I had few friends… well, let's be honest… at this stage in my faltering and fragile adulthood, I had no friends. None that lived locally anyway. My friends were all some luggage and a train ride away. Work colleagues were about the only hope I had of experiencing a social life.

Most Friday nights, after yet another exhausting week at work, I'd sit and wait to catch the train home. Invariably, I'd be the only one at the Victorian red-bricked train station that was perched on the city's industrial edge. The city was undergoing a process of massive urban renewal, but raised high above street level, there was a quiet timelessness about the station. Typically I'd finish work around seven, which meant that the bulk of commuter traffic was already home, settling down for the weekly pizza and DVD.

In all weathers I'd sit on the uncovered platform, awaiting the vessel to take me into the bowels of the eerily silent suburbs, with their toy store warehouses, parks and substandard Italian restaurants. Yet every Friday – week in, week out – as I made that sad solo journey home I was deafened by the pulsating sound of several bars around the station. One of which had the temerity to be under the station platform itself.

As I sat and waited for the train of social failure, I'd hear shrieks of laughter, glasses chinking, joyful voices and music beating against the perpetually grey city sky. Every Friday (and the odd Saturday I had to work too) I'd board the train. The train doors would open and stay open as it waited for a minute or two before pulling off. It was as if the driver was allowing me one final mournful glimpse into the life I didn't have. As the train pulled away I'd listen to the sound of happiness fade as the landscape changed around me. Sometimes I would swear that the sound of the wheel on the track had a, *'you're alone and lonely, you're alone and lonely, you're alone and lonely, you're alone and lonely,'* rhythm to them. This was hard to ignore, when leaving such vitality behind.

That wasn't a good feeling. I was young. I wanted some fun too. I wanted to stay and party. Yet, as work colleagues rarely went out, or stayed out when they did, opportunities were scarce. Accordingly, when I did occasionally call home to say I'd bumped into friends my parents knew I was lying.

Every time I called with that lie I would often tense up in anticipation. I must have looked like I was touching cloth in the phone booth, but I was merely bracing myself for the day when they asked, "what friends exactly?" True, I could reel off a raft of names, but we all knew such a roll call would be meaningless. I think that was why they didn't bother to ask. They spared me one more lie. Quite what they thought I was actually up to, I've no idea. Later in life my mother said she hated the idea that I was, "walking the streets looking for love." Either she knew exactly what I was up to or she thought I was a rent boy.

On this particular night in question I'd been out with work. It was a rare late night. These were like gold nuggets in a mountain stream. It was also a decent one where everyone was having fun. It was a lovely summer's evening and I had allowed myself to feel that dangerous, destructive feeling – hope. What's more, we were in the bar beneath the train station! I was cocking a snook to my mundane routine. My night ended, however, when I had announced around 10.30pm that it was time for me to leave and get my train. I always found this a very humbling experience. It was amazing to see how the group evolved quite happily without you.

"You off then? Okay, have a good weekend…" The conversation would change, someone would take your seat, the circle of people would contract and you were seamlessly forgotten. At the time that hurt. No one ever said, "Oh don't go, stay longer and you can crash on my couch…" Why I ever thought people I spent time with, merely because we got paid to do so, should care about me I've no idea. But I did and there we are.

I climbed the stairs high up above the palace of frivolity and went to sit on the platform. The cacophony of exhilaration rose like exotic steam around me, accentuating just how crap my life was. When the announcer declared that the train was running late I made a decision – I was going to go back to the bar. I didn't care where I ended up, but I wasn't getting that last train home like every bloody week. It was a summer's evening and if the worst came to the worst, I'd sleep at the station. Besides, there were plenty of bars that would keep me busy and warm until the first train.

So, with the obligatory call to the parents to say I'd bumped into a friend, I was back off to the bar. With muted surprise, I was soon back in the fold. Tonight I was going to have fun. It was a summer's evening, barely dark and the city beckoned. Within a few hours I found myself alone again, as everyone made their way home. The last train was gone, the clock had long since chimed midnight and there was a long wait until the next train home. The city was large, the weather mild and I was alone.

"What you doing now?" colleagues would ask as I stood alone in my work outfit with my rucksack filled with empty lunch boxes slung over my shoulder.

"Oh, when I left earlier I called some friends, so I am meeting up with them in a bit," I lied. I hoped that in so doing I would A) give the impression I had friends and B) suggest I had a life. In much the same way my parents could spot a lie a mile away, I suspect my colleagues could too. I almost expected them to say, "what friends?"

So there I was, the city was my oyster. The allure of a long night partying dimmed. What had looked like a blast now looked like a torturous marathon until the first train home. The reality was, I was tired and had nowhere to sleep. A hotel was too much for someone on my salary and taxis would cost the earth. No, this was an exercise in perseverance, grit and survival – which some may think a rather odd collection of emotions for a Friday night out…

There was one universal truth about nightlife in Manchester and that was the gay bars had the latest licenses. In fact, thanks to the gay bars, I could stay indoors and safe all night. It therefore made complete sense to make my way there. This had nothing to do with the fact they were gay – you understand. It was merely that they were open late. I was still very much at the stage where I'd happily say to your face, "what would I want to go to a gay bar for?" then wonder why you snorted, rolled your eyes and walked off. So I headed off to the hedonistic playground that was quaintly called 'The Gay Village.' It had a doctor's surgery, a post box and I dare say it had its fair share of butchers, bakers and the odd candlestick maker too. As I trudged through the city streets with scantily clad women tottering in high heels being pursued by men in gauche patterned shirts and way too much cologne, I played out how the night would unfold: I'd find a quiet corner, perhaps get a newspaper, read, have a coffee and wait until the sun came up. I suspect that was my conscious mind telling my subconscious mind not to get any dirty gay ideas. My subconscious mind would then grab a bottle of whisky, lock my conscious mind in a room and set about getting filthy gay ideas. My conscious mind would then bang on the door screaming 'stop it, you'll hate yourself in the morning,' before sliding down the door sobbing.

Then – a genius idea! Why wait in a bar only to be kicked out at 3am and then join a long queue just to get into a club? Why not go to the club directly?

There were few clubs of any note in the city. There were a few sleazy ones that I had no intention of going in to (because I was scared) and a few high-octane camp ones that I had no intention of going into (because I was terrified). Then there were a few mainstream ones in between. Ones that you could, to some degree of innocence say, "It's a gay club? I never knew!" and just about pull it off. Although pleading innocence would have been difficult as they were often called things like Cruz, Throb and C.O.C.K.

All was well until I started getting harassed by a 'gentlemen' who wanted to know my affections more intimately. A lot more intimately than I wanted him to. I may well have been going to gay clubs. I may have been telling myself it was because they played the best music and stayed open late. I may even have been a sporadic regular, but despite doing all of that, actually doing something with a guy in one of those clubs was a massive no-no.

As far as I was concerned everyone was a spy for my mother. I may not have been brought up Catholic but she certainly made me nervous of an all-powerful omnipresent being that judged me at any opportunity. I don't mean God, I mean her. In her world of omnipresent judgmental beings it went A) Her B) God. In truth, had God found me in one of those clubs I would have been far happier than if she did.

As I stood by the bar I often rehearsed what I'd say if ever she walked in and spotted me. Honestly, I did. Now, it might strike you as odd that I actually believed there was a chance that an older woman would travel into a city she wasn't *that* familiar with, tracking down the gay district and then systematically trawling all of the clubs called Throb and C.O.C.K., purely on the speculative off-chance that her son may be inside one. You may think it odd, but I promise you it was not beyond her ability or will. At the time this seemed perfectly plausible. I had grown up with her telling me that she tracked me as I went about my day-to-day business. She told me she hid in bushes to track me in school, took days off work to make sure I was doing what I said on school trips. Let me assure you, I thought she was everywhere. In fact, the very first time I had sex I checked the cupboards and under the beds before getting started.

Despite all of this I was fairly sure that had she ever managed to haul herself into the city, trawl all of the bars and then found me propping one up, I could talk my way out of being there. Had she walked in on me with my tongue down another man's throat, however, I may have struggled to justify that. I may have been here, I may have been queer but I was still getting used to it.

This gent was a drunk who thought that my arse was public

property. I told him politely it wasn't. His hands were all over me. I had to ask him to stop pulling my shirt out of my trousers as I ordered a drink. I turned down his offer of drinks, drugs and a place to stay for the night (although I did consider that). In the end, I decided that enough was enough and told a fearsomely huge security guard that I was being harassed. She wasn't happy to hear that, so a few words in my suitor's ear seemed to do the job. The threat of being thrown out (and heaven forbid) banned from a nightclub that played high-speed electro dance music was a potent threat.

All was fine until he came over to apologise. He then offered me a drink to say sorry. Which led to an apologetic grope and we were off again. I'd had enough and decided it was time to leave. There were other places with late licenses that were still cheaper than a cab or a hotel. If I wanted some quiet, I'd even heard that there was a gay sauna in the vicinity, which provided private rooms in which to go off and have discreet fun. My question was… did they have locks on those room doors? Frankly, if these places were open 24 hours, were obviously warm and charged a fraction of a hotel, I could merrily survive one night on a sticky wooden bench and forgo an en-suite and Egyptian cotton sheets.

So I set off.

My drunken admirer was not happy that I was leaving. So much so, he attempted a flying rugby tackle/piggy back as I was leaving. This proceeded to rip my shirt straight down the middle – and into several large pieces. As the formidable and fearsome lesbian bouncers ejected him from the building, I stood in the neon glare of the nightclub's foyer with its queue of expectant singles, looking at me standing semi-naked with one of my fledgling moobs exposed for all to see. I gathered up what was left of my top (and dignity) and set off into the night out of blind panic and acute embarrassment. I was fairly sure that the CCTV in the club's foyer was only for internal use only, but I was now on camera semi-naked in a gay club.

I sped off in the opposite direction of my drunken admirer, who had been dumped into a mound of bin sacks. I kept walking until I was in the relative peace of an emptyish car park. There I stood, looking around and getting my breath back. This wasn't how the night was meant to be and there was no way I could go home now. As I stood there clutching at tatters of my clothes I knew that I'd have to wait for the shops to open, buy a new shirt and then go home. What was worse, when asked how my night was, I'd have to say, "Yeah it was great thanks. A really good night." Was it too much to ask that I actually had a good time every once in a while?

I looked at the clock on the large municipal building opposite me: 2.30am. I had a six-hour wait until the shops opened again. I stood and wondered – should I attempt to go to another club where I may not get in or where the nut job may be or did I just find a quiet bench and wait for light to break? At that point the rain started to fall. Gently at first as if stroking my face in sympathy and then heavier, with disdain. I didn't move. I was stuck to the spot, left to evaluate my decreasing number of options. That was when she arrived into my life.

"Hello love," came a cheery voice penetrating the amber

gloom of the poorly illuminated square. "Are you looking for business?"

I stared back at this short-framed middle-aged woman and tried to work out how on earth her life had led her to this place. Why was she a prostitute? Did she enjoy it? Did she tell the careers advisor at school that she wanted to be a whore? Was she an enforced sex worker? Was she on drugs? Was she happy with her life choices? Did she enjoy a blissful work/life balance? Did she go home to a husband and kids? Where did she spend Christmas?

I stood motionless until I realised that whatever I thought of her chosen profession, she was the only one smiling.

"No thanks," I offered gently and smiled a half smile.

"Oh come on love, I give a fantastic blow job."

I wondered whether I should ask for references or query her customer feedback. "How was my cock sucking today? Call this toll-free number." Was there a guidebook I could check other user reviews? "Would have been five stars but the car next to us was getting broken into at the time which took the shine off…" "I would recommend Deidre any time, she always uses mouthwash between customers. Five stars for hygiene."

Besides, who was I to question whether she was good at it? I stood staring at her largely toothless mouth as she ran her tongue around her uneven gums as if to further demonstrate her point. It made sense in a way, if someone was going to be good at giving blowjobs it was surely a person who'd made a career out of it. She was a cock specialist. An ejaculation barista. Did she do a flat white?

"I am sure you do," I said graciously. "But no thanks." Whilst I prayed to God my mother would never see this sorry display, I knew she'd at least be proud of my manners.

"£40 and I'll take you to heaven." She threw back at me.

I snorted. Was she suggesting oral sex in a car park was akin to the rapture of meeting Jesus Christ? It also made me wonder just why a toothless woman, who looked like an extra from a Jack The Ripper costume drama, would think anyone's idea of heaven was car park oral sex. Not to mention a toothless woman offering a man sex in the so-called gay village. I could have ended it there and then and just said, "Sorry, I'm gay." I could have terminated this surreal scene by being honest but something prevented me from uttering those few significant words – again. Consequently I stood in silence.

It wasn't that I couldn't say those few words to a stranger from middle earth; I couldn't say them to myself. A spoken statement has far greater resonance than one repeated endlessly in your head. I ached to say it. I just felt crushingly unable to admit what everyone knew and what I was beginning to know.

"Again I thank you, but no," I offered instead. It seemed from her reaction that she thought I was playing hard to get but that with due pressure and persistence I'd give in. I decided to let go of my shirt and allowed each tattered piece to cascade down around my waist. "I've just been attacked," I said trying to let her down gently in some misplaced sense of British politeness and chivalry. "So I'm REALLY not in the mood." Probably best not to hurt her feelings… or be honest with mine.

Here was a woman who, in all probability, had seen it all. Despite this she looked genuinely surprised by the reality, which had literally unfolded before her.

"Oh love that's awful," she said looking at my shirt and then again up at me. "You must have had a horrible night."

I nodded weakly and teared up. I had. Then again every night seemed to be pretty horrible.

"Let me cheer you up," she said.

I smiled wearily, unsuspectingly nodding as I started gathering my clothes back in a bunch.

"Since you've had such a bad night, I'm going to show some pity and give you a discount. £30 huh? That'll put a smile on your face. That's a tenner off my usual price." She grinned broadly exposing her gums. Her pencil drawn eyebrows arched before she opened her mouth and, using her hand and tongue pressing into her cheek, gestured what a blowjob would look like.

I sighed, heavily, and with that the rain fell heavier still.

I AIN'T SMELLING OF NO FISH

I grew up in a small English fishing village. It was an unexceptional and sensationally unattractive working harbour on the North East coast of England. This small village was perched on an outcrop of land that jutted rudely out into the tumultuously grey and vastly unforgiving North Sea.

The harbour wasn't just the heart of the community, it was everything. Functional houses and developments sprang around it in a crescent, not so much panoramic sea views, as worker's cottages and sheds for gutting. It was from here that the village's limited prosperity came. The community was very strong but, as you'd expect, it was fishing-centric to a maniacal degree. If you didn't fish, you were there to teach, run a shop, have babies or gut the fish.

That. Was. It.

Unless…. Unless… Unless you were one of the two hapless, hopeless and tormented souls who had been thoughtlessly shipped in by the local council to drum up tourist trade. Hah! No one, simply no one, wanted to come and visit our village. It took some negotiation to get anyone to deliver milk. Why did they think people would holiday there? It baffled all of us. We may have been simple, but we weren't deluded! When taking a hard earned vacation, people would surely consider the sun kissed beaches of the Med or the majestic highlands of Scotland. We were offering the vacation equivalent of a deckchair next to the inferno where medical waste is incinerated – without the heat. I think it's fair to say delivering aid to a global disease epicentre or dental surgery may have seemed more appetising than holidaying in our village.

Were there any people on the planet who thought a freezing cold beach, a sticky smelly smoky pub and the odour of gutted fish would – or could – allure? The idea that you could entice ordinary folk to come AND STAY was a ludicrous folly. "Come see how we gut fish!" "Try your hand at removing a cod's entrails!" "Love slime? Why not holiday with us?" "When you think of dead fish – think of us!"

Suffice to say it failed – cataclysmically.

The notion that we could attract anyone with disposable income was a fantasy. We were, in many respects, living in a village that time forgot. It may have proved of some worth to a documentary filmmaker or palaeontologist, but tourists? No… We weren't there to titillate city dwellers desperate for some sea air, we were there to fish, to breed and then raise the next catch of fisherman and their wives.

Fishermen went out in wooden boats like they always had. People helped haul in the catch. Everyone lived by and from the sea. That was the end of it. Besides which, had any adventurous souls stumbled upon our village one stormy night, they would have soon fled in tears. Aside from the pub (more spit than sawdust) there was nowhere to eat beyond the fish takeaway or the convenience store that sold crisps. In fact, as the main take away only sold fish and chips and the smell of the fruits de la mare wafted across the small village on a recurring basis from all directions, it meant that no matter where you were you'd smell it battered, freshly dead or decomposing.

A stubby shopping street crawled through the village. Small local stores, where everyone knew the name of the people working there, populated it. It was the hive of the community and duly enabled the fishermen's wives to spend their money and their days talking about life in a fishing village. Meanwhile, their children attended the local school to paint pictures and play with multi-coloured bricks until such time that they too could fish or marry into the life.

Given that the small community was made up exclusively of seafarers and their immediate offspring, I wasn't entirely sure why my staunchly non-fisherman family elected to move to this educational and social backwater. Was it the smell of rotting cod entrails? In later years they confessed it was because the neighbouring village they had actually wanted to move to was too expensive. Which is like saying, 'we wanted to holiday in the Bahamas but we couldn't afford that, so we just dug a hole in the ground and covered ourselves in shit.'

Although initially suspicious of these curious outsiders, our arrival coincided with a spike in girls being born. As such, any family with boys was welcomed as a 'plug the gap' solution. We were, unbeknown to any of us, thus being lined up to become fishermen. As we lived exactly opposite the harbour, the boats and crews were impossible to avoid. We were forever being called across to marvel at some kind of deep-water goo. "Look at him, he's a beauty," they'd say of a lifeless mound of jelly and scale.

"Come out and fish," they'd call smiling with what was left of their teeth. I'd look at the kaleidoscope of stains on their chunky knit jumpers and breathe in their watery stench. I may have only been in the tentative early stages of my youth but I knew then, I ain't smelling of no fish.

As one of the few boys coming up to fishing age they were all after my services as deck hand, or whatever they did. Most days I stood there, as gruff men tried to get me onboard, literally and figuratively. I was caught up in my very own personal cod war. Who was going to get the newcomer as their recruit? It never actually occurred to any of them that someone would not want to be a fisherman. Their logic was, if you didn't want to be one, why move there? Good point.

Naturally, I was repulsed by this life. It stank. Everyone had fish scales and blood under their fingernails and seemingly had never heard of mouthwash. Or soap. Or shampoo. Their hair always look as tangled as their nets and smelled about as good. Not only that, but I'd heard that whilst out at sea, fishermen did their personal business over the side of the boat. That did it for me. I didn't care how salty fresh and exfoliated I'd be, I wasn't doing any of my poops over the poop deck... Or eating any more of their catch for that matter.

Small fishing villages needed things to occupy people beyond the stock in trade. Accordingly, alcoholism was rife. Men would sit in the street and drink from cans or bottles. There was (and still is) a rampantly romantic notion about a good sort of heavy drinker. Alcoholism only became bad when it made you nasty or angry or violent. In fact, it was only ever alcoholism if you became nasty, angry or violent. So long as your crime was to talk shit, declare your hitherto untold feelings over and over again, fall over or vomit, you were fine. Yes Jim sleeps in the street and urinates up shop windows, "but he's lovely with the kiddies."

The concept of agreeable alcoholism was something I grew up with. People drinking to excess were fine. It was expected and deemed very normal. It was a perfect grounding for the gay scene I would later frequent (even down to the gruff men hauling smelly tackle everywhere).

The fishermen would come back, unload their catch and then go to the pub. From there, they'd go home to eat their lovingly prepared dinners and then back to the pub. It was a very simple but extraordinarily hard life. They'd then go home to sleep, get up in the jet-black dark of a Northumberland morning and repeat the process again. The smell of alcohol was, quite literally, hanging in the air. Its pungent presence was never quite faint enough to be blown away by the sea breeze. It hung like a cloud of broken promises. Even to this day the slightest whiff of stale booze and I am transported back to my early days. Throw in the stench of rotting fish and I almost feel homesick.

My best friend in the village was born into this life. His entire family couldn't read and write and would often bring letters around to our house for my parents to read. Education was a merely a diversion. Fishing was their lives. As long as you knew your way around boats and nets, you didn't need be no writer…

Harry and I would go off and explore the coast whenever we

could. He knew he was being groomed for a life at sea and felt a crushing sense of depression at the fact. He envied me my get out of jail card. At least I could say no. He was continually kept out of school to learn the trade. Although we were only young, we knew what this meant. We knew that his future was his dad's present and it depressed us both. So we played and explored to take our minds off the inevitability of tomorrow. Rock pools, crags, hidden coves, we'd go off and explore the lot together. Maybe one day we'd find a better future.

Harry wanted to learn, he wanted to grow and he wanted to know. Yet if he was 'caught' reading he'd be asked, "what do you want to be doing that for?" I once answered on his behalf, "Err, so he can read the letters you get sent," and found my invitation to dinner was rescinded with immediate effect.

There was no reality beyond the village. There was no alternative. A child's destiny was sewn up at birth. There was talk about breeding more fishermen, (something that took on an entirely different meaning as I blossomed as a gay adult on Foreign holidays…). Their mission was to ensure there were always enough men to man the boats (and lifeboats) so that the industry would survive. Kids at the school would talk excitedly about how they were going to have wild adventures on the high seas, before luxuriating in the pub that looked (and smelled) like a public urinal but with a bar in it. I was always unsure of just how many exciting high seas adventures one could have catching mackerel, but as there were always plenty of memorials commemorating people who'd lost their life to the sea, I stayed quiet.

Young female teachers would look at us boys as one might rats in a cage and know that our futures were mapped out. Their job was to deliver us to the sea. They needn't bother with any of that fancy learning business. Absenteeism was rife, as kids would go out fishing with their fathers. As mine worked in an office I was often the only boy left in class with the exception of a small disabled boy who, like an unsaleable fish, had been tossed overboard.

The teachers would look at me with pity – the child who got left behind. They'd come up to me and comfort me as if I were grieving the life I'd never have. In reality I couldn't have been happier. I'd hear them talking about how they'd have a word with 'Jim' or 'Neville' or gruff old men with nick names like 'legs'. These men would fix it for me so that I didn't feel the acute pain of rejection, isolation and loneliness. They would find me a place and get me out hunting mackerel before I was lost to debilitating forces of aspiration and education.

Their mission was not to educate me but to get me out to sea. Again and again they'd offer and again and again I'd say no. This was attributed to the fact I didn't know what I was missing, rather than the fact I saw no joy at going out to sea on a freezing November morning in a rickety wooden boat to catch slippery smelly wet things.

I was, therefore, the only able bodied boy left in a classroom of girls. Frankly I liked the attention. I wasn't aware at such a tender age, but the girls were being paired with future husbands. "Did you see the way little Milly-May looked at Billy. That's a match made in Heaven," they chunter. Milly and Billy – God help them. I don't doubt they did end up married, probably unhappily with a hint of domestic violence to add colour. They'd no doubt breed, drop their kids off at school and repeat the cycle. It was a soulless and dark life.

At the time I was blissfully unaware that it had been decided that I would inevitably become the fisheries manager, rather than a man of the brine himself. This was because I knew my alphabet and was therefore executive material. My future wife was thus harder to find. I was becoming aware that this background noise was going on but remained quite happy to keep myself busy and paint with my rainbow paint set. Oh the irony.

It was here that I had my first inkling that something wasn't entirely as it should be. I knew that I wasn't like the other boys because I was repulsed by the smell of fish (yes, I know…) but there was something else going on too. Something was happening that I didn't understand, yet was curiously aware of. The only time I was ever tempted to get into a fishing boat and go to sea had nothing to do with the boat, the adventure or the fish, but rather the handsome fisherman making said offer. Obviously, as a child I didn't make any connection, I was just tempted because he seemed nice. I can picture him now. Looking back, it makes perfect sense but those feelings scared me. I knew no one else felt them. I was a freak. I was alone. I had come so very close to stepping on to that boat. I remember people actually gasped as my foot rose towards the steps.

After that incident, I decided to avoid any future life as a fisherman. I had to run from that life and those feelings. In my childlike mind, those feelings came from that fisherman so I had to stay away from fishermen. Which was almost bloody impossible in a fishing village. My life emulated a ball in a pinball machine – I was pinging around randomly whilst trying to avoid people. It was getting tiring and I needed a plan. So I decided that I'd run away and join the circus. Sadly, there was a snag. There was no circus. So, instead I'd run away and join the marching brass band that seemingly paraded past our house every other week.

Living in a small community that relied on alcohol to cure boredom, there were often excuses to drink. As such we had festivals and parades every five minutes. This was usually made up of a series of stalls on the local green, a beer tent (naturally!) marching bands and a local band procured from a neighbouring village. These bands were the product of their own declining industry – mining. Mining was under political attack and was staggering around trying to stay upright. These would-be rockers offered lyrically political statements that ensured we remembered those who'd died of asphyxiation in mining disasters or by drowning at sea. They'd parade through the town before mounting a make-do stage and drunkenly singing their message to other drunken people. People swayed, sang along and stumbled about whilst children stole sips from unguarded pints of beer.

That constituted a celebration where I lived.

The day's festivities were then usually concluded by a Marxist trade union rep giving an erratically repetitive speech about the erosion of traditional industries, workers' rights and the dignity of men who made their money smelling of a halibut. Then, after his lukewarm applause, everyone went off to the beer tent to finish off the day.

It was during one of these parades that I decided to make good my escape. The idea of having a smart sharp uniform and a shiny trumpet was much more fitting than mackerel and the stench of blood in my nostrils. Besides, I'd noticed that they were not always in step and figured they could do with a rhythm drill sergeant. I'd drill some rhythm into those drummers, I thought. Besides, I adored the fluffy things they used to hit the drums with. I SO wanted a pair! I used to watch them parade past my bedroom window and think it looked ever so glamorous. So I slipped out of the back door and off I went.

It wasn't long before my mother had spotted my absence and gave chase. She caught up with me on the village green whilst I was fingering someone's Tuba. She ordered me back home. It was at that point I decided my time had come. Maybe those salty sea dogs had a point. I therefore elected to use some of the language the fishermen had taught me. I spun around and, looking her up and down, declared, "Why don't you fuck off back to the kitchen you stupid woman." I spun back on my heels and began plotting my time as bandmaster. Suffice to say she didn't fuck off home so much as kick me all the way back home instead. I recall thinking that she was jealous of my escape plan. One that, in retrospect, would merely have seen me swap a fishing community for a mining one. Assuming of course that the police hadn't returned a run-away four year old home with a tut and a roll of the eyes.

Life wasn't always a grim roller coaster of crushing alcoholism and lost generations however… sometimes said fishing boats would drag unexploded World War II bombs into the harbour. As our house was in the direct line just behind the sea wall, we could easily have been wiped out if one had detonated. It always seemed quite bizarre. Here we were in the grim, grey 1970s and yet we would have had 'Cause of death: World War II bomb,' by our names. The very latest in a long line of casualties of the Nazi regime.

Initially, dragging bombs into the harbour was quite an exciting event in an otherwise drab decade. After a time, the Army would still evacuate us, not knowing we'd all leave by our front doors and return through the back. These bombs rarely exploded, and come on, we'd just put the cabbage on for dinner. We had to get back or it would spoil.

Curiously, the Army never ever evacuated the pub… they would have had a real disaster on their hands had they tried that. The bombs were taken out to sea and exploded in a spectacular surge of seawater. We'd all gather round to watch from a safe distance, as if to pay our respects to the body of water that had taken so many. Whatever I felt about the village or the industry, the sea was a formidable entity. Something to be feared. To this day I hate harbour walls, jetties and the like. The sea would suddenly whip up and snatch someone from the wall into its depth as if it were a hungry prey.

In a maudlin village with little hope, talk of someone dying at the hands of the sea was only ever five minutes away. I learned, as all fishermen do, to respect and fear the sea. Today when I fly somewhere and look out of the window at the vast expanse of water, I often wonder what it's thinking. It's may be odd thing to think, but the fisherman knew how to survive and the first thing they did was respect the sea. It could be a cruel mistress.

Thankfully, and finally, we knew we had to get out. My mother hadn't been too struck on her child telling her to fuck off and realised the village was heading for Davy Jones' Locker. My scrawling 'GET US OUT OF HERE BEFORE WE DIE,' in my mother's peach lipstick across my parent's bedroom wall had also apparently helped nudge their decision-making too. If we didn't leave, we'd be lost to the sea and to a declining industry that was, sadly, wiped out. Whatever happened to those men and women who could only fish? What about Harry? I often think about them. I am 100% incompatible with that lifestyle, but I had the utmost respect for the hard work they put in. Our fishing industries needed more protection than they got. They felt betrayed and, largely, they were.

Yet back then, it was about getting us an actual education and so it was time to move to the city. I was wetting myself with joy.

MICHAEL, ROW YOUR BOAT ASHORE

I met my first girlfriend at primary school. She was called Jane and I felt a great deal for her. She had dark hair, a lovely smile and we used to have great fun together. She was petite and I always felt like her protector, towering over her as I did. Not only that, but because we were always the best behaved kids in the class, we got to tidy the library up at the end of the week instead of going the tedious end-of-week assembly. In retrospect, getting us to clean and tidy the library and dressing it up as a 'reward' was a canny form of child exploitation and cheap labour, but we thought it was ace. Every Friday afternoon, as regular as clockwork, Jane and I were duly sent up to the library – unsupervised. It didn't take long before we'd devised a system. Thirty minutes roaring around the place cleaning and thirty minutes kissing. We were about eight and boy-oh-boy, it was a glorious way to end the week.

I used to look forward to Fridays. It was naughty and wrong, but wrong in a fabulously wrong way. Despite my tender years I had told myself that the feelings that made me feel different when I was four/five were gone. There were no alluring fishermen here, just Jane. This was the business end of life and Jane and I were to be together forever. I knew it in my heart. For almost an entire year this pattern was repeated and we thought it would never end.

Some of the other kids used to make fun of me and tease me for being a 'poof,' but I didn't care. They weren't getting jiggy with a saucy young slip of a lass behind Wind in the Willows every

Friday afternoon. No, they were in the school hall singing songs, holding hands and swaying to the deft touch of Mrs. Edgar's piano playing. Had I been your typical bloke I'd have told them all about what I was doing between rows R–Z every Friday. I'd have boasted and shut down their argument, but what Jane and I had was special. I did what any gentleman should do and kept it to myself.

Then one day came the bombshell that changed everything. Her stupid, selfish parents had decided to relocate. And yes, that meant she was going too. When she told me that she was leaving I felt actual crippling pangs of pain. There was a distinct wrench in my stomach. That night when I got home, I remember my parents had bought me a single that I had said I liked. 'Baby Jane,' by Rod Stewart. It felt like I'd been stabbed. That song reminded me of Jane back then and it still does now. I wondered if life would go on. I didn't know if life could go on!

Jane was as distraught at leaving, as I was of her leaving. So it was with great trepidation that we awaited our final Friday together. Such was her concern for me that instead of a sad, mournful last afternoon together, it was all rather surreal. Jane had decided I shouldn't be left alone and so had hand picked another girl for me. She was, I was told, briefed on what the library routine was and that I was to continue the tradition (in her honour?). It felt very wrong – and not in a good way.

Yet who was I to argue? I blush to think of it now, but that last Friday afternoon, we spent it kissing and cuddling – all three of us. The thugs and bullies who regularly taunted me as being a limp wristed poof, were joyously unaware that a few doors away I was

44

having a threesome. I was a playa! I wasn't out there singing Matthew Row Your Boat Ashore I was getting it on.

Despite this, life was never the same again. The library was just a room full of books after that. Fridays continued as normal, but they lacked the depth. I contemplated getting into trouble just to skip my weekly snog-sesh. The tonsil tickling was a formulaic end to a week not a thing to look forward to. I may as well have been doing biology. I was almost relieved when we moved to the next school and the child labour masquerading as treat was discontinued.

It was a few years into my time at the next school that friends and well-wishers spotted my solitude and decided that I needed a woman in my life. I also suspect that my fellow pupils were beginning to get the distinct whiff of Lavender. Accordingly, a woman had to be found. I was about 12.

Consistent with all school sport team selections, all the best candidates had already been picked. This was survival of the fittest in its most brutal form. Typically, all of the prime catches had been reeled in long ago, which left the odd, uncomfortable, cross-eyed and un-coordinated hopefuls praying for a swift death. The law of school pecking orders duly hooked me up with a woman who, like me, was one of the last left standing.

Perhaps the cooler kids thought because we were both social outcasts we'd naturally be good together. Maybe they thought we could spend our days chatting about ostracism and acne. It could quite easily have been a containment strategy – keeping the lepers quarantined. As long as they knew where the diseased ones were, the good-looking bright young things could walk the quads of the school in safety. I do not have any elevated sense of my own value, but if I was going to go out with a woman, it was NOT going to be her.

This plan was set in motion over time and required a degree of co-ordination. Unbeknown to me a rumour had been started that I had a thing for a girl called Claire. I most certainly did not. I would have preferred to snog some of the fishermen's daily catch than I would her. Claire may have been a nice girl, but if I were ever to dip my toe into the lady lake, it wasn't going to be with someone who made Tina Turner's Thunderdome mullet look understated. It was the 80s and yes hair was big, but she'd gone much, much further than everyone else. Having been ignored by boys throughout her school tenure she had decided to make herself impossible to ignore. Up went the barnet, out came the hairspray and the result was a privet hedge of hair stuck to her head. It was so large and sticky that it could ensnare low flying pigeons. Her hair, therefore, looked like a giant regurgitated hairball.

To compliment her dynamics, she was built like a rugby player. The clunky braces on her teeth acted like a storage unit for food and her skin was as oily as a Madras curry. Her forehead looked like the Pyrenees in acne and she was wearing correctional glass for being moderately cross-eyed. Sadly for her, when she smiled it looked like the opening to a cave, as various items of undigested food dangled at the entrance. She may very well have matured into a stunningly beautiful swan, but back then she was a very much an ugly duckling and everyone knew it.

This, they evidently thought, would get me back into women. Bless her, but if anything was going to drive me into the comforting arms of a man it was the sight of her, head tilted, her mouth open, expectantly hoping for my tongue to push through the leftover lasagna that dangled from her braces like culinary stalactites in a cave. It should also be pointed out that I was no catch. I was quiet, nervous, shy and although I wasn't exactly bottom of the league I was never one of the cool kids. For all I knew, she could have been thinking, 'Oh god, not him. Do they think I am *that* desperate?'

I was in the same cookery class as her brother. He was very supportive of his little sister. So when the shy – might be gay – boy in the class needed a woman, who better suited than his fur ball of a sibling? He would continually ask when I was going to do something about this possible love interest. Not wishing to be rude, or point out that I rather scrape my genitals against a cheese grater than touch her, I would dodge the question wherever possible. I didn't want to hurt their feelings. Her brother was a kind child who had refrained from teasing me. Accordingly, I didn't want to let it be known that I would rather French Kiss a Red Setter that had just finished licking it's own arse than kiss his sister.

One excruciatingly embarrassing Wednesday afternoon I was in my cookery class, showing everyone just how to make perfect pastry when in marches her older brother, a gaggle of friends and a startled looking Claire. She was obviously as surprised as I was and possibly as horrified.

My heart sank. Something was up.

We were told that our 'will they or won't they' relationship was driving everyone mad, so could we just get it over with? 'Will they, won't they?' As far as I was concerned it was 'they won't, will they?' I smiled an awkward and embarrassed smile. The girl, who was evidently flattered to get any attention, stared down at me (yes she was also freakishly tall) with a look of a guppy fish at feeding time. I stared back up at her and watched a morsel of food fall from her brace to the floor. The girl's brother had elected to give us our dignity and made everyone form a protective circle around us, but turn their backs to us. I was hoping Claire and I could do the same with each other, but alas, I was face to face with chompzilla. Where the hell was Jane now?

She grabbed her hands together and looked to the floor coyly. I think it's fair to say I was infinitely more nervous than her but the emphasis lay squarely with me to make the first move. I could sense that impatience of the group was growing. They wanted to hear slurps and groans as the waft of cheap margarine based pastry crisped in the background.

"Look," I said finally. "I appreciate what you're doing but this is showing no respect to Claire. If she and I are to get together we'll do it when we're ready not when anyone says so. It's important to me that Claire feels wanted, not that she's a sideshow." Okay, I may not have been quite that eloquent and mumbled in panic, but that was the gist. At that moment, I could see that Claire was about to pipe up that she was perfectly happy with the arrangement, so I swiftly grabbed her hand and called for the group to turn around. Addressing her elder brother I said, "I just want the best for your sister – don't you? This isn't showing her any respect is it?"

It wasn't, but my speech was far from altruistic. Standing there staring at her brother whilst feeling her gravelly hot breath on my neck, I prayed that he'd agree. I hoped they'd think I was a gentleman, rather than a gent who liked men. Her brother nodded a rather sorry nod and escorted everyone away. Claire waved goodbye to me with an expectant smile and I began to regain the use of my heart, which had stopped for the preceding few minutes.

The cookery teacher, who had been taking someone to first aid for a burn whilst this was all happening, returned to assist us in removing our respective Quiche Lorraines from the ovens. Re-entering the room, she stopped momentarily to stare at my sheet white face.

"You all right?" She asked, as I stared into the distance and felt blood return to my lips.

I nodded frantically, unable to speak.

"Don't worry," she said, "It'll be a lot better than you think! We just have to make sure it's not squishy in the middle."

It took a few seconds to realise she meant the cheesy delight in the oven not the cheesy relationship being foisted onto me by a social network that wanted answers. Claire's brother evidently thought that I was better than no boyfriend. If I did start going out with his sister, I could be welcomed into the boys club and those awkward questions about me wouldn't bother anyone anymore. Maybe he was thinking about me as much as her? People were definitely having doubts about me and buying time with Claire may have just confirmed those. I didn't have the courage to tell Claire that it was her brother I fancied…

It may have seemed like I had the perfect opportunity to hide behind another mask, to kiss this explosion of hirsute womanhood and shut everyone up, but I knew then A) she wasn't Jane. B) There was no way I was going near her without at least eight soldiers for back up C) It was too high a price to pay and D) On balance, I would rather have the eight soldiers or Claire's brother. It was a stupid litmus test of sexuality, 'do her or make us think you're gay', but it was a good barometer. I didn't give in then and I wouldn't give in again. Well, not for a few more years anyway.

I was about six when relatives came to visit. They bought me a perfectly expensive and jazzy shirt. I apparently looked it up and down and said, "I don't do paisley."

That would, in most people's eyes, have convinced them that something was slightly out of kilter with their angelic choirboy. For years I used to see the looks in people's eyes. A look that said, "there's something wrong with him."

It was often more than a look. People would say things like that quite deliberately within earshot or to my face. I've heard relatives questioning my 'normalness' to my parents and directly to me. People would, for no reason and totally out of the blue, say things like, "Doesn't the idea of two men being together make you sick?" What an odd thing to ask a young boy in the middle of the Magic Roundabout.

I would think about two men 'being together' and A) not have the faintest idea what they meant, B) knew many men who went out to the pub together, C) knew many men who worked together D) knew many men who went to the football together and E) as we were force fed 'The Likely Lads' (a TV show about two Geordie men on the pull), knew the idea of two men being together seemed perfectly ordinary. So quite innocently I would say, "No, why would it?" and return to watching TV. It was around this point that people would puff their cheeks out, sigh and say, "Well, we tried." They remained convinced that I was beyond help.

Had they actually told me what they were banging on about I may have offered something more substantive on the issue.

There may be gay men out there that make it from cradle to grave without anyone knowing, guessing or suspecting. That might be a good thing for them or a tragic fact. In my limited experience almost all men who try to hide their sexuality give themselves away at some point, or as is typical – almost all of the time. There are certain signs and imperceptible clues that people pick up on. People aren't fools; they soon notice when men enjoy having sex with other men – that's a 'sign' apparently. I'm talking about all the other stuff. Small things. Signs that say – hey, he may be a flaming homo. Signs that make people ask the question.

There are the guys who are as camp as a row of tents and who think that no one has guessed – when everyone on the planet clearly has. There are the ones who are 'confirmed bachelors' and people have their doubts but can't be sure. Occasionally, there are a few who come out and take everyone by surprise. Naturally, I was 100% sure that I was in that last category. If I ever revealed my true feelings, the shock would have been seismic. People would have fainted, birds would have fallen from the sky, cats would befriend mice and fish would be seen walking. In reality, of course, people would just look over their glasses and say things like, "Oh darling, we knew years ago. When you were four and you fancied that fisherman." I was totally sure that my sexuality was hidden behind a cunningly crafted and complex veneer of butch manliness. This was a pitifully cruel delusion. I was, frankly, as fruity as a cherry lollipop. Everyone but me could see it.

I had always known that something was different. I knew that I wasn't the same as the other kids. I also knew that whatever I was feeling was largely and universally frowned upon as a deviant state that would lead to my ruin. Accordingly, I was desperate to stop people thinking I was different so I tried my hardest to immerse myself in a mask of brusque manliness. Have you ever seen a camp child try and be butch? Think 'Are you looking at me Punk?' but with jazz hands…

To ensure my disguise was watertight I would monitor myself doing everyday activities like walking, eating, talking etc. I tried to ensure that I had a masculine walk. I wanted people to look at me and think 'he's butch.' I wanted a proper man's gait. I'd see myself reflected in a shop window and try to walk purposefully like a cowboy who'd hopped off his horse and was ready for a gunfight. In reality, I looked like I'd just shit myself and was walking gingerly to try and stop it sliding down my trouser leg. Butch? I thought that I ran like an Olympian, when in reality my run was nothing more than a motorised mince. I saw that the (rather dishy) angry kids ate with their mouths open. Despite being horrified by this rude transgression, I knew I needed to do it. So I tried. I managed for a while but I blew it by asking for a napkin. Then there was the time I saw a spider in class and flapped like a distressed pigeon, which didn't help. In short, I was the archetypal gay man who thinks he's fooling everyone, when in reality, he fools only himself.

As I couldn't see what everyone else could, I thought I appeared 'normal'. I was perplexed, therefore, by everyone's reaction to me, particularly at school. They were obsessed by me.

Like most people who are thrust into the Darwinian battle of daily survival at school, it didn't take long for the bullies to spot me on their blood soaked radars. Seemingly they didn't think I was quite as butch as I did. They didn't see me as a cowboy ready for a gunfight, but rather a gay man dressed as a cowboy in arse-less chaps singing YMCA.

Every walk down a corridor, path or street became a journey requiring significant strategic vision. It was always backs to the wall (ironically), walking in the middle of crowds, avoiding certain nooks, expecting a smack around each and every corner, trying to see where someone could hide and jump out right down to identifying a bully's silhouette in the distance. Day-in-day-out I would be assaulted, both verbally and physically. I fought back, but as I went up to bigger and bigger classes and schools it became more difficult. It had an edge. There were more of them, they were much harder, better fighters and sometimes armed. Never the less, I stood my ground. I fought back every time. I may have been a bit of a Nancy boy, but I was a Geordie and if you attack me, don't expect me to stand there and just take it. What made it worse; some of the chief perpetrators were in my class. During lessons they would throw things at my head (I don't mean paper darts either – we're talking weapons). Hit me as they walked past, try and kick me, throw me to the ground and of course, stab with whatever implements were to hand.

I tried to learn. I did. I really tried, but it was impossible. The teachers turned a blind eye to all of this. In the hardened North of England this was all regarded as good, honest character building.

What doesn't break you makes you stronger – which is a rather fatal method of survival. It did ultimately make me stronger, but I know many who were broken by it. It's therefore not an adage I subscribe too. The teachers thought that a good dose of abuse and violence would sort us out. Make us men. Accordingly it was allowed to continue unchallenged. They never wanted to challenge the perpetrators. I often wondered how much of that was from fear itself. Where were my fishermen friends now? I wish they could have popped in. They'd have leathered those bullies.

As a result, alone and vastly out-numbered, I began to hate school. When I went to the bigger, meaner school the sports changed from rugby, badminton, tennis, cricket and athletics to a choice of football or football. It was a bloody religion. I always remember that the cowards ran away from you in rugby but towards you in football.

My parents, with whom I did not share one iota of said hassle with, sensed my disquiet – particularly in football. They tried to give me a boost. Do something that would make me enjoy the sport, understand it more and ergo make me more popular. Suffice to say they weren't miracle workers. They bought me the replica kit of one of England's most successful footballers, Kevin Keegan. They bought me the top, the shorts, the socks and the boots. The lot. It probably cost more than they could afford. I was told that once wearing this magical kit, I would be just like the great man himself – but for his curly perm. With the kit on, I would be transformed into a player as skillful as the man himself. (I would have thought the inability (or desire) to play the game in question would have separated us from one another – but there we go.) The next day, my heart beating with trepidation, I turned up to my next sports match and duly changed. I did allow myself a few moments of bombast as I slipped into Kevin's officially authorised silky smooth kit. 'I'll show them,' I thought.

The various garments tried on at home in a dim light had not, sadly, exposed the truth. The shorts and shirts had a sparkling lamé quality to them, a fabric that a drag act may have considered too gauche. I changed in front of my aggressors – eleven on the opposing team and if I was honest ten others on my team – whilst trying to stand tall, but my God I sparkled. Boy, oh boy did I sparkle: like a mirror ball falling down the stairs. Every time I turned even slightly, the sunlight beaming in from the narrow roof top windows into our stinking, sweaty tiled changing room, caught my 'kit' and made me look like I was exploding from Liberace's piano.

"For fuck's sake," came a voice I am still not entirely sure wasn't the teacher, "Look lads, its Wonder Woman!"

I stood, iridescent in Kevin's glow, as a wave of laughter engulfed the changing rooms. Crude wooden benches laced with bags, kit and uniforms swayed back and forth as they rocked with laughter, vibrating with the hilarity felt by each team as this rather sad lonely child twinkled before them. Some fell to the floor clutching their sides.

"It's Kevin Keegan's kit," I shouted back defiantly at the sea of howling disbelief, a hand on my hip in defiance. It didn't do my argument any good.

"Give us a twirl," someone shouted until this became a chant. 'Twirl, twirl, twirl, twirl…" They bellowed and screamed in unison. The teacher, I am still sure, was leading the chants. Assuming I stood a better chance of being 'one of the lads' if I obliged and joined in, I duly twirled.

This was a mistake.

A huge mistake.

In twirling, I had transformed myself into a disco diva of blinding, glittering gayness. There was the school poof twirling around (hands outstretched…) and spinning and sparkling like a spandex'd gay rotisserie chicken. This did nothing to make any of the lads think I was butch and one of them. Whereas I thought I was joining in, they saw a gay boy sparkling and twirling like a girl.

"Are your socks made of silk," they asked as I kicked my bag under the bench.

Emblazoned down the side of my shorts and shirt were the letters KK. A man, who in later life I would love as manager of Newcastle United, but who, at that time, I loathed. WITH. A. PASSION.

"Does that stand for Kiss, Kiss," they all bellowed, knowing full well it didn't. The sound of kissing noises made a crescendo replacing the howls of derision. If half of the people in that room hadn't tried to kill me on more than one occasion, I would have taken the ribbing. I don't mind that! However, when it's merely a prelude to something involving fists – funny it is not. I turned to look at my boots to ensure they were at least ordinary. I bent down to get them, and as I did, a shaft of sun crept in through the small windows and caught my sparkling arse. Gales of laughter swept the room again as everyone, young and old, student and teacher broke down and wept.

I stood up sharply, twinkling like a glitter ball at a Village People concert. I was dazzling. I knew then and there that all was lost. I would never ever be one of the boys. My life at the school was over. I glanced again at the boots. Last night they looked normal. Today they looked as if they were made with diamonds. I shuddered but sat down to put my red, white and blue socks and boots on. Given that the city's major rival football team plays in red and white, turning up with a red and white sparkling figure skating kit made me as popular as yet another kick in the cobbles. I protested that it was red, white and blue and that I was a patriot, but this fell on deaf ears. As I stood, I sparkled, I dazzled, I glitzed and I cemented my reputation as a Nancy boy who should be kicked repeatedly.

I asked the teacher if I could be excused games. "No," he laughed before telling me to, "take it like a man."

In years to come I would do my best to follow that advice but back then, I knew it was a plain evil thing to say. "If you don't want to play football dressed up to the nines as Wonder Woman," he said, "change into something from the lost property box." I walked over to the wooden box in the corner of the room as the clatter of ordinary manly black boots led the way to the pitch. I picked my way through a box of urine stained clothes. A string vest and some denim shorts were all that I found that were vaguely suitable. I had a choice. I could play football in the freezing winter snow in a hardened North Eastern school as Wonder Woman's effeminate sidekick 'Kiss Me Kevin,' or dressed as a redneck rent boy. I elected to stay faithful to Kevin and played to the best of my ability as a sparkling, sequined star. Suffice to say I never wore it again and rapidly changed my allegiance to follow rugby.

Kevin, at the very least, you owe me a pint.

THE INCIDENT WITH THE SHAVING FOAM

As a child I was petrified with anything that connected me in any way, shape or form to being a man. The idea would make me feel sick – literally.

Looking back I can see why, I think. I knew that I wasn't 'normal'. I knew that I wasn't like the men around me. I wasn't like those who'd shaped my early life and impressions of men, and by that, I mean men who smelled of that intoxicating hybrid of alcohol and fish. I wasn't gruff. I didn't like getting my hands dirty, whether figuratively or literally. I felt like a fraud. Like I should have been in a category all to myself: Man. Woman. Child. Me.

The notion that I would inevitably grow up into a man freaked me out to the extent that if any kindly family friend ever referred to me as a 'young man,' I'd throw a strop. I just didn't want to think about it, deal with it or contemplate it. I wanted to push it as far from my mind as possible. If I could have stopped the aging process I would have. This inevitability gave me cold sweats.

When men became men, they got jobs, wives, had kids, washed their cars on Sundays and enjoyed football. That was the anti-me. I remember a friend and I were discussing getting old. I can still hear him saying, "Well I'll get a job and earn enough for the wife and family." It wasn't what he wanted. That was what we were expected to do. His lot was to provide for others, wash the car on Sundays and like football.

I knew that when I eventually grew up to be a man I would

<u>have</u> to get a job, a wife and have kids. It's what men did. I knew that my square peg would struggle to fit into that round hole and I began to panic. When I should have been playing on my bike or climbing trees, I was indoors planning how to dodge marriage for the rest of my life. The most immediate way to achieve this was simply to deny I was a man, or at least a man in the making. I recall once, whilst on holiday, playing with my brother and a few other children. It was a game of chase or something, one of the other holiday makers said, "Come into my room, I have an idea."

We were staying in a small seaside hotel. It had deep lush red patterned carpets, a permanent smell of lamb gravy and a sea view from the highest communal toilet (if you stood on the edge of the bath and craned your neck out of the skylight). I went into his room. The rooms were always a bit musty due to poor ventilation and people drying their pants on the radiators. The damp always made the floral flannelette bedclothes a bit sticky.

His room was tidy, it had a double bed with a double wardrobe and a sink against the wall. On the sink he had all of the usual items one associates with a bathroom. His stuff to one side, his wife's to the other. There was a smell of soap in the room. It was a reassuring smell. Clean people were happy, good people.

"Hold your hand out," he said. I did as I was bid. There he squirted a large dome of shaving foam into my hand. The idea was that I could run up and give one of the kids a bit of a pie in the face moment. I stood there with this huge, towering man. As we stood there, he was squirting liquid manhood into my palm (Oh, stop it…). I watched as it layered higher and higher. As I watched

I became increasingly agitated. My heart was racing. What if someone saw me? How could I explain this? This dumb foam, put simply, was representative of the responsibilities and choices that my later life was to have. The one that I had been doing my level best to avoid. Men shaved. Boys didn't. This was like holding a ton weight of responsibility in my very hand.

I knew from the media and those around me that gays should be stoned to death. Gay men caused AIDS. AIDS killed innocent people; therefore gays were killing innocent people. Not only that, but any gays not infected with AIDS were latent pedophiles. They were evil people who lurked in parks and touched you places that made you feel ill.

I had this horrible, nagging feeling that I may be one of those people. I didn't feel evil or nasty, as it happened. I didn't know how you did all of that other stuff, but I did like playing in the park – was that a sign? I just knew that the minute I became a man, the very day after I started shaving, I would inevitably become of these social pariahs. This horrible, achingly depressing feeling continued at pace – as soon as I was officially grown up, I too would be ready for death row or life in the shadows. The only solution was to get married to someone who was either so in love with me that she couldn't see the obvious or lied to herself too. Either way my future was all about being trapped, being unable to breath, to live or to love.

I stood there, staring at this white fluffy future life of misery. I knew that I couldn't just freak out, as it would scare every one. So I said thanks and ran off, as if playing the game. His room was on a lower floor to ours. Instead of re-joining the chase, I legged it upstairs as fast as my legs would carry me. I held my arm out, the toxic foam as far from my body as possible. My free hand clasped the foam arm as if I'd cut a jugular and needed to keep it still. I stumbled up stairs into our room and washed the offending substance from my hands. I was frantic. Made worse when I heard one of my parents coming towards the door. I desperately swilled the sink in a chaotic attempt to wash away the evidence. My father walked in and saw me.

"Didn't you get any foam?" He asked, seeing me standing by the sink, all flush. Seemingly the guy had secretly given it to all the children to make a bun fight out of it. (Either that or he'd a shaving foam fetish.) My father explained that my brother had given some child a perfect face splat and they wondered where I was.

Yes I'd been given some I mentioned coolly, whilst not looking at my father, but I had needed the toilet so had to wash it off to go to the loo. I was very good at coming up with excuses that always seemed plausible enough. Ones that probably wouldn't stand up to significant scrutiny but certainly ones that had enough power to get you out of trouble there and then.

It seemed so very odd. So genuinely pointless. Why bother? What was the big deal? Everyone else was doing it. Yet to me it was so significant, it felt like my hand was burning with shame. (I could make a joke, but I'm not going to…).

Having been brought up (to a varying degree) understanding Jesus' omnipotence, I knew that whatever I saw, he saw. Whatever I felt, he felt. He knew I was having gay thoughts and that meant I was destined for the furnaces of hell. There was no way I could control these feelings, there was no way I could stop them. I did everything possible to try. Bizarrely, I over heard some woman in a shop say that men weren't men unless they kept their wristwatches on whilst in bed. Don't ask me what the hell she was on about – but sure enough that's what I did. I woke up about eight times in the night to check if the watch was still on and then to see if I felt differently. One-night became one week, one week became a month and then I thought 'fuck it.'

I prayed every single night. Every. Single. Night. I prayed in tears, in desperation and in increasing pain. I had to convince Jesus that I was worth saving. Couldn't he just turn me straight? HOW HARD WAS THIS?

Water: Wine.

Me: Straight.

If he wasn't replying, they said, it was because I wasn't praying hard enough. That I didn't believe. Maybe it was because I had already done too much, too much evil that I wasn't worth saving? I read the bible every night (from an early age) and believed that God would never forsake a child.

> He called a little child and had him stand among them. And he said: "I tell you the truth, unless you change and become like little children, you will never enter the kingdom of heaven. Therefore, whoever humbles himself like this child is the greatest in the kingdom of heaven." And whoever welcomes a little child like this in my name welcomes

me. But if anyone causes one of these little ones who believe in me to sin, it would be better for him to have a large millstone hung around his neck and to be drowned in the depths of the sea.

Matthew 18:2-6

So you know, I *was* Heaven. I was the future. But then it said I should honour my father and mother. Which I did. I was the best-behaved kid known to creation. That said, my parents made casual references to my future wife and having kids. I knew that would never happen, I knew that was not my future. So did Jesus know that too? Did he know I was just playing them along? Did he know I was humouring them and thus, by definition, not honouring them?

So there we had it. There was the problem. How could I honour my father and mother without getting married? Jesus knew and I knew that wouldn't happen. I was thus pre-emptively breaking a commandment and enabling Jesus to send my prayers to voice mail.

That particular circle of life was agonizing. I wanted for all the world to change. I wanted to be 'normal'. I tried wearing the watch overnight, I'd played football (badly) and I'd prayed until sleep took me away from prayer. I was convinced that as soon as I did become a man, there was no turning back. That was it, I was off to hell. If I didn't stop it as a boy, there was no stopping it. It was now or never. And for that, I lived most of my childhood in some degree of anguish. When you live a life as somebody you're not, it changes who you are. You became a flake, a construct of imagined ideals. You get lost in a world of expectation rather than reality. It's a dangerous temptress as it so often fails to deliver.

Expectation is the root of all heartache – Shakespeare.

I had no idea who I was or what people wanted me to be. No wonder I wasn't that popular. It was a miracle I got up in the morning at all.

Everything, simply everything, took on a greater significance. If someone at school was mean to me, I couldn't shrug it off, as it had to be dissected and understood. It had to be analysed. If I could understand 'why' that was happening, then maybe I could find a solution to this problem. I tried to find the route cause of my feelings, those deviant feelings. Everything was dissected in a child-like manner. Were my choices in music, cereal and clothes all clues? If I ate something different, wore something harsher or watched something more aggressive, could I change? Was watching musicals, singing along to the original cast recording of Cats and dancing to disco a sign? I examined every aspect of my life, desperately searching for answers – answers that seemed so willfully elusive. Not only to me, but also to Mungojerrie and Rumpleteazer, they were a couple of curious cats…

Kids can be mean. They say stuff. Everyone knows that. Despite this, I took what they said to heart. Everything had the significance of the gospels. Every day I continued, burdened with fear, pain and a miserable life filled with heartache. It was around then that I started to have 'those' dreams. They were exceedingly timid, but to my innocent mind and me they were unbridled filth.

My first was dead simple. I was kissing my PE teacher, Mr. Green. I hadn't hitherto felt anything for him. He was the bastard who made us play football in the snow and watched us all in the showers, so I was shocked it was him in my dream as much as I was shocked that I was having these dreams at all.

In the dream I kissed him. That was it. I also had a very sloppy, inaccurate and slightly weird view of kissing it seemed. But still, there it was. I awoke in fear. These feelings had now infected my dreams. Like a noxious substance they had seeped into my subconscious mind and polluted my thoughts. Previously, my dreams had been the only place where I could escape my life and feel safe. My dreams were my only sanctuary. In fact going to sleep was a defense mechanism. Yet now they had been invaded and tainted by this toxin. I remember seeing Mr. Green that week and staring at him for answers. I found none.

These dreams continued. Then… it started to happen. Puberty arrived and it arrived early. My voice broke and hair stared to grow. Not only was I the first in my year to get pubes, I was the first by some noticeably wide margin. So what did all the kids start saying? They said that it was only gays that got hair around their cock. If I had been wiser, stronger, defiant I could have ignored that or rolled my eyes, but I began to wonder, was it true? Was this biological proof? Was this God actually hastening my path to manhood so that I may be punished early? The PE teachers would cram us into mass open plan showers. A large tiled pen with an entrance at one end and an exit at the other. We all had to go in and wait under the water. All these boys crammed together as if naked commuters on a packed underground train. We were so penned in we touched, rubbed and generally felt one another up without trying. The PE teachers would watch, comment and even invite certain boys to come to the front. Despite this claustrophobic intimacy, wherever I stood, there was a miraculous exclusion zone around me. No matter that they were grasping each other's cocks whilst gasping for air – no one wanted to be near 'the pubes.' I was Wonder Woman and I had curly growth.

I used to stand, lukewarm water splashing around me, scolding me as I stood burning scarlet in shame. People stared, laughed, abuse was shouted and punches thrown. I prayed, I prayed hard that I wouldn't get an erection. That would be the end.

The abuse became so intense that I knew I had to avoid PE. Accordingly I started up my little forgery business, forging notes to avoid gym class. I am not sure whether they knew or not, but they allowed me to bunk off (I was hardly a loss at football). Only once they did challenge me. They asked why my mother wrote like a twelve year old? I still remember looking as cool as I could, "She's stupid," I said. "It's embarrassing," I added and just walked off with my head lowered.

I have no idea whether they bought that story, but it brought a near end to my days doing sports at school. Mercifully, it wasn't too long before three other uneasy, unwilling and terrified chaps also joined the early development club. The boys began to realise that maybe, just maybe, all this hair growth was normal after all. This was certified when our teachers, notably Mr. Green, stripped and joined us all in the showers one day. Then we could all see what a grown man's tackle looked like.

No one thought I was gay now. In fact there was a very brief period when I was hailed as an untouchable. I was clearly a man and they were merely boys. I was (by definition of being first) evidently the manliest. Oh the delicious irony. Naturally, that lasted only long enough for the critical mass to get hair and then it was back to the status quo.

Some time after this development a new boy joined the school. He was probably the campest person I had ever seen. He was like a massive camp lightening rod. All attention, almost overnight went straight to him. I felt sorry for him, but in truth I was happy for the break. He didn't help himself though. He'd mince, scratch, pirouette, bitch, insult and just do everything possible to attract attention. For Pete's sake, he wore a chiffon blouse to PE lessons… even I saw that as a suicide note. He'd frequently tell everyone (teachers included) he was superior to them. His father was rich and so he could, "buy the shitty little hovel you no doubt live in and make your family my slaves." He attracted little sympathy!

I do recall once when, in a moment of sheer weirdness, he attacked me. That wasn't odd. He attacked loads of people. I walked into class with scratches over my face and blood cascading down my cheeks. I was asked who'd done it. I just about said his name when a gang of boys went out and promptly beat him up. I was never sure why anyone wanted to stand up for me, but I didn't mind. For once in my entire life, I felt like I was part of something, something that would look out for me. I was so grateful for that intervention, it made me feel safer.

Soon after that day, the boy left our school. Word ripped through the school that he'd committed suicide. He hadn't. I saw him shopping. Yet this spooked the teachers into action. Fearful that I may follow him and it would all come out, they wanted to make sure I was okay and asked about the intimidation and bullying I had put up with over the years. Immediately it revealed to me that they had been aware all that time. They knew yet said and did nothing.

I felt irritated. Here was a 'too little, too late' insincere attempt at assuaging their guilt. So I told them: You knew. You knew all along and you did nothing. I can still see their faces. I can still see how they looked away. They couldn't look at me. I told them clearly – don't expect anything from me. Don't expect any help or support – you left me to rot. If they come knocking, I will spill the beans… I felt extraordinarily empowered after that. I hadn't faced down the bullies but I had confronted their enablers. After that, when I was getting abuse in class, I'd stand up and simply walk out. The teachers had no authority over me. It felt odd. It wasn't liberating, but it did give me a sense of purpose. I wasn't going to put up with that shit any longer.

Imagine if they had offered help earlier on? Imagine if someone had reached out? Imagine if one of them had dispelled some of the stupid myths and beliefs about being gay? Imagine how much happier my life would have been? Instead of spending a childhood aging, I could have smiled every once in a while. People say I was born middle aged – that's the reason why.

Yet it was my defiance that proved to be the turning point for me. Oddly enough it wasn't any sense of empowerment that changed my attitude, it was their shame. It was the odious sight of them turning away in embarrassed recognition. I genuinely loathed them for that. I soon realised then that people wouldn't protect me. No one was there to look after me, so I had better do it myself. As a result, I switched from being scared to being a bit 'fuck you and the horse you rode in on.' It was (and is) a dysfunctional defiance. That same insolence moulds and shapes me today. It is a personality trait that has offended and isolated more than it has ever attracted.

Many have said I am provocative, aggressive and so on. Sometimes they have a point, other times my reputation precedes me. Suffice to say; when I go away and analyse the comments (as I still do), I think I know the origin. I understand the source. It was the need to be as seemingly strong as an old oak. It was the necessity of showing that I was not going to be bullied or cowered again. I was going to put on an act of unending defiance. I just haven't worked out how to stop that – or whether I can (or should).

It's because of this journey that I've been able to contemplate writing this book. I just hope that someone, anyone, reading this will think 'I relate to that!' In so doing, hopefully, they will be spared the pain of isolation, loneliness and discovery that I went through. I hope they can learn from me and lead happy fulfilled lives. If you do, drop me a line. I like letters…

PENPALS

I was a keen writer in my youth. I had pen pals all over the country and across the globe. Similar aged children would send me pictures of the Amalfi Coast, Melbourne, Amsterdam etc. and I would reciprocate with a picture of our local shopping centre, shortly after a storm, when a rainbow seemingly landed in the benefits office. Locally, it was believed to be where all the gold lay.

I loved the excitement of getting a letter. Various coloured envelopes from across the world would plop onto the doormat and I would tear them open desperate to know what trivial things were happening in someone else's life. The sense of anticipation was all part of the thrill. When would the letter come? Would the lovely postman bring me international greetings today?

I know I am going to sound old, but in an age where everything is on demand, instant and downloadable, we miss out on that sense of anticipation and longing. I think that's a shame, although I appreciate that I am probably just being a fuddy duddy. (And using the term fuddy duddy confirms it...)

I wanted to ensure that I never had too long to wait, so I had pen pals everywhere and wrote to them on a regular basis. I probably had twenty or so at any one time. Typically, they were girls, as boys didn't usually sit down at a bureau and write long letters on purple paper about their lives. I did have the odd male pen pal but they were always short lived. Then came my Dutch pen pal. I was probably early teens when we started to correspond. It all started innocently enough. Lots of stories about school, our local towns, families, music tastes etc. It was all fairly dull.

Then came a letter where he explained to me in considerable depth and eye-watering accuracy his recent experience of masturbating whilst travelling on a bus. This wasn't what I'd expected. I was doubtful I'd see that featured in the Smash Hits letters section anytime soon. I didn't really know what to make of this revelation. Was I supposed to reciprocate in kind? How could I? I never travelled on buses.

My reply glossed over that rather curious development and stuck to the usual things – Whether WHAM! were getting better, whether Simon Le Bon suited shorter hair and whether the Pet Shop Boys would be as big as Culture Club. These were the issues that mattered to straight teenage boys, not inappropriate displays of genital gratification.

He replied to say that he could sense that I was shocked.

I had been.

He explained that he was bisexual and that in the Netherlands things were different. Things that would be deemed socially unacceptable in the UK were perfectly permissible in Holland. I didn't doubt that, but having a wank on a bus? Even if no one was offended, it wasn't exactly classy. I also doubted that Dutch commuters would share his open-minded view. He went further, explaining how he'd done it at the cinema too. Now I don't know about you, but when I was watching Marty McFly go back to 1955, I didn't naturally think it was time to knock one out. That was just odd.

I suspected that our epistolary relationship was nearing an end. I had nothing to bat back with. He was satisfying his sexual desires in public places whereas I had acne and thought I was living dangerously if I had a Cherry Coke and a bar of chocolate at the same time. I doubt that would have set his heart racing. Besides, I had only just discovered the solo pleasures of the flesh. Knowing that Jesus was eavesdropping on my every thought, I had held out for as long as I could, but the inevitable *had* to happen. Yet despite this, I doubted whether me sharing the fact my first ever wank was whilst watching the Liverpool-based soap opera Brookside, would be quite as exciting as bashing one out on the top deck of the No.43 to Groningen Centrum.

I can remember that first time clearly. I was up in my room watching my grainy black and white portable TV. It wasn't like I'd just heard the theme music and found myself with a semi. I just settled down to watch it, when the urge took me. It was an exciting time in the Corkhill house and I was rather enamored with one of the family. As I lay on my bed watching their antics, the desire grew and grew until such time I decided to end years and years of waiting. So there, in my little bedroom staring at the small screen of a portable TV, I joined in with that all-so popular teenage pursuit of masturbation. I doubt there will be others who managed it whilst looking at Billy Corkhill or timing their first ever climax to coincide with a dramatic story revelation that shook the plotline. I was sent sprawling back into my pillow as the relief of many years of pent up frustration broke free, whilst simultaneously, lunging forward to see what was going to happen next. That was rather typical of me… Despite this, I wondered whether my Dutch pen pal would find that story comparable with his antics on a bus. 'So yeah, I knocked one out watching TV.' I'd boast with a knowing smile. He'd stare back at me. 'Was this in superstore in front of loads of horrified onlookers? Were you in Rumbelows window?'

I'd be forced to look to the floor and mumble, 'Nah, just at home in my bedroom.' It didn't have any edge and my stories didn't make my world sound exciting – because it wasn't! He asked me if I was keen to get letters from a friend of his too. I had my reservations. Would this be more public transport indiscretion? I decided to take a chance and said yes. Maybe he was normal? It turned out that his friend was a bit older and worked in a bar. He too (like everyone in the Netherlands seemingly) was bisexual.

One day I got a letter from this other guy that explained in blunt, but characteristically detailed fashion, how he was horny and drunk. How he wanted to fuck someone and (I remember this clearly) "I would love to be inside you right now." That came as a shock. To someone who wrote letters on scented, coloured paper detailing my favorite singers on the Band Aid single – in order of best voice and hairstyle – this was a bolt from the blue. Not only that but I wasn't sure what he meant. Inside me how? Like a kiss? What other way could it be? (I was that naive).

Then, because of my genuine innocence/stupidity I wanted to seek counsel on what he could mean. Be inside me? I had no idea what that might relate to. So I did what every other sane teenage boy would do. I asked my parents. I can remember asking them what my Dutch pen pal meant when he said he wanted to be inside me. We were eating breakfast. Everything stopped dead. I heard half a wheat cereal brick land with a splash into a bowl of milk.

Still perplexed, I watched their reactions as they looked at me, at one another, at me, at one another again until one said, "Where did you hear that from?"

Curious about their reaction, I told them. Swallowing hard on their morning repast they asked to see the letter and each in turn read it in silence.

"So what does he mean?" I asked like an idiot.

They looked back at me as if unsure of my stupid sincerity. This letter affirmed what I had been getting up to. It surely confirmed everything… didn't it?

"What?" Was all I could say, looking at their panicked faces.

"I don't think you should write back to him." My dad said, eventually.

"Oh," I offered confused. I knew these letters were a trifle dull. What he did at work, what he was feeling (usually himself) but surely that wasn't a reason to abandon someone? Then the thought occurred to me, maybe he meant something else. Something beyond my comprehension. "Was that rude?" I asked finally. They both nodded, not entirely sure how to explain anal sex to a socially backward teenager who was also probably gay.

I asked whether I should write and explain why I wasn't writing back, but my father advised silence hereafter.

"Well he has our address," I said matter of fact. "Let's hope he doesn't show up and ask why I am ignoring him. He did say he was happy to visit."

I think I can genuinely say that my parents lost all colour in their faces. The idea that a marauding Dutchman wanted bottom-based fun with their daft teenage son, and was prepared to fly to the UK to get it, was evidently a terrifying prospect. Had I realised then what was actually happening I dare say I'd have lost sleep too. As it was, I just trotted off to school as my mother went to <u>that</u> kitchen draw and had a pill from it.

My first ever 'gay' experience was with a guy at college. He was theatrically camp, pencil thin, immaculately tailored and the quintessential 'gay'. He wasn't my type, but when there is only one port in a storm...

Despite being as gay as a flute he fervently hoped that his dad, a builder, hadn't twigged his son enjoyed cock. The fact that his gayness could be seen from space was probably a stumbling block to this. His father had long since resigned himself to the fact that whilst his sons would follow him into the building trade, Joshua was going to be the exception.

The notion that he was letting his dad down caused him genuine pain and probably countless nights sleep. Every time I visited their house, Josh would do everything to keep me out of sight, as if the fact he had a male friend would only confirm his father's worst suspicions. Either that or because I was a dubiously camp male friend. Had I walked with the co-ordination of a breezeblock and had the vocal dexterity to match, he may have slept easier. Instead I would squeal and say things like, "I love that pelmet on those curtains. I bet they're only drip dry."

I did try and reassure him that it was ok to have a male friend, after all, his brothers had male friends. He'd just sigh and tell me that was very different.

"They're knuckle dragging cave dwellers that just go out to get drunk," he said by means of distinction. "They keep asking me to join them but I can't think of anything worse." He'd add with a shiver.

There was a gulf between Josh and his family, which I found very sad. I thought that his brothers were actually trying to reach out and help. They knew. The postman knew. The blind woman over the road who suffered from agoraphobia and hadn't left her house in 50 years knew. Maybe his brothers cared more than he knew. Then again, maybe they were as boorish as Josh said and they just wanted to see their little brother drunk. I don't know. But Josh tried his best to keep his life as secret as possible – which only made matters worse. He was painfully gay.

It also didn't help that he was also a lightening rod at college. Someone that theatrically camp is bound to attract attention. The fact we were friendly to one another confirmed his sexuality and so, I assume, also mine. That said, no one ever mentioned sexuality. It was never discussed; it was the ultimate taboo for my fellow college students. Everyone embraced this left-wing notion that every person was equal whatever their sexuality. They'd say soothing things about gay people and then go and discriminate against them in their day-to-day actions. It always made me feel quite vexed. It was the hypocrisy of enjoying the soothing balm of self-righteous equality in discussions and then overlooking prejudice in their day-to-day lives.

They were knobs.

On one occasion after about a year or so of friendship, we were spending some time with one another but not so much that we saw each other as good friends. Accordingly, we never discussed 'it'. We talked about music, our families etc. but never the huge pink elephant in the room.

Josh looked down on me, a lot. In fairness to him, he looked down on everyone. Everyone was beneath him. He thought himself superior to everyone, which was always quite irritating. Yes he was well educated, articulate and had money behind him (albeit new money…) but he wasn't in any real way superior to me or anyone else. In fact, his attitude made him quite the social outcast, which he took to assume was related to his sexuality. I once saw a greetings card that said: 'It's not homophobia, it's just everyone hates you.' I wish I'd seen that back then, he needed to understand that.

Josh had experienced things that, frankly, should have ended in a prison sentence. In his mid to late teens he'd had a full-on sexual relationship with his music teacher. A thin bearded man who, from what I could see, used to take Josh's father's money only to play with his son's instrument. Josh was very guarded about this and I was the only person who knew about it. The relationship had been fairly frenetic and all very 'real'. Not withstanding it was illegal then for anyone under twenty-one to engage in gay sex, to be shagging your teenage pupil was national newspaper scandal level. Their relationship was, as far as the teacher was concerned, physical. My friend thought it was more than that and became very bitter (and very hard to deal with) when they broke up. That happened when the teacher got another pupil that he preferred.

Josh had contemplated informing his father that the teacher was screwing both of them. Josh physically and his father for the fees. He decided against doing so as he was sure his father and brothers would likely end the man's life. It was a dark, brooding situation. Not only did Josh carry the pain and regret that he was failing his father, he'd had a secret love affair which, if ever discovered, would end very badly for everyone.

Josh, being old beyond his years, declared that he was coping with it all, that he was emotionally up to the immense challenge of living every part of his life behind real and emotional doors. It took a far heavier toll on him than he was aware and I would be stunned if it didn't cause him pain today. Not only that, but there were no people to turn to. The college chaplain might inform the Chancellor. The college counsellor may have been a point of call, however, this was a time when 'Section 28' was becoming law. Section 28 prohibited any schools from 'promoting' homosexuality. This included talking about its existence. Even saying, 'I know you are gay, but don't worry you'll be fine,' to a suicidal pupil would be considered promoting it and was thus illegal. At the time there was a McCarthy style witch-hunt in the teaching profession for anyone who dared to promote tomorrow's AIDS carriers. (Do you think I exaggerate?) It was law for 15 years. So being gay didn't exist for Josh, many others or me. As a result he lived his life with pedophiles and bullies. We all did.

It was a dark time for young gay kids. Especially ones who were being emotionally groomed and physically abused. Josh knew what he was doing up to a point, of that I am sure, but I doubt if he'd ever have been in that situation had he felt free to be who he was. He thought he could handle being in a 'relationship' with his teacher when in fact he was just being used. That enormous sting of rejection that inevitably followed did tremendous damage.

So yeah, this is what it was like being gay in the late 1980s! Against this backdrop of dirty old men, religious puritans and the much maligned builders of Britain, Josh and I had been getting on. We'd started to share some worries about our feelings. We weren't entirely open and free flowing, but a channel existed. In some respects it was a wonderful relief to be able to say these words out loud. You were terrified to talk about this with just anyone for fear you'd be reported to the educational Stasi. Conversely, however, talking about it also made the feelings real and that was the last thing either of us wanted.

One afternoon, after a few weeks of getting along well, he asked if I wanted to babysit with him. His charge would be in bed early enough and we could watch TV and talk. His employers had said he could invite a friend over and had ordered a pizza for us. I agreed, seeing nothing sinister or odd about it. Friends helped friends babysit. They are largely girls who do this, but that was just gender stereotyping!

So one Saturday night with the child fast asleep (actually asleep when we arrived) we were left alone in the house with a steaming hot pizza and unlocked booze cabinet. I didn't drink alcohol and was quite anti-alcohol, so the contents of said cabinet didn't interest me. Despite this, I noticed that Josh was drinking, something he didn't usually do.

Within no time at all, the pizza barely warm, he said he wanted to open up and share his feelings with me. I slumped back into the sofa in this stranger's house and grabbed a slice of pizza so kindly paid for by our hosts. I sat and I listened whilst continually topping myself up with fast food. I must have drifted off as I missed it at first, juggling with strings of molten mozzarella. His words were delivered, but seemed to take an age to reach my comprehension. When they did, I was left to splutter "Sorry?" as pepperoni protruded from my mouth.

"Do you want to or not?" he asked briskly.

I thought about what he'd said. The words seemed blurred in my memory and yet at the same time their emotional energy cut like a razor. Basically, he wanted us to get jiggy.

I was frozen in every conceivable way. It wasn't because he'd asked me; it was simply that I finally had an opportunity to explore and experiment. This guy knew what he was doing. He'd done it before. I had zero idea what IT was or would be, but whatever it was, Josh knew.

We sat in silence.

The terraced house with its traditional Victorian layout and period features seemed to look at me and raise an eyebrow. It was dusk and I was miles from home. I could have said no and left. Said no and just sat there in awkward silence. I could have played for time or… or… I could just say yes.

The idea of doing something, anything with another man was mind blowing. The magnitude of what had been proposed couldn't be accurately measured in the emotional soul of a confused teenager. Especially one who had been brought up on a diet of all things gay are evil. This was up there with discovering Hitler lived in your attic or landing on Mars to find a Starbucks already there and open for business.

In that small living room, on that street, in that town, we were both being excruciatingly honest. More honest than I had been in my entire life or would be for many years to come. I didn't seek to feign offence, deny my feelings or even run from them. I seriously considered the offer of going upstairs and having "some fun."

Images raced through my mind of naked bodies writhing together. I knew that this could answer a lot of questions. I also knew that it would change my relationship with Josh forever. If all went well would we become boyfriends? The notion that two men could go out like a regular couple seemed utterly abstract to me. Men and women went out, men and men had shameful sex beyond the glare of public view before going home to feel the pang of loneliness. Men couldn't be romantic. That was for girls. By extension, if a man was romantic he was really a girl and should just have the operation. Although this may seem archaic, that was how popular culture tried to make us feel. Somewhat like Iran today.

The notion of becoming boyfriends was so alien to me that he could have suggested that we walk bare foot up the Eiffel Tower, backwards, naked and covered in honey and I would have thought that proposition more sensible. Yet, when I considered what it might mean or lead to, all I could think of was the bodies together. The answers. The possible satisfaction. I turned to Josh who was perched on the edge of the old sofa. "Okay," I said, after what felt like weeks of consideration.

He seemed somewhat surprised and raised his eyebrows

theatrically. Given how genuinely pantomime camp he was, this was probably just his default reaction to anything and everything. I dare say he looked like that when he peeled a banana. We both stood up hesitantly and walked nervously to the stairs. The people who had gone out for a meal had no idea that in their bedroom, next to the room housing their sleeping child an 'aberration' was about to occur. If the house was haunted we were about the give the ghost a first…

"Hold on," said Josh and walked into the kitchen. He grabbed a bottle of spirits from the top of the fridge, whipped the top off and drank several mouthfuls of the stuff in no time. "Want some?" he asked.

"No," I said, irritated. "I don't drink." I couldn't believe that he'd forgotten my stance on alcohol. Here we were about to engage in a truly life changing situation and he offered me booze! "Why did you offer me some, why are you drinking?" I asked moodily. In that moment I felt a genuine annoyance at this small, seemingly meaningless action. He knew that I didn't drink and why. So why ask?

He looked at me startled. "Dutch courage," was his matter of fact reply.

I didn't say anything but the damage had been done. There may have been innumerable drunken nights lying ahead in my future, but that night I was sober and wanted to be. I wanted the experience to be attributed to desire, fun, exploration, discovery, adolescence, stupidity – anything but drunkenness. This had to make sense, it had to mean something.

It never occurred to me that he could be nervous. I never considered that he too might be scared about what it might mean. Being taken advantage of by an adult is one thing, but someone of your own age makes it all frighteningly real.

He apologised and pushed passed me and headed up stairs. I followed, still irritated but trying instead to focus on the writhing bodies that enjoyed their fun in my mind's eye. We got up to the top of the stairs and after (responsibly) checking on the sleeping child, pushed an old wooden door open to the bedroom. It was a rather small space with a dark wooden bed frame, dark blue sheets and a large wooden wardrobe. There were net curtains at the window affording us privacy for the underage homosexual voyage of discovery that was about to stain the royal blue sheets.

I sat nervously on the end of the bed whereas Josh had almost dived onto the bed, seemingly mistaking its blue for an infinity pool. I began to have my doubts. Should I? What if someone walked in? What if my parents found out? Did I really want to? This man was nice enough but he wasn't my type and he thought he was better than me. Was he using me?

"It'll be alright," he said from behind me and very softly caressed my back. I was more aware of the world around me at that point than any other moment in my life since. I could have told you if a baby was crying in the next town, let alone the next room, I was that alert.

"You knew this was going to happen," he said, presumably to re-assure me. I hadn't, so it came as a surprise that he thought that. "You know I've always fancied you." Again, more news to me. I know that I've acquired a reputation for being as blind as a bat when someone is flirting with me, but this was something else. "I've told you before, you're a bit of rough. A craggy diamond, I like that." He offered, temptingly…

He continued to caress my back as he spoke; it felt like he was trying to wind a child – only in very slow motion. The writhing bodies gave way to a sense that I was having liniment rubbed into my back.

Me – a bit of rough? I was as rough as a powder puff. Surely he was being ironic. To discover that he meant it was both shocking and impressive.

"I've changed my mind." I said and turned to him. "Sorry."

He pulled his hand away and stared at me angrily. "Why?" He asked.

The truth was I didn't like his patronising tone. Bit of rough? Who did he think I was? In what was to become the first in a life-long series of knee-jerk emotional reactions, I elected to make my first time with a man slightly more meaningful than with a guy who had to get drunk just to touch me and then say I was a bit of rough. I am sure his dad and brothers would have found that analogy quite hilarious had they known I was labelled a bit of rough.

"I don't know," I lied. "I just… I think it'll make our friendship weird."

He looked down at the bare varnished wooden floor. The room, which was already small but felt smaller because of the dark colours, closed in further still.

"It'll be even weirder if we walk away now. Come on, it'll be totally fine." He said and returned to the expectant caressing once again.

I stood up. "Sorry," I said and promptly left the bedroom.

I travelled down the stairs alone and stood in the hallway unsure of what to do. He appeared at the top of the stairs shaking his head and walked down towards me sulkily. I knew then that our friendship was over. I knew that we'd never speak again. I also knew what to do if I wanted to save it – I had to use my body.

We sat in silence as the pizza remains grew stone cold. After some time, I stood to leave just as homeowners arrived back, bursting through the door with smiles on their faces. After checking on the baby, the father said. "Right lads, I'll drop you home. Okay if I take you separately as I've got loads of shit in the car?"

Josh looked at me and then at the man. "That suits us fine," he said smiling weakly.

With that, my first gay friend and experience – the tender touch of an expectant teen – was over. We never spoke again. He never looked at me again. It was as if I never existed. I felt the sting of bitterness that coursed through his veins. Yet I felt no sense of injustice, just sadness that he felt so bad.

In the days that followed I knew I had been right. I knew I was right to stick to my belief that the first time had to be special. Even in the depths of future denial I still maintained that view. I wanted it to be meaningful. Maybe not exactly making love, but I needed it to be a little bit special, not just a night of throwaway sex.

Oh dear Lord, was I really that naïve? What a fool…

A NEW DAWN?

Moving away to University felt exciting and liberating. I wasn't in the slightest bit nervous. I didn't even think about it. Even when I turned up at my new home, a Victorian villa that had seen better days, only to discover that I was to be spending my first year sharing a bedroom with two other guys. In fact, when I got into my room and discovered that my bed (yes, they were allocated) was actually a rickety camp bed behind the door, I still remained upbeat.

This may have dismayed others, but to me it just felt like I was about to embark upon something new and exciting. Things that terrified others looked rather appetising to me. I arrived, gradually met the other guys who would be living in the house with me and surveyed my new bedroom.

In the interests of full disclosure, I should point out that I didn't have a typical student experience. We didn't have rats, damp bedsits and evil landlords. It was a bit more Baywatch than Boot Camp. Our campus overlooked the sea. As did my bedroom with sweeping views across the coast from our delightful bay window. So wonderful was it that we arranged our only comfortable chairs facing out so that we could all just drink in the spectacular view.

We each brought something communal to the party. I brought a TV, one of the guys brought a HiFi and the other brought copious amounts of body hair that he shed when he sneezed. We shared a bathroom with the two guys in the room next door. There were five of us, one bathroom and ten of us sharing the small toilet.

After all the introductions, the agitated laughs at bad jokes it was off for a week of social Fresher frivolities that had been planned. This included the usual three legged pub crawl, trips to night clubs, a revue for the Rag charity but also such wonderful experiences as a boat-based pub crawl where we visited many pubs along the river and then partied on the boat and had BBQs on the beach.

It sounds terribly posh doesn't it? I don't think it was.

Well, maybe a smidge.

It wasn't long before I realised that actually, this wasn't going to map out the way I had imagined. The excitement and elation I had felt arriving soon gave way to massively powerful depression. I just wanted out. But where? The Pet Shop Boys song, 'This Must Be The Place I've Waited Years To Leave,' was always on the black stack HiFi and it seemed to sum everything up. I had waited years to get to university and now, I felt like I had to leave.

It is no exaggeration to say that after a few days I was shaken to the core when an overpowering, hitherto dormant, depression awoke within me. It was unbelievably powerful. By the end of my first week I was in tears most nights. Frankly, it was embarrassing. I was embarrassing. I cringe now thinking about it. I am happy to confess I must have seemed like a total knob. Yet I couldn't control the bloody thing.

It wasn't long before I realised that no matter how hard I tried, I was not, nor was I ever going to be, one of the lads. I had hoped, in some strange unfathomable way, that when I got to university everything would sort itself out. Like a sofa bed – as soon as I had room to stretch, the transformation would astound. I had taken to Jane when I left the fishermen and I had hoped, in some juvenile sense of optimism, that moving to Uni would eradicate the feelings at college. It had never occurred to me that the exact opposite would happen. I never gave houseroom to the possibility these feelings wouldn't simply melt away when I was allowed space to be… It didn't take long to realise that instead of simmering down, every emotion that had been tucked neatly away was being turned up to boiling point. My sofa wasn't turning into a bed it was turning into a homosexual.

All of the other guys had years of life on me. Having to keep my confused sexuality hidden, buried and in the shadows as much possible, I had never lived. I was young and very, very naive. I hadn't kissed anyone (discounting the girls at school). In fact, I hadn't even had an alcoholic drink. I hadn't kissed the barmaid, never mind had a sniff of her apron. I lived in a little curled up ball of fear. Scared of the outside world and terrified of the world inside. Whereas most kids kiss behind the bike sheds, date, have those silly teenage fumbles and explorations, I had none of that. One guilty abandoned back rub in a small terrace was hardly in the same league.

The guys had full and meaningful times in education. Socially they'd spent their time with their mates talking about girls. I hadn't had any of that. I'd spent my time with no one wanting to talk to me because they couldn't make out who or what I was. Even if I had joined in, what was I going to talk about? I wasn't actually aware of my sexuality so couldn't talk about it. I knew I had those feelings, but were they real? Besides, I wanted to fit in more than I wanted a boyfriend (dear God) so I would have ended up making an unconvincing attempt to talk about tits. Like a comedy letch, I would have 'fwoared,' at 'ladies with big boobs'. I would have been growing as a man and talking like a child. Seducing straight from the Carry On films. It would have fooled no one.

I was surrounded by these worldly souls that seemed normal and cool. I was desperate to fit in. As anyone who has shared similar experiences will tell you, the minute you try to fit in is the minute you stick out – like a very sore, throbbing thumb. We were all on the verge of turning 20. Even the dullest kid had been allowed (and enjoyed) those rites of passage from childhood into adulthood, yet humbly and innocently I'd gone without. I felt kind of cheated. Why couldn't I have had a decent experience growing up? I went to one teenage party and it was as chaste as a prayer meeting. I had tried to host a teenage party but the house got trashed and within an hour I had to call the police. So, you know, that had passed me by. Emotionally I was closer to early teens that early twenties.

I was desperate to be the person I thought the people at university wanted me to be. They drank alcohol and got drunk, so that's what I did. I held off for a bit, as I didn't know what this magic elixir would do to me. When I did succumb it hit me for six. The years they had on me showed. I was like a teenager with his first beer. I was a loud obnoxious tit. A very annoying one at that.

In fact, I was a teenager with my very first beer… All of those embarrassing parties at school, those secret drinking sessions with your friends trying not to get caught by your parents or the police, all of that was missing from my emotional timeline. I had hit puberty, skipped teenage life and was suddenly in a bar surrounded by men and women and far from home. I was genuinely out of my depth.

Secretly I hoped university would be a springboard that would propel me into adulthood and normality. I soon felt the pang of pain when my double hop somersault led to the same springboard hitting me on the back of the head as I fell, concussed.

At first the booze buzz was amazing. I was happier than ever. It allowed me the drunken hope of a better tomorrow. I engorged on this feel-good stuff. When drunk everything seemed possible. Sadly, however, my naivety soon discovered that alcohol had dangerous side effects… it smashed the locks from the door of my inner closet. Feelings that I had more or less contained for years burst forth in a messy fountain of attention seeking exaggeration. The Student Union bar was like the gatekeeper to a carnival of distressed emotions. I was drinking to keep up with guys who had been drinking for years. I was hopelessly out gunned. As soon as I reached a tipping point of inebriation I was on my own personal Pride parade. I was all for dancing down a street waving banners and flags. Alcohol was the liberator. Sobriety, however, was the evil bastard guard who kept the keys to my cell and who always tracked me down in the morning and locked me away again.

These feelings came as a genuine shock. What were they? I

hadn't ever allowed myself to feel these things. I hadn't allowed myself to experience these emotions so what were they, where were they coming from and how on earth could I stop them? I had hoped in some far off quarter of my mind that I may be able to ask people who maybe, just maybe, had been through it before. All universities have LGBT societies so I could ask them about these aberrant feelings that were stopping me from being one of the lads. Tragically for me, however, I had enrolled into the least gay campus in Western Europe. An LGBT society you say? Ha! There was no society, come to that, there were no other gay students. Not one. No one to speak to, no other beacons and no hope. It was just me with a big fuck-off neon pink arrow above my head that said 'emotionally volatile, closeted gay – beware.'

Typically there was a trigger point and the depression would hit. When that happened, I went from loud, annoying and a bit too in-your-face to the one breaking down in tears at the end of the night. Like an emotional teenage girl who had just discovered her favourite boy band was splitting up, I found myself in the highly unfavourable position of being an unpopular emotional wreck. It didn't take me long to assume my role as a bit of a social pariah as a result. I was dealing with basic emotions like a 13-year-old, yet I was surrounded by 20-somethings that thought I was a liability. They weren't wrong.

To their credit, my housemates would ask what was wrong and terrified anyone would find out, I lied and moved away from their attempts at comfort. They were puzzled. (I was behaving like Joshua did with his brothers, so maybe now I understood.) Here they were being good mates and trying to help but they just saw rejection for their efforts. In fairness, it doesn't take too many times at being rebuffed before you begin to lose interest and sympathy. I was just desperate to protect this dark, scary and dangerous secret. I knew that whatever it was, it would rip a hole right through my life; just at the point it was potentially getting interesting. At no point did I realise that hysterical tears, going on long walks to be alone and emotional blubbering were in themselves a whole heap of gay.

Everyone used to say that the way to 'forget' your problems was to get drunk. More to forget? More to drink! Therefore that's what I did. This created even bigger problems, even greater scenes and gained me a rather unflattering reputation. I certainly don't bloody well blame anyone for that!

A friend of mine said he heard a description of me around this time. I was likened to a housemate's rather dangerous teakettle. 'Unpredictable, quick to overheat and likely to break down at any moment.' Harsh, but spot on. I hate that description. It's 25 years later and I remember it word for word. I hate it because it was so true.

I used to see these guys (all male house) who all seemed well adjusted and settled. They were grown ups, sane, logical, ordinary and here was me – a whistling teakettle of uncontrollable emotion. I'd have given me a wide berth if I'd met me.

I decided that I needed a coping mechanism. Something that would give me the opportunity to remove myself from emotionally combustible situations. As such, I used to excuse myself from every evening's end and go for a long walk just before the marauding emotional darkness turned up with a bottle. In my sozzled mind, this was a masterstroke. I would walk and walk and walk and any emotions I had could be worked or walked out. I would walk for hours some nights. Anything that happened thereafter would be in the privacy of the darkened dunes. Either that or I would walk for so long that I was too exhausted to feel anything worth causing a scene over.

This was time for reflection; an attempt to understand what the hell was going on and also to try and save any dignity I had left. As we were within easy walking distance of a river and a beach, that's where I went. I'd sit by the sea and listen to the waves. I'd sit by the river in the sheet black of an estuary evening, with the birds breaking the silence of the night and just let the sounds soothe my nerves. A train would often travel on the headland opposite. Little rectangles of speeding light would fall onto the river, cascading a multitude of patterns on the water as the train took its occupants to some place exciting. The sound was minimal over the estuary but the sight was almost magical. Inevitably no one was around, so I could be alone with my thoughts and myself. If anyone had seen me they would have thought me odd, but the solitude of the night was my best friend then. Once, lying on my back in the sand dunes looking at the stars, trying to concentrate on the beautiful therapeutic waves rather than the chaos in my head, someone walked right past me and frankly I nearly shit myself. The beach at night was supposed to be mine. I would walk to the farthest side of the beach and just be.

I'd sit, sometimes sobbing, just trying to work out what the hell was happening to me. Even then I knew, but I didn't know... Couldn't I just turn that off? Couldn't I simply ignore it and wait for it to go away. The other guys coped, why couldn't I? What was wrong with me?

In the end, I became hyper responsive to any emotion. I began to pre-empt my emotions massively. If I thought a depressive surge was imminent, I would just get up and walk away. It was a survival technique more than anything. In no time at all, I had gone from an emotional liability to a loner who would just vanish for a walk. My plan to save my reputation served only to enhanced how odd I was. No one else did it. So I was alone in every sense of the word. People would ask me where I'd walk to and I'd tell them. 'I walked to this point, that place or I just sat by the sea.' Sometimes they'd ask why and I'd just go quiet and they'd change the subject.

I suspect they all knew, but either way they probably thought I was a fruit loop. I know I would. In all honesty, it was a miserable existence. And I had three years of this to come...

NOTHING LIKE A DAME?

Realising that I was not going to address these feelings by moping by the sea, I decided it was time to get proactive. I couldn't talk about this with anyone. There was one guy in my year that everyone thought was gay but he was a bit weird and deeply closeted. Besides, I was already sharing a bed with him.

Then it hit me! The only reason I thought I may be gay was because I hadn't enjoyed the warm, tender flesh of womanhood. It was like a thunderbolt. As soon as I lost my virginity and actually slept with a woman then surely, SURELY everything else would naturally fall into place. Wouldn't it?

I mean, what did I know? I had never had any sexual experience with a man. Yes, I had the odd stirrings and Scouse based soap experiences (as well as some confused fumbling), but on paper I was as straight as any other bloke. I just needed some experience. I hadn't kissed a woman for God's sake! How could I think I was gay until I had done that and decided it wasn't for me? I knew deep down that as soon as I experienced the soft touch of a lady's lips, I would be sorted. It was so obvious; I sat and wondered how it could have eluded me for so long? I wasn't afraid of my gay feelings; rather my straight ones bemused me. The guys would laugh when I told them what had happened. Then as soon as I had my girlfriend and my hilarious story was told, I'd win my dignity back and be admitted into the guys' club. Simple as that…

To prove this point, I started relationships with women in

earnest. In those early tentative years, I had one stable monogamous relationship. We may have had few things in common but we humped like rabbits.

As far as I was concerned, if practice made perfect, then so long as I did it often enough something in me would change. It wasn't a conscious thing, a decision to lie, it just seemed like it was what I needed to do. As a theatre student (another clue?) we were being taught that the way to successfully 'get into character' was to immerse ourselves into the role entirely. To be at one with the character – you had to be the character. Stanislavski's method of character acting meant that I had to become the character I wanted to play. So… as I wanted to be a straight man with an uneventful life, I needed to rehearse and practice as often as possible. I needed to be a straight man with an uneventful life. I'd think like the character, act like the character and hump like the character… then I would BE that character. So very obvious.

Obviously, I could have taken a Brechtian approach and we'd have had sex with all the lights on and narrated our actions without getting emotionally involved, but I doubt that would have been as popular or helped as much… (One for the drama buffs x)

Although I wasn't aware of this nonsense at the time, I was trying to make myself straight by playing a role. Stanislavski genuinely warned actors that they could irrevocably become like their characters if they did this immersion successfully. This was not about playing at something any more; this was potential life changing personality re-education. A sort of DIY gay conversion therapy.

This was powerful stuff and you had to treat the method with great respect. Accordingly, that's what I did… I mean, you have a headache – you take some painkillers. You have cancer – you get chemotherapy. You have sexual feelings for men – you take a woman to your bed three times a day until symptoms desist. Then, bingo, you're in character and free to enjoy a standing ovation. So… that's exactly what I did.

I set about finding a girl to make me a man. As I'd decided I should discard my timid, shy naive persona; I donned an arrogance and swagger that I was told the ladies loved. They must have done because they were very keen. My ego swelled as I had many women who expressed an interest. Already I was beginning to think my life was changing. I had just adopted a straight man's swagger and already they were flocking. This was a dead cert winner of a plan. Maybe this was a sign?

I had decided that one of the best ways to attract a woman would be to dance and dress evocatively. I would have the strut and the look. To that end I dug out a pair of old jeans that were tatty and torn but fairly figure hugging. Sadly, under each back pocket there was a wide tear in the denim. Each rip ran from one end of each jean pocket to the other – on both sides. It was like wearing two skin coloured smiles across my arse. Yet, despite that, this is what I wore out. Although the wind whistled around my arse, I danced, cavorted and writhed in full sight. This was the real me! 'Are you watching ladies?' I thought as I gave it everything in front of almost everyone in the college.

It's fair to say this caused a stir. People would comment on how bold I had been etc. Crucially, it worked. It wasn't long before I met a woman.

Of course, thinking about it now, maybe my choice of seduction spoke greater volumes than I was aware. Perhaps, just perhaps, it wasn't the best start to a heterosexual relationship to be seen dancing to Madonna's Vogue in arse-less chaps. Yet another clue? I rather suspect without knowing it I had probably just outed myself to everyone in that town. Oh, did I mention that I also vogued whilst I danced? Not to mention that I mimed along to all of the words too?

Yeah, I'll stop talking…

Actually, I was amused when I was told that my attire was too risqué by nightclub management and was asked to cover up my arse rips. I set about sewing rather glamourous fabric into the holes to cover my extremities and offer some added verve to my look. The fact that I A) sewed glamourous fabric, B) had glamourous fabric and C) wanted to co-ordinate my look, should have been a massive bloody beacon of gayness. Sadly, whilst this beacon blinded everyone around me, I remained in the dark. I think it is fair to say that a guy wearing arse-less chaps who vogues and sews glamourous fabric into his pants is probably not going to enter a long-lasting heterosexual relationship. Just a hunch.

Astonishingly, it was through this rhythmic display of tart glitz that I met a girl. (I know…) We'll call her Sarah. She was a rather nice girl, a part time Goth who had occasional halitosis. It wasn't long before I'd perfected the art of holding my breath and kissing. She often thought my piggish grunts were wild expressions of an unfettered passion, when in fact I was merely gasping for breath and trying to stay alive.

The general rule of such character acting is simple… if it isn't working then you aren't immersing yourself deeply enough. You need to redouble your efforts and push yourself harder and further. No emotional stone should remain unturned. As such, we'd go to her darkened bedroom with its purple lace draped over every lamp and The Cure intoning some lethargic melancholy in the background and I'd set about my work.

My character wanted to enjoy this. To enjoy it, however, my character had to understand every facet of the process. Before I could truly enjoy it, the process of lovemaking had to be thoroughly deconstructed, re-constructed and then – and only then – enjoyed.

Seemingly, the stereotype that men are only being interested in their own gratification – in, out and off to sleep – is largely true. I, on the other hand, was not like other men. Oh no. I was on a mission to perfect the task ahead of me. I wanted to understand my character and what motivated him. I concluded that the best way to do that was to study my equipment, my performance space and those I was acting with. As soon as I had grasped the tools of my trade, I was on to a winner. Once I was familiar with every stage direction then I could indulge in some improvisation. Without being conscious of it directly, this was a process for me, a project, like flipping a house… It would be over when I stopped fancying men. To get to that point I merely had to understand, learn and implement heterosexual practices on Sarah.

My core work ethic has always been the same – if you're going to do a job, then do it to the best of your ability. Learn on the job, read up on the subject and improve. That's exactly how I applied myself to this task too. I read up extensively on what to do and what women liked. I had researched techniques and successful procedures. I would squirrel myself away in the library and read women's interest magazines to get tips of the trade. As a result, our typical sessions would last for five, six, seven hours or more… We'd make out to a chill-out CD that was forever on repeat. That's what I thought hetero sex should be like. That's what women in women's magazines said it should be like. So that's what I did. Sarah was genuinely exhausted some nights, whilst I kept thinking – 'I need to concentrate on that nipple work…' 'Tomorrow we'll see if we can get that elusive eighth orgasm…'

As I was learning on the job, it didn't matter whether I was actually having fun. Acting is hard people. This was character research that would lead me to a path of heterosexuality. She'd look at me as if I were an alien when I told her she shouldn't worry about pleasuring me; it was my job to keep her happy.

Did she complain? God no, but she moaned a hell of a lot… Night after night, week after week I tried to get closer and closer to my character. As I felt no different in my outlook, I simply put in more hours. This research project was not going to fail because of a lack of effort on my behalf. She thought I was a sex addict.

Unbeknown to me I was getting a reputation as a man who basically gave a woman a full sexual MOT. I rotated the tyres, gave the under carriage a full going over, buffed the interior, ensured the bonnet was polished and flushed out all the pipes. It soon transpired that my attention to detail had not gone unnoticed in the kitchens where war stories were traded over tea and toast. To everyone's incredulity, Sarah would explain that I wasn't interested in my own pleasure but would spend all of my time on her. Her friends were so amazed that they'd tell their friends. Who then told theirs. Before long I was being solicited by an array of women in black outfits who wanted me to give them the same precision tune up. It also didn't take the men long to start complaining that I was giving them a bad reputation as girlfriends were complaining that they were less attentive than me. Oddly, my character was being discussed quite extensively and the reviews were all favourable. It was an astonishingly odd situation to be in. Moaned at by men for being too good a lover and sought after by women. Little did anyone know it was just an act…and that 'anyone' included me.

I was always coming up with different ideas and variations on our routine. How about edible body paint? What about a nice yogurt to smear and lick? Costumes? I suggested these as kinky twists in our nightly marathons of lovemaking. I thought it would keep us both interested and excited. Sadly, she declined. I tried to entice her with the prospect of me fishing out various yogurty summer fruits with my tongue, but it was not to be. She wasn't interested. She was a traditionalist. The prospect of having an organic gooseberry fool smeared over her lady garden, with me using my tongue to search for gooseberries, didn't quite appeal.

So I had to continue as before. Sarah liked the tongue-based part of my research. In fact an hour could slip by quite easily.

Well… for her. I had lock jaw a few times. Once my tongue had a strikingly powerful muscle spasm that evidently hit the spot because I thought she'd have to be peeled off the ceiling. Conversely, I thought my tongue was about to drop off…

My commitment to my part was never in question, but I was beginning to have doubts. After six months of intense physical workmanship, I began to wonder: how much longer was it going to take? Sarah had already pointed out that I was staring at men in a nightclub – not that I was aware of it. Increasingly I was finding the sex tedious. This was an experiment in sexual cleansing and it was showing no signs of success. I liked Sarah. She was a very kind and considerate person. She was always very tender and was always thinking about me, making small gestures to show her affections. I had never had that before and found it rather strange. Why was someone making such effort? I enjoyed our conversations and we did have a good time together. Just as I was beginning to think we should only be friends, she started to suggest she wanted more from our relationship. I don't blame her. I would have too if I had been her, but at that point we were drifting apart. I think that's why she asked for greater unity – to disguise the fact there was little or no 'us' anymore.

We'd met each other's families. When she came to visit my parents I looked upon it as if it were just another friend staying over. Heaven alone knows what stress and panic she experienced beforehand, getting introduced to the future in-laws. For my parents I suspect it was one of the few moments in my life where they dared to dream that there would be a happy ending. All that gossip and tittle-tattle that followed me round as a child would evaporate under a cloud of family albums and grand children's portraits. My parents were so happy that we were together they even allowed us to share a bed. Bless them! Yet despite this positivity and excitement, I always recall her stark words to me a mere hour after I had met her family for the first time. "Mum says you're nice but we'll never last." Not exactly cheering, but they could obviously see what lay ahead.

Towards the end of our relationship we went away for the weekend. We went to London. It was snowing. There was a moment where we stood in the middle of Parliament Square, the snow falling silently and not a car nor a person was about. We had this historic landmark to ourselves. We stood in the middle of the road, the snow was falling, the sights were captivating and I knew that the feeling should have been magical. She went to kiss me and I pushed her away. I can remember explaining that I don't much care for public displays of affection (which I don't) but I knew deep down the reasons why. It was because I didn't want to be seen. I knew then it was a lie. I knew I was conducting a deceit. Don't ask me how I still didn't realise why, but I didn't. Suffice to say we'd reached the end of the line. I hadn't meant to mislead, I certainly never lied, but I thought much like Dostoevsky's The Idiot. I was simply that, an idiot. Unaware and unable to see the trail of emotional destruction my actions were having. So we split up. I was told by a mutual friend that she missed the sex, but had a lot of course work to catch up on as she'd let her studies go when we were together. I considered that a win-win.

I decided that perhaps my research needed variety. Instead of playing at being in a relationship, I needed help being with women of all types. In short, I needed experience being attracted to lots of women, not just one. That's how men rolled, so that's what I needed to do. Thankfully I still had offers on the table.

I am well aware of just how much of a cock this makes me seem, but genuinely I had no idea what was going on. It's only looking back that I can see what was actually happening. These encounters were not emotional and I would tell the women that. It was never my intention to lie, deceive or dupe anyone. They told me that they were modern independent women and reassure me that they were just after physical encounters too. I soon learned that women lie to men to get what they want, just as men do to women. These women lied about not having emotional attachments, just as men lied about having them. Typically, they are both lies.

It all became far too complicated and involved. I touted myself as a simple guy who was up for no strings sex, women would say that's what they wanted and then declare their love for me. It got very messy.

One woman portrayed herself as a dominatrix. She'd heard the stories about me and wanted to 'tame' me. Show me how it was done. I was intrigued and she was certainly very forward. She came to my apartment after meeting up in a bar. I had barely had time to lock the front door when she started undressing me. Within minutes we were in bed together. She pushed me down to the bed, and straddled me with the words "I am going to ride you cowboy."

I lay back and tried to think of anything that would enable me to offer her something to actually mount. In due course there she was fully in situ. I lay there and waited to be ridden hard. Nothing. Count to ten… nothing. I opened an eye and looked up at her, there she was, frozen stiff. I sat up, she was still on top. I was beginning to wonder when the bucking bronco was going to kick in.

She looked at me nervously.

"What's wrong?" I asked. Was this all part of the game?

"Nothing," she snapped defiantly.

"Well it's not a stool," I replied sarcastically, waiting for the cowgirl to get busy.

She looked terrified and lost. I raised myself up and saw sheer panic in her eyes. I reached out to hold her and she slipped down next to me. She was cold and shaking.

I was still confused, what had spooked her? It couldn't be something I'd said?

It transpired that I was her first.

The bravado was an act. She was actually a timid person in every respect. She had assumed that if she pushed me enough I'd react and take over and that she would lose her virginity to a man who knew what he was doing. She hadn't realised that she'd gone too far, got me to the point where I thought, "oh go on then…"

She lay there crying, fearing how foolish she was and what others would think of her. I felt so atrocious for her, for what she'd experienced and what she was feeling. I knew things had to change. I comforted her as best I could and attempted to make her feel better. We dated for a while, but once the term ended, so did we. She was the last woman I ever slept with.

The experiment had failed and despite some very happy travelers on my journey, I felt even worse. Instead of curing the condition it had simply made me feel even more lost than ever. Yes, I had a reputation as a perfectionist in bed, but a lot of women also thought of me as a bit of a twat. I never wanted to get into a relationship – I never wanted to commit. Although the sexual traffic was usually one way, in their direction, they wanted more. I was unable to offer that. Although I told myself that's what I wanted, I always ran for the hills. Seemingly I'd let Stanislavski down.

I learned that most women gave more in bed than men. A lot more. A lot of women don't just perform a physical act; it's also an emotional one too. The physical satisfaction to these women is (to a greater or lesser degree) linked to their emotional state. A lot of women told me that they could be like men, that they could fuck someone and walk away no problems. I believed that. Maybe some can, but the ones I met enjoyed it more when they thought it was more than just sex.

I may have always been honest with the women, and I was, but they didn't believe me. They thought they could change me and got angry when they couldn't. Later on in life when men lied to me, I was left feeling as bad (or worse) than any of the women who had ever wanted more from me. Yet, I finally knew how they felt. If there is such a thing as karma, I experienced it first hand. Women wouldn't make me straight any more than the countless prayers I made as a child had. Surely now that I had all the evidence I could possibly amass, it was obvious I was gay. All I had to do was admit it and move on yes? Yes… Yes…?

MY FIRST. ISH.

The very first time I was intimate with a man was in the dying embers of my time at university. I had spent a long period of time in reflective celibacy after my previous forays and when it happened it came out of a non-event. I wasn't looking for it and if I'm honest I think he was just trying to get out of a taxi fare home, but perhaps I do myself a disservice.

It was some weeks since I had taken the boldest and bravest step in my life to date. I told a friend I thought I might be gay. The evidence was overwhelming. I had gone to his house and stood at one end of his room. It was early (ish) and he was still in bed. The room was in darkness, which suited me. I told him I had something really bad to tell him. I had silent tears rolling down my cheeks. Sitting up, his pillow propped against a wall, he looked at me earnestly.

"I think," I began… "I think I might be gay."

I didn't want to say I was gay. I think 'I might' be gay still allowed for a, 'oh actually hold on, I'm not!'

I stood there looking at the floor, terrified to see his reaction.

"Is that it?" he said and slumped back down into his bed.

I was shocked. Was that it? The thing that was corrupting my entire life. The announcement that was the hardest thing I had ever contemplated making, let alone actually having the courage to do it. Yeah, that was it, thanks.

"Yes!" I said surprisingly irritated.

"I thought you were going to say something bad, like you'd got off with my girlfriend." He said before vanishing under the covers.

It struck me as vastly peculiar that such a thing was a confession he'd expected to hear. It was him who had told me I had the reputation for the simmering temperamental teakettle. His girlfriend was very straight-laced. Oddly, I was offended on her behalf that she'd be unfaithful to him. Never mind that I would.

"It's a bloody big thing," I said finally.

His head remained under the duvet, but the words crept out from their place of warmth and slumber, "Only to you."

There, then and at that moment I had the sharpest smack across my face ever. Was that the case? Was it genuinely only a big deal to me? Did everyone else not give a shit? Was that possible or was he only saying that to make me feel better.

The silence that followed drew him out of his bed and he chatted with me about the implications. It felt surreal. At this point I was in the last few weeks of my last year. I had managed to survive all three years successfully convincing no one that I was straight. All the girls, the sloppy public displays of affection, the crude attempts at being 'normal' had all come to naught. No one knew who I really was (because I didn't know either). Accordingly, it was nigh on impossible to get to know me. In a sense, because I was trying to be someone I wasn't, I was actually pushing people away from me. My quest to behave like a normal person was actually making me abnormal.

Looking back I realise that had I just been myself, warts and all, it would have been nowhere near as bad as I feared and I would have made many more friends as a result. Maybe 'is that it?' would have been a universal reaction. But hey.

In fact, if I've learned one thing through all of this, it's more important to just be yourself than someone you think others want you to be. Easy said, more difficult done, I know. However, being yourself, good and bad, warts and all, is far more important than investing years of energy trying to be something else for others. Fuck them. So if you are reading this and are in the closet – blow the bloody doors off. It may get worse before it gets better, but you'll be a damn sight stronger to fight the challenges when you are just being yourself.

Back then, however, I wasn't only trying to be a person others wanted me to be. I was trying to be the person I thought I wanted to be. Also, lest we not forget, this wasn't a time of general gay acceptance. Being gay was still taboo. When I was at university the age of consent was not the same for straights as gays. Anything I did would be have been illegal and I could have been sent to jail, if reported. Being gay was still a relatively lonely and occasionally paranoid experience. You were either out and (seemingly) as strong as an ox or quietly alone. As there were no gay groups at university there wasn't anywhere to go. The police could stop you on the street and search you if they thought you were gay and off for some illicit outdoors fumbling.

I was only stopped once whilst out walking. I was carrying a bag of records. The police demanded to search my bag and proceeded to mock my taste in music. They took out each record and lambasted me. "Oh my God," one said looking into the bag, "you like the Pet Shop Boys? Why?" He then looked up at me with his face crumpled with disdain.

I set about trying to defend my love of the Pet Shop Boys whilst they mocked me for liking 'girls' music.' I set about explaining the boys' genius and range, but they just made noises that made me sound like I was a whiny girl. "We'll let you go and see your GIRLFRIEND," they said with laughter as I packed my records away. Thankfully, that was all the police harassment I experienced – at that point.

From where I lived there was only one gay bar and that was ten miles away. It had blacked out windows and no sign above the door. One would be forgiven for thinking it was a sleazy den of unbridled filth, yet it was just an ordinary boozer. Had they opened the windows up, people looking in would have wondered why the gays were drinking somewhere so dull! Yet the darkened windows made people think that all manners of sleaze were happening – which added to the distrust/prejudice. In a nutshell, if you were gay, you were on your own. As such, opportunities to meet people, to talk, to express your feelings were spartan.

Sadly, given my track record as an abnormal normal man, an emotional wreck and a social pariah, at my final summer ball I cut a rather lonely, pathetic figure. The balls and such like were always celebrations of heterosexuality. They were occasions to get drunk, have fun and cop off with the person you'd been fancying all year. Either that or it was a place to mistily rejoice in the magic of a carefree university life with your long-standing soul/best mate.

There were probably four gay students at my university at this point and the ones that were out were very out. I mean very out. The other few remained hidden away. The ones who were out resided in a very protective unit (or clique) that shielded them from the world. They sneered at me. I was scorned. I think I can see why now, but then I thought they were just being mean. Maybe they believed I knew I was gay and was snubbing them or was in deliberate denial. Maybe. In reality I had no real grasp on what was going on despite the obvious evidence. I found them and their attitude a bit intimidating. They embodied everything I feared about my feelings. There was no way I was going to embrace that. Besides, they all appeared to have immense confidence. I didn't.

Three years on, I stood alone and unhappier than ever. As the night drew to a close the couples filed out, the party boys raised hell in the bar, I stood in the shadows by the back of the hall and just watched and wondered what if…

I remember thinking that we lacked the panache of the Americans when it came to hosting such events. Yes the place had been done up, there was so much crepe paper we were an aggressive sneeze away from an inferno. However it looked like a Primary School Christmas Party. Trainee primary school teachers had cut lots of silly hippy words and phrases out of sugar paper. These were the same people who thought saying things like 'Mr. Froo Froo visited me yesterday and was so sad he cried tears of blood,' was a perfectly good euphemism for getting their period.

I stood, leaning against a tower of crash mats. They had been stacked neatly and shoved behind a large lush red velveteen curtain in a forlorn bid to retain the ball's mystical magic. The back of the hall, where I stood, was in shadow. The focus of the multi coloured lights that flickered and speckled their festive joy were directed towards the area earmarked for dancing. Music pumped out as the remaining dancers gave it their all, determined to see the night out to the very end.

I was (as was often) gripped with an all-pervasive sense of doom and depression. I was as miserable as sin. I wondered if I would ever be happy. I didn't see a life as a happy gay man or as a happy straight man. I wanted something that seemed so illusive – happiness. It genuinely felt that it was impossible to be happy and gay which was depressing as I was beginning to acknowledge I wasn't straight. Whatever was happening, I knew that I felt like shit. Smiling at people as they left I wondered if I'd ever be able to offer a genuine smile? I watched as people left and surveyed the last three years of my life. What a fuck up. I was sober and dismayed. This was a wreck of an opportunity. I wasn't sure what else I could have done, but I felt like I should have done something.

My sole survival technique had been to believe that it simply had to get better. By the sheer laws of probability I had to find some snatches of happiness somewhere at some point. Didn't I? If odious people could find love, then surely I could. Even if it meant I too was odious.

Just then, out of nowhere, a guy came up to me. I knew him, sort of. I knew he was the ex boyfriend of one of the guys who was out. He had left university but still lived locally. He popped up to various functions and events from time to time. I had spoken to him a few times but that was all. In total we'd probably spent 10 minutes in each other's company.

"You look bloody miserable." He said. I jumped. I hadn't been aware anyone else was near me.

I smiled a weak, watery smile.

"Having fun?" He asked playfully.

"The usual." I answered, dryly.

In a strange way, because I never considered the possibility that anything would ever happen with anyone, I just thought he was being chatty. Why else would he be talking to me?

We chatted for a while about the night, the DJ, the people, the lights, the curtains, the floor, the weather, dry skin, deep fat fryers – pretty much anything meaningless.

I began to think all might not be as simple as it looked. He was still talking to me. Why was he still talking to me? We stood in silence and watched inebriated twenty-something's dancing slowly and meaningfully to Whole Of The Moon by The Waterboys. The lights had been lowered to bat cave levels with a few tracing spotlights to suggest said moonlight. We stood in silence watching this scene and I began to wonder what was going on. Was he still there? Quick look. Yup.

The song ended and melancholic students, some in tears at the realisation that this was their last ever ball in the place they had come to regard as home, wandered out. The lights came up and, still singing choruses from their favourite songs and linking arms, the hall finally disgorged its last few revelers. Their singing was often out of sync, but they didn't care.

"Oh well," I said, as if I were caught in a conversation with a charity canvasser. At that point most people wished me well and left, but he stood rooted to the spot. In the light I could see something that I hadn't noticed before, a look. Hidden deep in his gentle brown eyes was a person talking to me. Talking to me without saying a word. It was as if I could see everything he was feeling. The vulnerabilities, the pain, the searching. Did I have a spooky insight or was I merely looking in a mirror? I wasn't sure, but I realised something was happening. I wasn't sure what, but something was.

My mouth was now as dry as the desert. I was panicking. I tried to speak but couldn't. I was literally transfixed to his blink-less stare. I am sure it looked weird but I was hooked in a tractor beam of emotion. I tried again to speak. My tongue was rasping in dry desperation. Nothing.

Finally, after about eight attempts I managed, "Do you want to come back for a coffee?"

Given that I lived in a small shared house with eight students, all female, I was pretty sure coffee was all it would be. Besides, what else could it be? To my astonishment, with a very gentle smile, he agreed. Was he taking advantage of me or was this real?

We left the building together, which in itself was very daring. We walked side by side, not sneakily out through the fire escape, but through the paper chain festooned halls, bathed in the full glare of fluorescent strips of light that always irritate the serenity of early morning darkness. People dumped large handfuls of shredded paper into black bin liners and watched as we left together. They all

knew he was gay and suspected I was – so this was bold. The fact
we were just going to have a coffee never crept into their minds.
The fact I was the only person thinking it was just going to be a
coffee might seem quaint.

We walked in silence back to my residence. A place we called,
ironically, a cottage. It was actually a converted garage. It was not
uncommon to find students bringing friends back for food and
drink, so this wasn't out of the ordinary. However, having someone
that hadn't been seen before and (usually) of the opposite sex in
the small hours meant something else. Had anyone walked in on us
making coffee then technically they wouldn't have thought
anything of it, but it was obvious to them that it might be more
than coffee.

So we made coffee. We sat and chatted and then went into my
room where there was (quite genuinely) more comfortable seating.
I sat on the bed. It's what I did, so that my guest could have the
one comfy chair. I didn't read anything into it as I always did it. I
never dreamt it would be a come-hither.

He came in and sat next to me.

There we were. Two men sitting on a single bed, our backs
against the wall (ha-ha) looking across my empty cavernous room
with me wondering what was going on. The occasional slurp
punctuated the otherwise perfect silence.

I finished my coffee in scaldingly record time and, jumping up,
asked, "You fancy another?"

He shook his head. I ran out of the room and into the kitchen
where the kettle was around boiling point. I made another coffee

and returned to find him where I'd left him. If anything he looked more comfortable. Having returned, I was now standing in the middle of the room. I was all at sea. Did I go and sit back on the bed? Did I sit in the chair? Did I go to the loo to buy some time? Did I down this drink and make another coffee? Did I offer to call a cab?

"Are you sure you don't want another coffee?" I spluttered.

He put his cup down and roundly said no. .

Okaaaaay. So. Erm. Ah.

"You coming to sit down?" he asked, seemingly aware of my inner chaos and turmoil.

I nodded like a toy dog bouncing up and down on the back shelf of a car. I had no idea what was happening, what I wanted to happen or what could happen. This wasn't so much a shock to me as an earthquake in personal evolution.

THERE WAS A MAN ON MY BED.

With manly bits and a hairy chest (I imagined…).

This wasn't something I had ever encountered before. I sat back down slowly and with such trepidation that I actually dropped the remainder of my coffee on my trousers.

I actually did that. For real. I sat there looking at my trousers with the coffee burning its way through the fabric with searing ease. I couldn't take them off, what on earth would that look like? I sat transfixed as the pain sored.

"You gonna take them off?" he asked.

Was that a come on? Was it concern? Was it just the blindingly obvious thing to do?

I jumped up again as the pain landed with a burning thud and quickly dropped my pants. I stood there, trying to kick them off over my shoes. It must have looked like I was attacking a small pile of laundry.

At the very moment I had wriggled free and kicked them across the room in the direction of my laundry bag, my bedroom door swung open. I jumped back up as if I had been caught red handed with the Mona Lisa. We both looked towards the door. A friend of mine, who had not seen me leave the ball, popped around to make sure I was well. Her face was scarlet when she saw us both. There I was standing with my trousers off and a gay man on my bed. It didn't take a mathematician to put two and two together on this one.

I looked up startled, curiously guilty and in need of an explanation. "I got them wet." I said to her.

That didn't help things.

She nodded. The guy giggled.

"Coffee." I added.

"Er, I'm fine thanks," she said.

"No, coffee – on my trousers." I said desperately.

She nodded. "Right. Well so long as you're okay, I'll be off."

She wished us both good night and departed. My door was a fire door, which meant it took an endless amount of time to close. We both watched as it made its way to being closed. When it finally did so, it seemed to close so with a judgmental thud.

"Well, that'll give her something to talk about," he said finally.

Still I stood in the room, my trousers gone, but my socks and boxers still on and a feint stinging on my thighs. If this was to be the first time, it wasn't quite how I had imagined it.

"Shall we go to bed?" he said matter of fact.

Shall we go and see a movie? Shall we have a coffee? Shall we close the window? Shall we go to bed?

All fairly innocent questions, but here was a man on my bed, wanting to get into the bed – with me. Together. Side by side.

"Um, yeah, ok." I said.

"To sleep." He said, as if to reassure.

"Sure!" I said, breezily, as if that's all I had planned anyway.

That's when I wondered if I was just a convenient taxi substitute. Surely, surely, he didn't just expect to come home with me and then go to sleep? Like we'd known each other all our lives. Was this a ruse or was he actually that full of himself?

He was good looking and he certainly had been around, but…? He stood up and undressing to his pants, he got into bed. I remained still. I walked over to the door and belatedly turned the lock. *Note to self, do that earlier on in future.* Did he just want a bed for the night?

A one-night stand?

A long-term relationship?

A cheap alternative to a taxi?

There and then I'd have settled for advice on how to get my shirt off gracefully rather than looking like I was trying to wrestle myself out of a Lycra body stocking. Then, like some socially awkward geek, I looked down at this man poking out of my duvet and whispered, "I'll just brush my teeth…"

With him staring passively back at me I did exactly that. I had no idea what was about to happen. My heart was racing so much I was sure it was leaving visible heart shaped imprints on my skin, but hey, I wasn't going to forgo a minty fresh breath.

Having finished, I wandered over to the bed. He lay there silently. He was looking at me. I got in as delicately and un-suggestively as I could.

"Good night." He said.

I turned the light out and lay there.

WAS THAT IT?

This wasn't a bed and breakfast matey. If I had got as far as being in bed with a nearly naked man then there was stuff to happen before sleep.

I sighed heavily. It wasn't meant to carry any meaning it was just a massive sense of relief and frustration. Here I was, sort of, and I hadn't burst into flames.

"What's wrong?" a voice chirruped up.

I didn't know what to say. What did I want? What did I expect? I didn't know. I made some attempts to give an answer, but it was just the odd sound or word. He knew what I was saying, I think. Either that or he was just finding me annoying. So he turned over and began kissing me.

This was the first time.

It was a bit of a shock as I was still wondering why I'd sighed. It felt different, more forceful and obviously more abrasive than a women's kiss. I spent the entire thing trying to evaluate what I was feeling. Having had some many silent worries and concerns, wonders and questions, this felt like the perfect time to answer some. Soon, the novelty, the wonder and the excitement had passed into pure emotional analysis.

It was a bit rougher, was this better – yes or no?

He was quite heavy – did I prefer this – yes or no?

There was definitely more tongue, did I like that – yes or no?

So it continued.

He finished and looked at me. "Better?" he asked.

I nodded. I wasn't sure whether he could see me in the darkness but it's all I could muster. I was also aware he hadn't brushed his teeth and could clearly taste coffee. I wasn't sure what had just happened. He hadn't moved and I still couldn't remember what my name was. He was well aware that this was my first time. I was rigid with fear; I had lost the power of speech and was essentially clueless. Yes, I had a theoretical understanding of what could happen but still, this being my first time it would have been nice for the more experienced hand to take the lead. What happened next was, in retrospect, the perfect introduction to the next few years of my life. He was more than happy for me to tend to his needs and desires but less so in returning the favour. Me? I was just a willing newbie with a bed.

As before, I looked upon this as a project. I was on a mission of research. I had to analyse everything.

- o   What was that like?
- o   Did I do that correctly?
- o   What did I think of it anyway?

- o   How was I feeling?
- o   Did I feel repulsed?
- o   Would I do that again?
- o   Was this what I had been waiting for?

Now. Let me tell you that I prize myself on being shower fresh at all times. This guy did not. At all. In. Any. Way. The more excited he got, the more was revealed. When the curtain was fully down I genuinely thought he'd dipped his cock in cottage cheese. It wasn't knob cheese, it was pebbledash.

It may be true that I was undergoing an exploratory life process to see how I felt about being gay, but I drew the line at that. I wondered if I needed a hod carrier to shunt some of those bricks to a safe place. I may have been a sitting duck for a cheap bed and sexual exploitation but I was no chump and I wasn't chomping on that. I tried professing not knowing what to do, in the hope that he'd reciprocate and let me in on the fun, but alas, he wanted to go to sleep, one way or another.

Yes I had a body lying there that I could pretty much experiment with, but there was no feeling, no intimacy. It felt very cold and crude. At the point I knew I would get nothing more from the procedure, I hastened a conclusion to proceedings and accordingly we went to sleep.

Well, he did. I lay there listening to him snore whilst feeling a bit lost. Was this normal? Was this how it should have been? I recall seeing the sunrise before giving in to exhaustion and falling asleep.

Later that morning, after a broken few hours sleep, I could hear the house waking. Doors banged, footsteps ran overhead and chatter could be heard.

I got up as he slept. How did I manage to get him out without anyone knowing? We'd have to walk past our only communal space. If anyone was in it, they'd see us. There was always leaving through the window, but that would look even more sinister.

I sat in a chair and just looked at him. My head hurt and I smelled different. I had never before had a real one-night stand. Not really. I also remember there being a lot more tenderness with women. Where was that? Was that not part of the gay bargain? Would I have to accept that my future sex life was to be as cold and disconnected as my emotional life? Was my path hereafter going to be made from an unsatisfactory patchwork of meaningless moments – a sort of relay race of regrets? After a while he stirred and I told him to stay in bed whilst I went and made coffee. I walked into the kitchen to see the housemates comforting one of the girls.

"You okay?" I asked genuinely worried.

She nodded and looked away. The rest stood around her as I set about making one coffee. I couldn't make two.

Seeing that sufficient comfort was being offered I set back to my room. When I returned he was dressed. "Thanks," he said and took the coffee from me.

"You're welcome." I offered semi sarcastically, feeling a bit moody.

Just as before, we sat in silence. After he drank his coffee, he said he had to go. We both stood and I went to escort him from the premises with as much stealth as possible. He kissed me again and smiled. It was the only warmth I had seen since standing alone in the hall. I was beginning to believe that this was an effective tool for him.

We both walked towards the door. I stopped and turned to him. "Do you think I am gay?" I asked, matter of fact.

He looked at me vacantly. Hadn't that been obvious?

"I thought at the very least you were bi," he replied coolly.

With that I opened the door, and checking all was clear, hurried down the echoing hallway to the door. I pushed him outside and with fleeting thanks said goodbye. I turned, ran back to my room, grabbed my towel and headed for the shower. I wanted to smell like today, rather than ugly disappointment from the night before.

If anything, this had raised more questions than it answered. The experience had felt as wholly disconnecting and unsatisfactory as standing alone watching others happy. I stood in the shower, as steaming hot water cascaded down on top of me. It felt like one of those scenes from a movie when people try to scrub away the scent of a mistaken encounter. I scrubbed, I stood. It felt like a massive let down. I felt like a fraud. Was this what all the fuss was about?

The end of the year had arrived. People had the option of hanging around for the odd week or they could just go home. As it was my final year, I had elected to stay. It would be nice to hang on for a bit longer, have the town to myself. My year group was all meeting at a sea-front pub for a farewell pint later that afternoon so

I wanted to be ready for that. I was sure that given the late night and late starts, the gossip wouldn't have reached them by then. Besides, after that drink, I may never see most of them again. This was an end.

I dried myself down and looked at my body with slightly mournful eyes. What a weak frame. What a pathetic set of longings. I felt exposed in every sense. I stayed in my room for the rest of the day unwilling to face the world. It was only when I had to leave that I made my way to the pub. With all the forced joviality in which I was now well versed, I managed to traverse one final fake fling.

The call came for everyone to be in a massive group shot. I elected to stay out of it. People thought it was odd but I felt like I didn't want a record of my time there. I wanted to vanish, not to exist. I felt invisible so behaved accordingly. With hugs, goodbyes and pledges of eternal friendships made, I made my way back to the house where two of the housemates were sitting in silence.

"Is Karen okay?" I asked.

"Yeah," said one of the girls. She was Northern, blunt and sometimes rude.

"What was wrong with her then?" I asked curiously.

There was an awkward silence. I looked up from my coffee cup. I was facing away from them but could hear them mouthing things to each other.

"What?" I said tartly.

"She was just tired," said one finally. "She, err, didn't get much sleep. That's all."

It was a very decorous way of putting it. Karen's room was next to mine and her headboard abutted the wall by my bed. Seems we were a lot noisier than I thought in that echoing house. Not only that but the wall that separated us was not as thick as the others, she'd heard everything. Every cottage cheese thumping minute.

She left later that day, without a goodbye.

After she had gone I sat in the house alone. Again it was silent. I began to appreciate the fact that I could have physical relations with a man. The million-dollar question was, could I have an emotional one too? It seemed like I was destined for a shit life. Hated for wanting to be loved and abused for trying. Didn't seem fair somehow.

After my time at university finished, I had the opportunity to stay and work on campus. What's more, I got paid for it. It was crap money, but enough to keep the wolf from the door.

Being part of a very small high-profile team meant that I could go nowhere without being known. The spotlight was on me even more than before. Students saw me as one of them rather than staff, which suited me. However, as I wasn't actually a student any longer, I cared a little less about the scrutiny. It should have been a fun year. It should have been the year I could kick back and relax. It probably would have been, but for some of the out gay students who I was forced to work alongside. One in particular was almost a militant gay. He was so out, he was almost in again. He'd spent the preceding years giving me daggers for what he thought was my self-hating lifestyle or at best deliberate denial.

I knew that I had to win them over if I had any chance of making my life tolerable. To that end, I initiated several conversations. I made coffee for him, offered him drinks, bought him food, chatted and generally tried to be amenable. Although not deliberate, I was bribing him to like me. For whatever reason the ringleader was not happy to accept me as a confused/closeted gay man. He never told me why (despite me asking) so I had to presume that he thought I was gay but ashamed of it and thus consciously not out. As far as he was concerned, I knew something was different and I suspected I was gay. In his mind, as soon as I

suspected I might have a touch of lavender about me, I should
have been parading down the street wearing a pink T-shirt
emblazoned with the word 'Poof' in glitter. As a result of my
reluctance, I was someone he didn't like and so he spent the rest of
that year ensuring that my life was as miserable as the preceding
three. In short, my quest to win him over had failed.

I think it's one of those funny things that often the worst
prejudice you experience is from the very people you would expect
to embrace (or at least tolerate) you. I remember once, (when
drunk) saying to him. "But why do you continue to hate me when
I'm…" and I couldn't finish the sentence. In fact I just started to
cry. That was the most open I had ever been with anyone – since
that Victorian terrace and two terrified teens. He just said, "Oh,
I'm not putting up with this," and promptly walked away. This
sense of latent anger always surprised me. I had never done
anything bad to this man.

So I knew I had to endure my time with him stalking around,
constantly undermining me and making my life more difficult. In a
peculiar way it was around then that I started to learn one of life's
most valuable lessons. By trying everything I could to get him to
like me I was subjugating my personality for dubious rewards. Why
should I change who I was just to get validation by a rather
viperous queen? In a desperate bid to be accepted, I was betraying
whoever I was. There was no chance that I could learn to love
myself when I couldn't just be myself. How could I ever discover
who I was if I was forever trying to be someone else? All of this
just to be liked!

This steep learning curve set the undertone for the year. Initially, when I was trying to be all things to all people, I was largely all over the place and profoundly unhappy. This in turn made me drink, which in turn unlocked more hidden fears and caused more problems.

Soon my walks around town, the beach and the river were not missions in head clearing but rather search and rescue missions. I'd search out some bloke hoping he'd rescue me from the malaise for which I was in. In all those years, across all those walks, I never once met anyone. NOT ONE.

Once, rather curiously, I had literally bumped into a woman who was sitting in the darkness listening to the waves and we'd got chatting. She was very attractive and had a great body. She was a student I knew only by sight. She knew of me and I knew of her. So we chatted knowingly for some time. We shared our war stories and had a laugh. Then just as I bade her farewell for the evening she just asked, "Do you fancy a blow job?"

I was rather dumbstruck by this and laughed. I wasn't very interested at the prospect and assumed, incorrectly, that she was joking anyway. I said yes just to see the look on her face in the hue from that evening's full moon. It was when she turned on her heel and headed further into the dunes that panic set in. Surely she wasn't being serious?

A million thoughts flashed through my mind. There was a weak voice that piped up, 'maybe this could be your way back to women.'

Could it? I appreciate that some people would think that I

could just lie back and think of some bloke, but to me this was a step backwards. It was there in those dunes that I knew for sure that women were never going to be my bag ever again. I mean, if I was turning down a beautiful woman who was offering me no strings sex, what chance did I have?

As we arrived at the deep banks of sand with long tall grasses waving in the breeze and I was desperately thinking of a face saving way to get out of it. Surely this was most men's dream? A very attractive women offering guilt free, no strings oral as I reclined into the sand, yet there I was feigning a limp, dragging my leg across the sand in a bid to say I'd stood on some glass and had to go home…

Just as we reached a large moonlit clearing she turned and asked "Will you still respect me in the morning?" Having been racking my brains for a get-out of jail card, suddenly I had been presented with one. A very odd, peculiar and uncomfortable one – but I knew I had to take it. I looked at her. She had a perfectly kind face and I didn't want to hurt her feelings, nor out myself, so I just said "No."

It was at that point that I saw the look of shock on her face. This was a step too far for her, so she said "Forget it then," and we both walked from the dunes to the road. I felt the need to escort her home, which I did, both of us walking in silence. I walked her to the door and she opened it and disappeared in without a glance back. Lord knows what she thought of me. I stood staring at the closed door. Wouldn't life be easier if I just said I was gay? Ironically, I'd probably be way more popular. If I'd been honest with others and myself I would have pushed fewer people away. Yet I still thought this was the best (and only) path to tread.

Within my new guise as elder student figure I was often invited to many house parties. New students who had yet to label me as a closet case were happy to see me at their parties. It was a fun at first and it was delightful to have positive attention. Not that long after the incident with the girl in the sand dune, I was at a party near the beach. Duly I set off for some peace and quiet (I wasn't actually drunk this time, I just wanted some space) when a guy asked if he could join me. I said he could. He was new and was finding it all a bit much. I knew where he was coming from. He was gay (albeit not out) and I assumed he just wanted to talk about his feelings (that was kind of my job). We walked, we talked. He asked to sit. We sat. In fact we sat in pretty much the same moonlit clearance that I had been some weeks before feigning a limp and saying I wouldn't respect her in the morning.

He told me about his life and I listened. It was often the role that one had to sit listen, nod and laugh or comfort as the need arose. I am not sure how it started but we started kissing. Things started to go from there…

It was the first time that something spontaneous and genuine happened to me. Against the noise of the parties, the abuse, the passive aggressive cold shoulders, here was a tender moment. It felt very odd and divine. I was terrified that someone would come upon us and out us once and for all, but that also added to the excitement.

Fun though it was, I knew this guy was a bit drunk. So I said we should stop. I didn't want him to wake up the next morning with a 'what have I done?' feeling. So I told him – should he want to do that again, he had to be sober. This irritated him but he could see that my motivation was at least genuine. We started walking back to his. He then asked if he could be my boyfriend. The question floored me. I shuddered to a stop, staring at him. We stood on a quiet road that wound its way down to the beach past bungalows containing blue rinsed old people.

"I'm not gay," I said rather pathetically. "Sorry," I added and set off up the hill. I assumed, bizarrely, that would take care of the matter.

"I JUST HAD YOUR COCK IN MY MOUTH," he screamed at the top of his voice. It was so loud I think I heard a flock of birds take flight in the neighbouring county. The odd bungalow light came on and more than one net curtain twitched.

"Keep your voice down." I hissed at him.

"WHY?" he shouted again. "DON'T YOU WANT PEOPLE TO KNOW YOU'RE GAY AND YOU LOVE COCK?"

Well, yes, that just about summed it up actually. Was that too much to ask? I walked back towards him. "Were you never confused? Were you never unsure and worried and scared?" I whisper shouted right in his face.

Evidently there was sufficient anguish in my face to convince him that shouting about cock, as several octogenarians reached for their speed dial to the police, was not a sound move.

He nodded and smiled. He had a fantastically broad smile. A very kind and warm smile that made me feel oddly relaxed. Not turned on, not sexy, not lustful, just relaxed. I had never felt that before.

We headed back to the party that was breaking up. One of his housemates was making that staple student party food – toast. We stood in the kitchen, all three of us, silently eating toast. It felt extraordinarily normal. We then drank awful instant coffee from chipped mismatched cups under the luminescence of industrial strip lights and chatted. We laughed at the party's antics until his housemate bid us a good night and left us in the brightly lit kitchen. The clock ticked, the fridge purred and we smiled at each other.

He stood up and took my hand, without arguing I followed. We headed up to his room which, (rather annoyingly), was on the top floor. We didn't exactly creep, we just walked. Someone saw us walking into his room together and I am fairly sure they didn't think we would be discussing politics. We dispensed with the small talk and headed to the bed where we began kissing again. After a short time we were naked and under the sheets. This felt more natural, more real and more ordinary than any encounter ever before.

"I've some condoms," he said finally. That had never crossed my mind before. This meant that I had the prospect of actual real man-to-man sex. That was new, scary and unchartered territory. If I had taken a quiz in the mechanics of sex right there and then I'd have failed. I wasn't exactly sure how it worked. I was the woman on the stool, startled, unsure and paralysed. I stared back, a look of terror on my face. "You'll be fine," he said and reached for them.

There, in that student attic bedroom, after an aborted seedy sand dune BJ (and some toast) I had my first real and meaningful sexual encounter. Oddly, as we both knew it was my first time, we both narrated our every action. It felt like we were doing the soundtrack to a nature documentary. We kept asking each other questions and reassuring one another – in whispers. It was sweet in its own way.

Afterwards we just lay there quietly until the silence of sleep took us to another place. Then, as light fell through the thin patterned curtains draped over a narrow latticed attic window, I looked at him sleeping. This was now the second time I had woken next to a man.

This time I studied his body. The hair. The freckles. The nipples. The armpits. The stubble. The smell. Everything. One of the things that had struck me was just how fine and soft his hair was. The hair on his head, arms and legs etc. It was silky soft. I had expected it to scratch and bristle but no. It was as if even the smallest of my preconceptions was being challenged.

I wasn't staring because I was aroused or for any sexual reason, I just wanted to dissect what I was feeling. Why did his frame make me feel the way I did? Naturally I found few answers.

I found it almost impossible to just accept my feelings and enjoy the result; I still thought I had to understand. Fundamentally that was my problem from the start. If only someone had told me not to waste time over-analysing things and to just enjoy what I was doing and who I was. Ha, if only…

For the very first time I didn't feel dirty or guilty. I did feel a bit awkward and embarrassed. He woke as I lay there and gave me a huge smile. We lay there for a bit chatting. It was odd. I didn't feel the need to get up and rush away. I didn't feel any compulsion to flee. I was happy to lie there and chat. Then, with the inevitability that always follows a night of secret passion, the coldness of a business like departure finally arrived. I got dressed in silence and we both listened at his large wooden bedroom door for sounds of life. He went and checked the scene and when clear signalled for me to creep down the stairs.

This wasn't entirely to avoid being found out, it was simply because students gossiped all the time. If you didn't want your sex life discussed and dissected you kept it secret – if you could! However, in such a small community this was largely impossible, as someone would see you at some point.

We got to the front door and I turned briefly to say goodbye, as I did, he kissed me. This was a shock. It was a statement. I stared at him and again there was that smile. We both knew that we would never be an item. He was at the start of his journey and I hadn't a clue what mine would be. We stood in the doorway. That stalking chill of a summer's morning rushed into the large hallway. He stood staring at me and me at him. There was a mutual appreciation, a shared connection, but nothing more. It made me wonder in that brief pause whether normality was actually achievable in my life. Away from waspish judgmental queens, away from society and its misconceptions, could I just be normal? Would I feel like this again? He mouthed 'See you later' for surely we would and then the door closed. I walked home feeling generally happy with myself. Something significant had happened.

In writing this book I decided to look him up. See where he is today. To my surprise (and joy) I see that he is famous now.

Bugger me.

Leaving university meant moving back home to live with my parents. Living there was nice enough. It was suffocating and claustrophobic but had nice bedding and a perpetually full biscuit barrel.

I got a job and started work in the city pretty quickly. Commuting into work first thing, then back with the hordes, was soulless. This was accentuated by the fact that the city seemed to be constantly buzzing, whereas my life was a very damp squib. I managed to do this two-and-froing like every other face on the train for a year. Soon after that dubious anniversary, the tedium of my routine, my life, the miserable solitude of the last train home and the fleetingly rare nights out began to wear me down. The time had come to take the plunge and move into the city itself.

Aside from any freedom this would grant, I just craved freedom of movement. Not having to worry about waking my family up after a rare late night, not having to see yet another disconsolate face on the last train and perhaps crucially, having a personal space I could invite people back to.

I soon found an apartment on the edge of Manchester city centre – affording easy walking to all of the bars and clubs. What's more, I had decided to be genuinely proactive (and bizarrely bold for someone who still told people he was straight), I volunteered at a gay men's charity. I had hoped that this would be an excellent opportunity for me to meet other 'like minded people' as the papers used to describe gay men hooking up. Just for friendship you understand – to talk about sports etc.

It was all rather exciting. From my apartment I could walk to a renovated cotton mill that was now home to funky 'work spaces'. I would go every week and would sit with a unique collection of other gays (usually only guys) and we'd stuff small brightly coloured cardboard envelopes with two condoms and two sachets of lube. These would be duly dispatched around the city's gay bars and clubs so that it would – it was hoped – help fight the spread of HIV, AIDS and various other Sexual Transmitted Infections (STIs). Although back them we called them STDs – Sexual Transmitted Diseases. You didn't just have an infection you had a disease. You were diseased! It was a more brutal time.

Every week we would talk about what had been happening to us all. At that point I had less to say than the others. I liked to listen. I used to imagine that what we were talking about was all perfectly normal, that we could just as easily be discussing curtains, as we were cocks. I told myself that this little group of guys was normal. I would tell myself that the outside world was not normal for rejecting us. This was just a mundane chat with a group of ordinary blokes. Then someone would talk about being cautioned in the street for wearing arse-less pants whilst brandishing a dildo and my fragile illusion of normality would shatter like a cheap mirror.

I had a great time there. It was always a high point of my week. Aside from anything else it helped me feel normal. Very normal. I was Radio Four, book at bedtime guy and some of them were drug taking rave attending whores. I'd listen to their stories as if I was enjoying an afternoon play. I'd devour their life experiences with great interest. It was a world I had never really encountered or could relate to. My attic night of intimacy and one-off fumble in the dunes seemed like I was helping an old lady home with her shopping by comparison.

There was a rent boy who was adamant he'd given up the trade. Every week he'd come and tell us he was temping at a bland office job. Then as sure as eggs were eggs, he'd digress to a story that told us all where he was getting his cash from. As one of the older guys there (I was early twenties) the staff would look at one another and then to me as if to say 'will he ever learn?' He would tell tall tales about his activities – being chased, attacked, hospitalized, the old men, the fat men, the unhygienic men, the mobsters, the threats, the injuries – all of which was in a day's work for him. He talked about how he'd started young – and I mean young. As his parents had thrown him out of the family home early, he soon learned the trade to earn a living and pay for food. He did what he did to live. He even actively sought out pedophiles to get some experience and some cash (honestly, he did). I found this mortifying. I couldn't believe my ears, but seemingly it wasn't as rare as you'd imagine. To him this was life. That's all there'd been.

He looked very young for his age and so used that to drum up business amongst that demographic. Naturally, our volunteer forum had to be non-judgmental so we all said nothing, but a look can convey a million messages. I was horrified about his life but admired his fortitude because he fought every day; he fought to live. Once, in a minute of melancholy, he said, "well yes, but you have to get on with it when you have no other choice in life." There was a somber silence that followed as we all packed our envelopes in deep contemplation. I hope he is happy now.

There was one guy who was being beaten up by his family for being gay. He would turn up in various states, with numerous bruises and broken bones, yet he'd always lie to protect his family. 'An ex had attacked him, but they'd broken up now… he was mugged but they had found the culprits… he'd been playing rugby and…' No one believed him, as no one was ever that unlucky (and no way did he ever play rugby!). We knew what was going on. Then one day he just spilled the beans after a pretty aggressive and violent homecoming. He lifted his shirt to reveal a set of black, blue and purple ribs. We were duly horrified. He said he couldn't go on. He was on the point of a breakdown. He told us about the horrors and, as one, we turned up later that week to help him move out. We didn't know him really, but he was being persecuted for feeling the things we did, so he was one of us. It was a strangely unifying experience. We helped him move out of his family home and into a place that kept him safe. His family shouted abuse at us all as we loaded stuff into one of the volunteer's car. Helping him felt satisfying, but ever so sad.

It was that afternoon after we'd all returned from our stint as removal men that I was introduced to a woman. She was strikingly good-looking, tall and had radiance about her. She came in to see the staff and everyone crowded around her asking her about her life. I hadn't seen her before but assumed she must been on maternity leave or maybe had gone to work elsewhere and was just popping in to say hello. I happened to walk past the hubbub and one of the staff introduced me. I forget her name – but let's say she was called Sophie. "This is Sophie," they said as I shook her hand and said hello.

There were fewer people around her as they'd sloped off to get coffees, grab biscuits, checked messages etc.

"So Sophie," I asked. "Did you work here?"

She smiled a rather lovely smile. "No, I used to volunteer here so I thought I'd pop in and say hello," she answered warmly.

I see. I hoped I was this popular when I came back.

My 'mentor' at the charity was standing next to me. "Sophie is post op," he said finally.

"Oh God really?" I said looking at her. "Are you okay?"

She thought this amusing. "I'm very well thank you, the operation went well."

"Oh that's good," I said finally, looking all concerned with a crumpled forehead. "So you're better now?" I asked.

My friend looked at me with wide imploring eyes. "Sophie is post op," he said again as if I had missed it the first time around.

"I know, you just said," I said looking at Sophie. "I was just asking if she was okay. I hope you're feeling better," I added.

She nodded. "Yes, all better now," she added with a beautifully broad smile.

"Good," I said. "Well, I'll see you later and I hope your recovery continues to go well."

I walked off as my friend sped behind me. He slowed my pace and stood in front of me. "Do you know what post op means?" he asked.

"Yes," I said with a roll of the eyes that screamed incredulity. What kind of twonk did he think I was? "You have an op, you get over the op, you are post op." I felt like I was being treated like a fool.

"Yes, that's true," he said smiling sweetly. "Look at Sophie." I did as I was bid. "When she started here, she was Steven."

I stared at Sophie. I continued to stare at Sophie. I began to realise why Sophie's voice was a bit huskier than most women I knew. I continued staring until Sophie gave me a wave.

I turned to my friend. "Post op?"

He nodded.

"I say!" I said. I glanced back at Sophie and watched her interact and walk. "But she looks like a woman," I added rather stupidly. "I mean like an actual real woman." I was shocked. I had never knowingly met a transsexual before and was taken aback by how good she looked. I stood staring, transfixed. She was extremely attractive – as a woman.

"She is a real woman," my friend said, laughing at my awkwardness.

"Well yes of course, yes indeed, naturally…" I said in my right-on, everyone has the right to be themselves way. I slid over to the photocopier and copied blank pages so that I could keep on staring. It seemed amazing. It also explained why she was so tall. She was stunning and delightfully happy – it was wonderful.

146

I had a great time there. Occasionally we'd go out for drinks, but sadly, it wasn't the social opportunity that I had hoped for. Instead it was just a good laugh and something positive I could do for the community. I liked the work as it did make me feel like A) I was contributing something worthwhile and B) it enabled me to feel I was making personal progress. It wasn't that long ago I was afraid to actually say the word gay, let alone sit with fellow gay men and talk openly about sex based issues. Not that I talked, you understand. In many ways I still thought I was going through a phase. I mean, what's gay about living in a city where you only frequent gay bars, enjoy sex with men and volunteer at a gay men's sexual health charity? You people have dirty minds…

Living so close to all of the action, it didn't take me long to throw myself into a hedonistic splurge of activity. Many years of doubt, reserve, fear and panic that had been locked into a box with a label that read, 'Do not disturb. Ever. EVER. No really – ever!' was about to be opened.

This was the first time that I was officially off the leash and I had every intention of making the most of it. I became a fixture at gay clubs and bars most nights of the week. This was a voyage of discovery; these were new uncharted territories for me. Was this a promised land of excitement, sex, thrills, spills and who knew, maybe love? I didn't believe that for one second, but hey, one could hope. I embraced everything that was on offer. The summer was bright and the city was buzzing. There was a real, upbeat positive feeling to everything. It felt like everyone was enjoying themselves. This had a profound effect on me. I began to believe that it was possible, just maybe, to be out, gay and happy. Maybe. Unlikely, but not *impossible*.

Those early months after I moved in to my flat were busy. Many guys would listen to me say that I wanted a relationship, that I was more than just a one-night stand. They would agree. They would say that we had so much in common. We'd go back, shag and then they'd leave promising to call. It's a story as old as the hills but I was caught up in the mindless hope – believe the bullshit – shag – sting of rejection – hope again – this time it'll be different – here we go again cycle.

There were some nice men. Men that I wouldn't want a relationship with, but who were honest about what they wanted. One of those came back my apartment for coffee and a bite to eat. Typically we ended up in bed. We were just about to get jiggy when he stopped dead and looked at me in the darkened room. "I can't do this." He said, mournfully.

"Oh," I replied. He was a rotund chap with thin dark hair and sad eyes. He sat there looking ruefully around my spartan bedroom. "Is there something wrong?" I asked.

Even by the faint light that was coming in through the curtains I could see a pain on his face. His eyes were deep, dark and full of sorrow.

"The thing is…" he began.

Uh-oh. In my experience things that needed an introduction were rarely good. "I can't get it up easily." He said, in a low doleful tone.

Okay... Well we've all been there once in a while. I told him so and said we'd give it our best shot. I was upbeat about our chances. In my experience when blokes stopped worrying it all kind of happened.

"You don't understand," he interrupted me. "I only ever get off when, when, when I shag a cowboy."

Say what now?

We both fell into silence.

A cowboy?

In Manchester?

Good luck mate!

I lay back in my bed, propped up on my pillows, looking up at him. I couldn't immediately see how we could resolve the situation. I wasn't exactly a cowboy and I wasn't yee-haaing for anyone. I just prayed he didn't mean getting on a saddle.

"Okaaaaay," I said finally puncturing the silence in the room as a city outside my bedroom window partied in a perfectly normal non-cowboy like manner. I could see how that would be a bit of passion killer given that we lived in Lancashire.

"I've…. I've… brought some stuff with me," he said gingerly.

Uh-oh. Uh-oh. Uh-oh.

I quickly ran through my mind everything he had with him. I failed to see where a saddle could be hidden.

"Stuff?" I questioned, suspiciously.

He got up out of the bed and rooted around in his clothes. From there he produced what looked like a small piece of old cloth. He stood by the side of the bed holding it out in my general direction.

"It's a face mask and a neck tie." He declared. I stared at the cloth in quiet disbelief. "Would you wear them for me please?'

I sat bolt upright, staring at these things that looked like they were fresh from some pantomime. He wanted me to wear a bandit's red polka dot facemask and a necktie – which could also double as a bandana. Was this for real?

I looked up at him, into those sad imploring eyes and back again at the Wild Western apparel. I thought about how I had been rejected, ignored, abused, attacked and left in tears. I had been treated appallingly, I had dubious charitable sex and I had fallen for every lie in the book. So what was one costume? What harm could it do? Yes I'd look like a twat, but this wasn't an audition, it was about being kind. It was about helping someone out – yet again.

"Yeah okay," I said.

He seemed genuinely thrilled. "Really? Will you?" he said excitedly. His sad eyes sparkling for once.

"Why not?" I stuttered, with a shoulder shrug.

He tenderly tied the mask around my head, a bandana completed the look. This was not a story Sherriff Andy would ever want to be in – with our without his toys.

I looked like the world's shittest cowboy, but he was ecstatic.

"What are you like with accents?" he asked.

"Why?" I snorted. My facemask lifted sharply like a skirt in my derisive breeze.

"Can you do an American accent? Like a John Wayne one?"

I couldn't. "No, I don't think so," I mean, come on! I was already looking like a tit. Give me some dignity…

"Pleeeeeaaaaase!" he implored.

"Howdy! Well gee zir," I said pathetically in what would count for a hate crime today. "We don't see many of yar cowboys around these paartz, what brings ya t'town?"

Suddenly he was as hard a phone mast. My American was as convincing as Dick Van Dyke's English, but gee zir, it had him standing to attention. At that moment this timid, soft, gentle fellow became a bucking bronco. There we were, me desperately thinking of things to say (I think I said 'do you want some re-friend beans' at one point, before stopping to think if they were in fact Mexican…), but he loved every bizarre minute. This was very much the Wild West Manchester.

Naturally, as with all rodeos, the bull has to be tamed. And in due course we came to a rest. After we were both done he whispered. "You can take it off now." I was glad. It was oddly stifling and hot under my little taste of the Wild West. We lay there until we fell sleep. In the morning I made coffee and toast whilst we chatted. At the door as he left, he turned and asked if he could say something. I prayed it wasn't in a Southern drawl, y'know.

"I just wanted to say thank you. You are a very kind man. You didn't have to do that last night. Many haven't. You were just lovely and I want you to know that you have made me very happy. Thank you for being so sweet."

With that he walked away. I felt genuinely touched. It was without doubt the kindest thing anyone had ever said to me. I knew it was going to be a good day and that despite my fears, the future could be better than today.

Later that day, still feeling a warm glow I set off into town. It was the Pride Parade and I wanted to take a look. It was a warm sunny Saturday afternoon and float after float trundled through the main shopping area. We had a rather detailed S&M float; semi naked dykes on bikes display, fisting, bondage, leather and an assortment of equally lewd and lurid acts.

As I stood there I saw my 'sexuality' portrayed like it was a sordid circus. I heard mothers tell their children to look away as it was disgusting and shouldn't be allowed. Some pointed. Some laughed. Some walked away. Some shouted support as other shouted abuse. It was a peculiar way to seek equality.

'I like being tied up and whipped with my cock out – please embrace me as your equal…' WHAT? It wasn't a gay pride procession at all. It was a kaleidoscope of sexuality. Essentially, all of the things on display straight people enjoyed too. It had nothing to do with being gay as far as I could see, just human sexuality. A sexuality pride parade, yes – but just gay? No! By getting decked out in leather and straddling a flat back lorry and driving through the city centre, these people weren't promoting equality and certainly not facilitating any understanding. They were demonstrating what was then known as 'sexual deviance.' This was not advancing the cause – it was sending it back decades. How was this useful?

I stood and watched in horror. This wasn't who I was. This wasn't who I wanted to be. This wasn't what I wanted people to think of if and when they heard I was gay. 'Oh you are gay, what float are you?'

I was no prude. If someone wanted to entomb themselves in rubber and be left alone for hours then good on them. If you like S+M, being whipped, leather – then bravo, but please don't say that it represents 'gay' people. It doesn't. It represents people with fetishes – of any sexuality. I genuinely felt that the very community that should be helping me come to terms with my sexuality was actively out there pulling the rug from under my feet.

I understood why they were doing it. Years of repression resulted in a giant rainbow coloured 'fuck you' but that wasn't pride, it was rebellion and defiance. The reactions it generated depressed me. It made me feel that no matter how good I felt, however hopeful I could be; I could never live amongst the general population and be accepted as a gay man. Even if I were happy with myself, I would still be rejected for being a deviant on a float. They'd just assume I was upstairs fisting someone who was clad in rubber whilst a tits-out dyke oiled her bike in my back garden with its shed that doubled as a dungeon.

That afternoon sent me into a spiral of depression. There was no escape. With the depression came the dark clouds and I was back in the bars and clubs seeking validation and support once again. The warm glow from that morning evaporated faster than steam from my coffee.

A night or so later I was back in the bar and got chatting to a rather charming man. It was always interesting who drank alcohol in bars and who didn't. If they were drinking a soft drink it meant that they were either A) driving and/or B) secure in their sexuality. Not drinking beer suggested that they didn't need to be several sheets to the wind to go into a gay bar. This man was polite, sober, complimentary and generally well balanced. It was a rather refreshing change.

After a few drinks, some of which he bought (very rare), he invited me back to his. I agreed. It would be nice to spend time with someone with manners. We went to his car and began driving the considerable distance out into the countryside, across the moors. At no point did I think he was about to murder me in the wilderness. He could have easily lured me out to my death without me even realising. No one knew my name so no one would have known who I was or where I'd gone. The TV report would struggle to find someone to interview, as people didn't want to admit they were in a gay bar. I could just imagine the presenter outside the bar saying, 'he was seen leaving a gay pick-up bar with another man.' My mother would have gone spare. In reality, anything could have happened to me but I was always trusting. (Gullible? Needy?)

After a while we reached a rather nice house. He obviously had money. Photo frames of family members were dotted around the place. We sat we chatted and then, in time, we entered the bedroom for some mattress Olympics.

The next morning I sat at a lovely window seat over looking the glorious countryside, whilst he very kindly made me breakfast. It was all very civil and polite. As we chatted, he saw me glancing at the photos. "They're my family," he said after a while.

"Ah," I said curiously. "There're lots."

He smiled. Handing me my breakfast, he walked over to a frame and brought it back to the table.

He was pictured with a young girl, maybe five or six. "She's sweet," I said tucking into more sausage. "Is she your niece?'

He smiled. "No, she's my grand daughter."

I looked up at him quizzically. At the very most he was early 40s. Grandkid? "How can you have a grand kid?" I asked. "Did you have kids in your teens?"

He laughed. "Not quite." He walked back to the kitchen and returned with some orange juice. "So how old do you think I am?"

That question was always loaded. You were always doomed to disappoint. "Forty" I said. I actually thought he was maybe 45, but I wanted to err on the side of caution.

"Good guess," he said and sat back in his chair watching me eat. "I'm 70," he said finally.

I spat out my juice. With it dropping from my chin, I looked up at him again. "You're joking?"

He shook his head. He walked over to photos and labelled every occupant of each frame. Son, daughter, grandson, and granddaughter – it went on. I sat in stunned silence. He looked about 45 and had a wonderful body.

"Shocked?" he asked with a degree of pointlessness. I nodded. "Am I your first pensioner?" He asked playfully. Again I nodded.

"But you'll remember the war," I said for some bizarre reason. It almost felt like I had enjoyed some illicit WWII sexual action.

"I do," he said. "I fought in the latter part of the war," he added, as if he was giving me today's weather. "Rock and roll, miniskirts, the 70s, ABBA, guys who think they are straight when they are clearly gay – you name it, I've seen it all."

My breakfast was being duly ignored and growing cold, as I remained stunned and staring at him.

"Look," he said finally. "Did you enjoy yourself last night? I think you did. I did too. So what does it matter?"

It didn't, but my god, it came as a surprise.

He told me that he could see I was struggling with my sexuality. He told me that I needed to embrace it to stop fighting it. He came out to all of his kids and they accepted him for who he was. He said I would never be happy until I accepted what was obviously true. He told me that the war had made him see that life was precious so why waste it being someone you shouldn't be? (Despite him getting married due to society and pressure in the 50s). He explained that he decided to be honest and live his life. I was fighting a losing battle, he told me. It would only make me unhappy and that the closet was a lonely place. Swimming against the tide was only going to wear me down and result in drowning – better that I swim with it.

Every word struck a cord, yet mysteriously I just said, "I think it's just a phase."

He laughed uproariously. Had I been him I would have too. He smiled kindly at me and said, "Okay! For what it's worth, I think you're gay and I think you will only be happy when you accept that. But if it is just a phase – then fine. At least we both had a good time last night. So that's good."

With that he drove me back into town and we chatted. Maybe he'd see me around the scene again? No, not this time, I reassured him. This time I was going straight for good…

He smiled again and wished me well. After that I knew I had to make a change. I HAD to get a woman. I had just had some under the sheets fun with an OAP (albeit a really fit one) and pretended to be a cowboy to get some intimacy – what on earth was next?

ONE LAST SHOT AT WOMEN

After my dalliance with the pensioner I was all the more convinced that all of this going to gay clubs when I was drunk and going home for dodgy sex with people that ranged from a solid 'one' to a drunken and questionable 'seven' on the shagability scale was just a dubious phase.

I mean, come on, how hard was it to be straight? I'd met loads of straight men and they seemed – what could you say – nice… personable… but largely a simpler kind of man. I could do simple. I played the lion in The Wizard of Oz at school and someone said he was simple at heart – so I had a pedigree of pulling off simple. Yes, I may have to learn my way around power tools and understand how to change car oil, but surely that was quite achievable (so long as I could wear gloves).

Okay, I volunteered at a gay man's charity, but many straight men assured of their sexuality would do that, right? So hey, maybe I just hadn't met the right woman. Maybe, this was just one of those clumsy mix ups that we'd laugh about on our 50th wedding anniversary after five decades of complete wedded bliss.

'The definition of insanity is doing the same thing over and over again and expecting different results.' – Albert Einstein

I decided that it was worth the effort to make one last, desperate attempt to meet a woman. Don't ask why. So I answered an ad in the local paper. Adverts then fell into two categories. Men seeking women or women seeking men. Usually they followed the same pattern: 'Tall leggy blonde seeks fun-loving man for walks on the beach and to keep her safe, 30+' 'Handsome, wealthy man seeks voluptuous companion to travel life's roads. 25+'

It always struck me as odd that the women always sold themselves out in the ads. They always wanted someone to look after them. Why not look after themselves? And why don't men just say they want big tits? 'Voluptuous,' please… Come to that, how many people live near the frigging beach? I lost count of the amount of people who liked walks on the beach. The beaches must be crammed with middle-aged divorcees enduring awkward first dates. And fires! Everyone seemed to want to curl up in front of a real fire. The solid fuel industry must have taken great comfort from those lonely hearts adverts, especially during the rise of renewable energy. No one said they wanted sex. Ever. No one said, 'Bitter divorced man seeks sex to help him get over ex-wife and to vary pedestrian masturbation routine.' People never actually said what they wanted. They didn't want naked horizontal jogging, oh no, they wanted companionship. That meant sex, but hey… I dare say log fires and walks on the beach also translated into some kind of penetration.

Now… if you were a man seeking another man, ah well, that's where things got tricky. This was when local newspapers would refuse a one line ad saying, 'GWM seeks sim for fun' for fear that these small adverts at the back of the local paper, curiously sandwiched between advertisements for stair lifts and the horse racing results, would somehow corrupt the youth of the day and turn them all into randy buggers.

An advert for 'Man seeks fun in Lancashire with like minded souls,' was an advert for a gay fuck on the moors. Polari (a gay slang from the 1950s) wasn't exactly used in these adverts but you could see why they might be.

NAFF – Not Available For Fucking

DISH – An attractive man

CHICKEN – A young man

LILLY – Police (from Lilly Law)

PALLIASS – A nice back

EEK – Face

TRADE – Sex

TROLL – Walk

OMI – Man

OMI-POLONE – Camp man

DOLLY – Walk

MANAGARIE – Food

An advert for 'OMI SEEKS DISH FOR TROLL, TRADE AND MANAGARIE. NO OMI-POLONES OR CHICKENS PLEASE. RSVP,' wouldn't corrupt anyone. You'd need to be a bloody code breaker to decrypt that. Is it any wonder they went after Alan Turing?

I decided that rather than a dish for trade, I'd simply settle for a fun loving girl who enjoyed, 'good times, cinema, theatre and walks on the beach' THERE IT WAS AGAIN. Did anyone actually ever get from the beach to bed? Were beaches just overcrowded with lonely singles on first dates wondering how they could bring up the subject of shagging without looking slutty?

Whilst we're on the subject, what's the point of saying you liked good times? Who doesn't? You'd hardly be looking for someone to make your life miserable, would you? "Lonely drunk girl seeks average/obese man for life of recrimination, bad sex, arguing, regrettable life decisions and general unhappiness." Not exactly the thing you'd pay 75p a word for (extra £2 for lines above and below).

'GSOH important.' What? Well duh. 'Poor sense of humour important. Looking for man who can't joke or laugh as I am uniquely devoid of joy'. Also, given that humour, like art appreciation, is subjective, that's a minefield. I know people who think they are hilarious when in fact they are just embarrassing. Maybe they think that of me...

How many people would reply to an ad that said, 'introverted loner seeks sim for awkward silences and occasional rows.'

'Love to laugh!' Do you? Really? Who doesn't? I mean, no one wants to date a clown, but everyone likes to be happy don't they? Surely a component part of that is laughter? 'Lovely curvaceous girl, 23, seeks man to make her feel ugly, weak, unhappy and to enhance sense of low self-esteem. Age unimportant as long as you don't like to laugh.'

Love to laugh... why state the bloody obvious?

My reasons for responding to such a lady were simple. I liked cinema, theatre and bloody walks on the beach. On the matter of beaches, I had probably done more walking on the beach than most. I doubted I would share those experiences with her. "Yes love, the last time I was on a beach I was with this bloke, he's mega famous you know. Anyway he was giving me a BJ and... err hello, where you going... hello!"

I posted a letter to the relevant PO Box number (we did that back in the 90s you know) and waited. I was fairly sure that I would get a reply and I duly did. In truth, I was probably the only person to reply who was under 70. Before long we'd agreed to meet. I wasn't nervous. I looked upon it as a bit of an experiment. I would learn something about myself one way or another (again).

She was a remarkably fiery individual. She was divorced and going out was an attempt, "to get over useless shitty men who just go to bars for a cheap night. I'm not cheap, you know what I mean? I mean these men they just think you're not a real person you're just some dumb blond, you know what I mean? I mean, I'm not some one-night wonder, I'm looking for something else, something meaningful, you know what I mean? I want someone who is gonna see me for me, not just a pair of tits and what I really like about you is that you are good listener as most men just want to talk about themselves but you are a listener. It's really rare and I really like it coz men, like my ex, all he wanted to do is talk about himself, you know what I mean?"

The fact that I hadn't been able to ask her what she fancied as a starter because she didn't stop talking may have contributed to why I was such a great listener. I nodded. It seemed like the logical thing to do. Keep things simple.

"I mean the men in my life they have, well they have treated me like I was like their possession, like I was just something to be used and I've had enough of that. I want a man to want to meet me because of what I'm like not what I look like, that's why" I put the ad in the paper coz I wanted you to want to be with me, you know, the real me. The me inside here, (she pointed at her bosom which made me look at it.) That's the real me," she added, making her bosoms wobble. I was transfixed by her fleshy ripples. I looked back up at her. "I mean if you don't love what's inside here how can you love me? That's why I did an ad without a picture, that's when I knew you were real, you know what I mean? You're someone who wanted to get to know what's in here, you know?"

More bosom ripples.

I wasn't sure that a twenty-word advert was capable of encapsulating an entire human character, but as was the norm, I nodded sagely. I was nodding because I had no scope for talking. She took this nodding as a gesture of wavelength sharing. That I was aware of her pain and hardship, which in a strange way, I did. Just not exactly in the way she'd have expected. I just smiled and made light work of a breadstick.

"The risotto looks interesting," I offered feebly after another monologue about the inner her. She looked at me quizzically. Like I had just lurched up and performed star jumps in the restaurant. "The risotto," I repeated looking at the menu. I felt the need to draw her attention back to the food. Besides, I'd finished all of the breadsticks – and all of the refilled breadsticks.

A waiter approached as quickly as he could. Like me, he'd been waiting for her to draw breath. "Can I get you a drink?" he asked so fast I thought he'd get a nosebleed. "Will you be having wine with your meal?"

My lady friend smiled at him. "Nah mate, I'll have a large vodka T, garlic mushrooms and a rare steak, cheers mate." The waiter, suitably dispatched, looked emptily at me. He knew what I was thinking and I knew what he was thinking.

"Right," I said "I'll start with the terrine and then the risotto please."

I recall those choices because I can still see the look on her face. You could see her wondering why I had just chosen a girl's meal. She narrowed her eyes at me in mistrust. Why would man purposefully choose risotto? Was I gay?

The waiter jotted the order down and said, "Interesting choices!" He looked over to my date and then back at me. She was distracted. She was rooting around in her bag for something as if she'd dropped a coin into a drain. I smiled a knowing smile, threw my eyebrows up as if asking him to pull the fire alarm. He smiled a knowing smile back at me and left me to return to my charming companion.

"The thing is," she continued breathlessly, before putting her bag away, "when you have been messed around so many times by so many men you start to wonder if all men are the same, I mean I know it's a cliché, but the truth is that a lot of men are happy to just get what they want from you without thinking about what you want, what you really want and need, do you know what I mean?"

I nodded. I did know. I wanted to share, be part of this conversation to tell her I knew exactly how she felt… but it was not exactly conducive to being on a date. So I returned to smiling and nodding. It's all she wanted me to do anyway. This wasn't a conversation; it was a one-way rant. I wondered how peaceful a walk on the beach would be with her. Sitting in front of a roaring fire with this monologue would be an invitation to hurl yourself into the flames.

It was at this point I surveyed my 'date.' I was resolutely sure that I would rather swallow a pint of vomit than kiss her ashtray mouth, but I didn't feel any clearer. It would take one hell of a man, comprising exclusively of hardened rough edges, to try and smooth this particular jaded gem. Did this mean that I wouldn't like any woman or just not this woman?

I stared at her chest. I felt that I could. It was rather formidable. Like a shelf. I imagined balancing a pot plant on it and chuckled. Fortunately this coincided with a joke of hers, which made me seem like a perfect listener when in truth, by now, I had started staring at the guy sitting behind her.

The date rattled along at such a pace that the only words I spoke thereafter were to the waiter. When the bill came I noticed her coquettish look. It was the only time she was silent. She looked up at me and fluttered her eyelashes – honestly she did. Well, she tried, She had so much mascara on it was like raising the Titanic, but there was a quivering movement.

Did she think that was going to make me pay for it all? Those bloody vodkas weren't cheap. It's not like I was going to lose anything by not paying. However the gent/gay/coward in me couldn't face the awkward silence if I'd said, "Shall we go Dutch?"

especially as that would probably necessitate me explaining that I meant going halves with the bill and not shagging amongst a field of tulips. I imagined the cold stare from her hard face, which seemed hewn from a mossy dank rock of life. It was chilling. So I paid.

She smiled knowingly. Then, as if the waiter had ceased to exist and at the exact point he was standing over me taking payment, she leant forward and without any volume control 'whispered,' "Take me home and fuck me." I looked up with a sudden, shuddering shock. The waiter gasped.

"Let me get your coats," he said and dashed off, leaving me alone with this voracious woman who wanted someone to see her for who she really was – albeit naked. I considered saying I was going to the toilet and doing a runner out of the emergency exit, but like a motorist slowing to see a car crash, I was transfixed.

She may have mistaken this for intent, but it was fear. I could feel a trickle of cold sweat navigate my spine as I sat staring.

"I think the waiter has a good feeling about us," she added smiling. Her yellow teeth and orange skin made a strange sight by candlelight. The waiter returned and looked straight at me, his eyes flash with concerns for my safety. I imagine he and I had the same connection that strangers experience when they huddle together for safety in a natural disaster.

We were outside the restaurant when she turned to me on the step. "Well, how a'but dat fuck?" She said in a baby-like voice that simply made me want to bring my beautifully original risotto up on the pavement.

I stood, gulping at the air, much like a fish after being reeled in. "Well," I said hesitantly, looking around the dimly lit street. Embarrassed diners exited through what looked like a disastrous first date or an impending domestic. "That's certainly ah um, a, a…" I couldn't think of anything to say. "It's certainly a bracing offer."

BRACING?

What was she? A wet weekend in Scarborough?

BRACING?

A walk along the seafront in a gale is bracing. A night of sickly sweet scented candles, warm cheap white wine and physical intimacy with a woman can never, ever, be regarded as bracing. In fairness, she'd probably delight many a man. I suspected having sex with her would be like shagging a tornado. Yet as we stood on that dimly lit street, I would have taken my chances with the storm.

"Bracing?" she said, rightly perplexed. She stared at me as if I may just be messing her about playfully. Was I having a laugh or was this something to do with that risotto?

I smiled and looked pitiful. I didn't need to fake it, I just did. In the back of my head there was a voice saying that one of the tips to avoid being ripped apart by a wild animal was to make yourself appear as small as possible. Standing in that doorway, I wondered if I looked as pathetic as possible, she might just give up and walk away lambasting the uselessness of men. Then, as I stood still in silence, I remembered reading something about frightening an angry unhinged beast. It was not to be small, but to make yourself look big and to throw dirt at them. I glanced at the large black municipal flowerpot, which housed an ornamental tree covered in fairy lights. It stood a few feet away from me as I stood shaking. I contemplated grabbing a handful or dirt, throwing it at her, before raising my arms up and roaring like a rather spineless ape. I doubted, however, it would do much to calm her down. I imagined her looking at the clumps of moss nestled in her rather fierce cleavage before she tore my face off. I wouldn't have blamed her.

"Is it my tits?" She asked, bizarrely.

I had no idea what to say. Was this a 'does my bum look big in this,' question? Could I try and reclaim some of my dignity by getting the answer right? What could it be about her bosom that would persuade a red-blooded man to avoid intimacy? Yes they looked like they could break a man's leg if they were vexed, but loads of men would love that.

"God, no!" I said as if offended by the question but desperately trying not to look at them. "They're… lovely."

LOVELY?

WHAT. WAS. WRONG. WITH. ME?

A light Victoria Sponge is lovely. A man who wants to stick his head between a pair of sexually charged tits rarely calls them 'lovely.' If I was hoping for lad status, I had failed rather seismically. As if to detract attention from my ham-fisted approach to the situation I looked down at them and smiled what I thought was a keen, lecherous lady smile. Her bosoms huddled together before me like two conspiring twin sisters. You could almost hear them talking amongst themselves…

"What's his problem?"

"Don't ask me, I said he was odd when he asked about the risotto.'

In truth, I doubt I looked like a letch; I probably looked like I needed to be winded. I cringe thinking about it. It was so painfully awkward. I stood there gurning at her tits.

"LOVELY?" she said, duly offended.

"Delightful," I added, as if to put the tin cap on it. She had delightful bosoms. Lovely…

TAXI!

Was it too late to throw the dirt and run off?

Saying to a very proud woman, who had gone to a lot of effort to get her life back on track, that sex with her would be bracing and that her breasts were delightful was probably about as passively aggressive homo non erotic I could have got. I stared at her nervously as the chill wind of the city swirled around us. She looked back at me trying to work out why a man would go out on a date with her and then do a runner at the prospect of sex – besides the fact she was terrifying.

"Delightful?" she asked in a tone that said, 'My tone maybe soft but my inner voice is telling me to snap you in half and then eat the remains with a glass of cheap Chardonnay.'

"Well yes," I said, "They're lovely, it's just…" I thought about saying I just didn't do it on the first date. That would sound pathetic and frankly unbelievable. What man has ever said that? Any mention of "I respect you too much," translates as, "I think you're as ugly as fuck." Should I claim to have an STD and was waiting for the ointment to work? Oddly, despite knowing that I'd never see her again, the thought of incriminating myself like that just seemed wrong, odd and unfair.

"Just what?" she barked.

I sighed a long sigh. For the first time that evening I felt like the real me (or at least an approximation of what I thought was the real me). I looked back up at her and could see that she could tell that something had changed in me.

"I'm sorry. There's nothing wrong with you at all. You are very beautiful and any man would be very lucky to have spent such a lovely evening with you. I lied to you. I, well, I…"

"Oh I get it," she said.

Did she? That would have been the very first time I had ever said it out loud for sure, so her guessing would allow the genie to stay in the bottle that little bit longer. I longed for her to say it, give me a hug of compassion and then leave me on the kerb to the lonely isolationist life that I had fooled myself into believing single life was all about.

"You're married aren't you?" She spat the words with venom.

I looked up at the illuminated restaurant sign that was bolted to the brick arch above the main restaurant window. Several diners had stopped eating and were now watching this drama unfold, no doubt keen to find out whether I was brave enough to turn that chest down – and how.

It would have been easier than anything to say, "Yes, that's it, married, yes." I could have stood, taken all the abuse and the slap that would have accompanied it, but instead, I still shook my head shamefully as if what I had to say was way worse.

"No, I'm not married." I added mournfully, looking sad. "I'm gay," I said finally. Years of denial, a million tears, a billion fears and decades wasted and I had finally admitted that I was gay. I glanced briefly at the diners, as if to say, 'happy now,' and could clearly see one say to another, "Told you."

My date was angered all the more by this revelation.

"Oh for God's sake!" she exclaimed, brusquely. "I'd have much more respect if you just told me the truth. If you don't fancy me then just say it, don't make up shit just to get out of spending any more time with me."

She began walking away from me, her shoe heels scraping along the pavement, each sounding like a lonely cry in the night.

"It's true!" I shouted in horrified defiance. She continued walking and whistled to hail a passing cab like a demented pressure cooker. I was incredulous. It had taken me bloody years to get to this point and she didn't believe me. "I'M GAY!" I shouted at the top of my voice. She shook her head and got in a cab. I stood and watched her drive pass, her parting shot was her one finger salute through the cab window as the cab whizzed past.

Really? How rude AND I'd bought dinner!

I was numb. I had just lost my confessional virginity and, as ever, I stood alone in the amber hue of the street. I glanced up to see her cab turn the corner. The tall buildings either side of me felt like they framed the moment. The large clock tower that straddled the theatre at the end of the street stood watching without judgment. It had survived war, civil unrest and bankruptcy. Open and busy again the theatre just stood there as if to say, "I've seen this all before mate and much more," and then chuckle at my misfortune.

I turned again to see the diners still transfixed. None of them spoke, none moved. I took a deep breath and shook my head. What was my next move? What would I do? I smiled at them weakly and marched off in miserable defiance.

COMING OUT… SORT OF…

However much I liked to dress things up, however much I continued to fool myself, no matter what I told myself, it was blindingly obvious I was never getting married and having kids. The reality of coming to terms with my sexuality was becoming increasingly inevitable. Not because I was happy with it or positive about my life, it was simple exasperation at the bloody games I had to play to remain hidden from view. I was fed up hiding from the world and myself.

I had been to too many clubs and slept with too many men for this to be a phase. Not only that, but as far as I could see, the world was still spinning on its axis and life continued. Would the reality be that bad? I was beginning to think that perhaps I would be happier if I stopped fighting the obvious and capitulated… a bit.

I wasn't going to do or be anything overt, I wasn't cabaret diva just yet (well…) I just thought that I could gradually become gayer.

Maybe I could drop the exquisite, devilishly successful butch masquerade that had fooled so many people for so many years. Instead, I'd casually let my pink veil drop and be a bit gayer – a tweak camp. One brick at a time in the long yellow brick road. After all, a little bit of fairy dust every now and then wouldn't hurt, would it? One day at a time. I could just turn my red-hot masculine inferno down to a softer shade of pink as each week went on. I'd allow others to learn to love the gayer me over time.

Teasingly.

Gradually.

Subtly.

So…

What better place to start than a work's function?

I duly decided that a massively important and fantastically glitzy one off function that my work was going to stage would be the perfect time to debut the inner more fabulous me. Naturally I'd need a few glasses of Dutch courage, just so that I could hit the ground running, figuratively speaking. I had quite a few glasses of courage as it turned out, which made me fairly invincible…

A fusty old man who was, in reality, a twat, ran the company. He'd sack people on the spot and didn't ever believe in employing women. He thought women were just baby dispensers who should stay at home and do the dishes and dust. When he took over the company he set about making various people redundant. All women. One day he walked into the leaving do of one poor girl he'd booted out and said, "What's this then love, your birthday party?" To which she very politely replied, "No it's my leaving do, you sacked me remember?"

This rather unpleasant large sweaty man, who rarely fitted comfortably into any suit, looked around at the appalled silence and said, "Oh yes! I remember. So, anyway, is there cake?" He really was odious. He waited, waited and waited and then when enough time passed he employed men to replace the women for whom he'd previously said there was no job. He did allow women to work in the sales department because as he said to me, "what man can resist a good tit?"

I felt like pointing out I found him entirely resistible and he was the biggest tit I'd ever seen, but I kept my counsel. I was always appalled by his attitude and his policies. He was a dinosaur from an era that I doubt ever really existed. A vile man whose sweat would stain his clothes and leave an odour trail that stretched from the ground floor to our office on the fourth. One of the unintentional upsides of working in an all male office, however, was the amount of eye candy on offer. It may have come about because of reprehensible means, but if life presents lemons...

This function was a one off. The company (like its owner) was as tight as a fish's arse. We got no pay rises. No bonuses. No flexi time. No more than the basic holiday requirement. No overtime – nothing. Even a Dr's appointment had to be made back up – whether (like me) you spent entire weekends working overtime for free or not. For them to push the boat out and actually spend money on a function was akin to a man landing on the moon, upside down, holding a gladiola and breathing without a helmet.

According to his status as a large middle-aged balding sweaty man with no likeable qualities whatsoever, he rarely bothered to show up in person for anything. He didn't want to socialise with us as he may get his hands covered in something unmentionable. At a Christmas drink (to which he was not invited) he told everyone that our one-off Christmas bonus (a £15 voucher) was, and I quote, "cheaper for us to give you lot that than it is for us to pay the tax on." It was a tax dodge.

Naturally, his attitude made us all feel warm, valued and squishy on the inside. However, as this was the company's 50th or

75th or zillionth birthday, he'd been wheeled from the asylum to attend.

Within about ten minutes of his arrival he was left standing alone and with a face like a slapped arse. He looked around the room at everyone assembled. It's fair to say we were all there to eat and drink as much of his money as we could. You could tell he was wondering if he needed as many staff and who the women that weren't waitresses were.

It was at this point that I decided it was time to spring into action. I made a bet with my fellow diners that I could make him laugh. After all, I WAS fabulous now and I had been drinking. Who doesn't love a drunken homosexual? What's more, who better to witness the new sleeker, gayer me than a man I'd met only once before? Who better to dazzle than the man who paid my wages and could influence future job references?

He stood alone holding a pint of beer, like someone clutching a nappy dripping with shit. Upon approaching him and saying hello, I saw him look me up and down. Was it my impertinence? Was it my gait? I was wearing a perfectly bland suit and tie so knew I wasn't offending his sensibilities. I didn't really mince up to him, but I may have offered a bit of a sashay.

"Hello smiler," I said with a beam. "Thanks for tonight, must have cost a bob or two. Hope its tax deductible…"

My boss appeared out of nowhere with that look on his face I had grown to know. Roughly translated it was: "Whatever you're doing or about to do – don't."

The big man looked at my boss as if to say, "and who is this vermin?" My boss set about indulging us both in a raft of meaningless small talk as I gently, but fabulously, swayed as if in a soft breeze.

I was also going through a period where I was getting offended at things I thought were happening or even worse – at things I thought were about to happen. My boss's intervention spelled only one thing to me: he was saying a big fat no to me being here, being queer and getting everyone used to it. That suggested immediately that he knew the big boss was a homophobe. A big, dirty, evil homophobe. What else could it be? What other possible explanation could there be? (My boss trying to keep me employed maybe? Just as a starter for ten…) I had nothing to substantiate this, I just 'knew'. I knew in the pit of my stomach, because in a flash of clarity as befits the drunk, I just knew….

I wasn't about to stand there and be insulted by a homophobic letch from the dark ages! Who did he think he was insulting me because of who I was? How dare he treat me like this, I wasn't going to tolerate this bigotry a second longer! Seeing my face crumple in drunken disdain (and knowing precisely what tended to follow), my boss stared at me, his eyes wide like someone had dropped a vial of tea tree oil deep into a cut. The big boss turned and looked at me again.

"Nice suit," I snapped sarcastically. "Grey. Mmm. I can see why you went with it. Good job you have a shirt on though, I might not know where the suit stops and you start."

I smiled broadly as if I had just paid him a generous compliment. My boss winced visibly and this man gave me a long, cold stare. I was aware that during this reproachful glowering that he hadn't blinked once. That made me transfixed with his eyes and eyebrows, which seemed to spur him on. I tried to focus on his pupils but they kept moving about and multiplying. At one point he had three.

I glanced back at the table I had been sitting on. I noticed everyone had their head in their hands or were looking at the floor.

"Ere," I said like Eliza Doolittle, nudging his arm. "You reckon we can have a float at Gay Pride? You can be on it. I mean there must be a reason you only like employing men…eh?"

"MORE DRINKS" My boss said and escorted me to the bar.

"What's wrong with smiler?" I asked genuinely. I glanced over at him – he was still staring, still not blinking. At that point I offered him a coquettish wave.

"What are you doing?" my boss asked. "You trying to get yourself sacked?"

The thought had actually never occurred to me. I looked at my boss who gave me a 'bloody fool' look. "Go and sit down, keep your head down and behave," he barked.

I was duly dispatched back to my table. I sat there feeling fabulously bitter. Not only was he homophobic, clearly he didn't like the workers. This was hatred and class war too! Workers unite. Rise up and fight. We must overcome… as soon as we've poured ourselves another wine. As I sat and drank I felt someone staring at me and I knew it was him. He was still trying to work out why he spent money employing weirdos like me.

"That was mad," said a guy at the table. He was from a

company that we'd just acquired. "And you didn't make him laugh…"

I nodded. "Yeah, but did I make you laugh?"

"Oh yes," he chuckled. "You made us all laugh!"

I sat and sighed. Maybe being fabulous wasn't my thing. Yes I was gay, but truth be told, I had all the panache of a cement mixer.

"Is it true what they just said?" He asked in a loud whisper. We were alone at the table. Everyone else had fled so as not to be tarred with my pink brush. They were all dancing to a cheesy pop song that tends to be wheeled out at weddings.

"About what?" I asked, not even looking up.

"You gay?" He said matter of fact.

I kept looking down. I had never been asked that question quite like that before. It was an aggressive question but not asked nastily. It was a sterile, matter of fact, "Does this bus go to Camden Town," emotionless question, yet it carried such weight. Simplicity could be startling. Stupidly I had thought my vivacious fabulousness would have already answered that. I never dreamed that I would still have to talk about my sexuality or be honest about it. I looked up at him and smiled. It was all I could manage, but all I needed to do. I looked back down again, feeling a bit foolish.

"I know how you feel." He said. His name was John.

It's well documented that I'm spectacularly quick to jump to incorrect conclusions and breathtakingly slow to see the obvious.

"No you don't," I said melancholically.

"I do," he replied with that matter of fact seriousness I had experienced earlier.

I looked up at him. "Oh yeah, how's that then?" I asked provocatively.

He just stared at me. A cold dead stare. Suddenly there it was. I could see that look. Something I had seen in many bars and clubs. That gaze of fear, that stare of pain. I knew then I was not the only gay at the table. As soon as he realised I'd seen what he wanted me to see, he looked away.

We sat in contemplative silence. "No one knows," he said finally. "I, I, it just can't be – okay?" he mumbled, as if talking to himself. "It would hurt too many people. I just, I just can't." I nodded. I didn't agree. If he had to upset his family then so be it. He had to be himself. 'Not everyone was like me,' I thought.

Almost as soon as I thought that, I was struck by the hollow, echoing absurdity of such a thought. Not everyone was like me? What was that then? Not out to family, sort of out to some friends, needing to be drunk to meet other men and acting like a pantomime dame to colleagues in the hope I would never have to actually tell them – like that huh? How could I hold myself up as some model of virtue? That was a joke. A rather pitiful tragic joke.

"I know." I offered weakly and continued looking at the tablecloth. "I understand." Considerably more than he could ever know.

There we both were, sitting silently at the table. There we both were, enormously unhappy and wrestling with our sexualities and what it meant to us. Him afraid of coming out for fear of hurting people he loved and me trying to work out who I was.

There we both sat, fabulous and feistily somber.

"Why aren't you two dancing?" someone shouted as they returned to the table.

"Oh, I don't know," I said pitifully. "I think the dance floor is for fabulous people, don't you?"

She looked back at me quizzically. We remained seated. In a short time everyone else rejoined the table. John offered me a final look as if to say 'please don't tell anyone.' I smiled. His secret was safe with me.

Everyone came back to the table and with their drinks replenished they settled back down. I was aware that some were wondering what had gone on in their absence, as we were as quiet as the grave and about as cheerful.

I sat staring solemnly at the cutlery that remained on the table. I traced the patterns on the knife. The swirls and twirls of steel engaged my focus. The fresh white tablecloth splattered with wine, crumbs and sauces. The effects of life. A mess. A total mess that needed a lot of clearing up. Yet as I stared, I was aware that whilst there was a mess, it also signified a good time. Happiness. Every stain, every crumb, every crumpled serviette showed where we'd had a good time. Was it possible to have both happiness and yet still be in a chaotic mess? This table suggested so. I looked up at John who was back to being the man he never should be.

I decided that I had had enough of hiding. I'd had enough pretending, of lying. I saw in John a kind of fear that I never wanted to feel again. It made me sick to my stomach. I never wanted to live a life in such terror. I saw the denial, I felt that pain. I saw an endless, tiring, futile future filled with more lies and deceit.

Worse still, I saw myself in his eyes. In that minute, at that moment, I was sure that if I didn't take action, now, there and then, I would end up just like John. I felt a sudden rush of nausea. It was now or never. This had to stop. This had to end.

"I'm gay by the way," I said very matter of fact. My head was bowed but I was as bold as I could be. I didn't know what to expect. I didn't know what to feel. Gradually I looked up to see everyone at the table staring at me aghast. "I said... I'm gay!" I repeated it but bolder, louder and frankly a bit camp. I thought they'd be pleased. Still they stared at me in shock. Surely they'd guessed?

"Well that's good to know," someone said over the loudspeakers. I spun around to see that the speeches had already started and everyone bar me was silent. I had just outed myself to the entire company. A room full of faces looked back at me. My eyes darted about to see bemused, shocked, amused and disgusted faces staring back at me. In that instant, I both died and came to life.

The speeches continued seamlessly and I sat, rigid, suspended in disbelief at my actions. I could get sacked. I could be shunned. Everything in my life was going to be different tomorrow. A new, scary and exciting era was truly beginning.

GYM AND TONIC?

After my date with the bracingly delightful breasts I had a period of general abstinence. I couldn't face anybody or anything. I would finish work on a Friday night and not speak to anyone until Monday morning. After a few weeks of this enforced solitude I found myself ordering several unnecessary things from the deli counter at the supermarket just to have some level of human interaction.

Sitting in my apartment on a Friday and Saturday night it felt perverse and cruel that only a few streets away a city throbbed, bodies writhed, people danced, drank and laughed. I felt like one of those Victorian urchins looking through the frosted window of a well-stocked and warm toyshop and seeing the joy others were having.

Essentially I was lonely. I hadn't made any friends. It's hard to make friends when you live a clandestine life, furtively slink off to clubs and refuse to discuss your private life. No bloody wonder I was alone. When my previous flat mate had moved out I had thought it an opportunity to have space and the place to myself. I wouldn't have to sneak men in and past their bedroom door now, I could treat the place like my own.

That worked well for a few weeks. I had the place and the space. However it was only ever relevant two nights a week at best. Not only was I paying double rent and double bills, I was doing so for minimal added privacy. Given that it hadn't been an issue when

I did have a flat mate it seemed like a waste of a chance to make friends. I started to think that if someone did move in I might be able to broaden my social circle. Not only that, but I could get someone to share the bills. I never thought it was a substitute for a relationship – I saw it purely as an opportunity to meet people and make friends. People used house shares all the time to make social groups work so why not now?

Not wanting to disturb my landlord with the tricky matter of subletting his home, I put an ad in the paper for a tenant. Initially, I put it in the gay press. Gay Times Classified. They just bristled with class. I had a few enquiries – mostly odd people. One asked if there was enough room for a sling and another asked if they'd have to supply their own waterproof sheets… One or two were normal. One of them, David, seemed perfectly respectable and wanted the room. We met at the apartment and I happily agreed that he could move in. To celebrate we decided to go out for the night – to go clubbing. I was so sure that he was who he said he was, that I didn't get him to sign the tenancy agreement before we went out for the evening. "Oh you can just do that in the morning," I said, happy to have someone seemingly normal – if a little flouncy – in my life.

The plan was for him to move in the day after we went out clubbing. Which made sense. Get to know one another a bit before we started living together. Out we went to a club and started to have a relatively jolly time. It was then I could see that he was a huge bitch. He stood slagging everyone else off.

I mean everyone. It started off amusing; the odd comment but soon became very tedious. Did he really have to have a go at everyone and everything? The bar man, that man over there, the DJ, the bouncers, the lighting guys, the guys who decorated the place, the people who laid the carpets – you name it. I dare say if the columns holding the building up had got in his way they'd have been berated too.

Who amongst us can't be the tart little queen when we want? However, you have to know when to do it, when not to and when to stop. I won't lie and say I get that right all of the time… but I am not so dumb that I don't get the hint when someone takes umbrage. Not only that, but if I was meeting a future flat mate for the first time I would be on my best behaviour – as I was. Initially I entertained this nonsense. I smiled, nodded and laughed whilst changing the subject at every given opportunity. Maybe he was nervous. I was.

Yes, he was right, the paint was not as neat as you might like, but we were in a fairly dingy club that had sticky carpets (for a host of nefarious reasons), so was this really the ideal place to start analysing the décor? It was never going to be featured in an interior design magazine was it? It was more likely to feature on Crimewatch, so really?

Then came the point in our brief relationship when I'd simply had enough of this negativity. I am not going to claim that I returned fire on everyone else's behalf, but this incessant bitching irritated me. I was trying to move away from negativity. I was trying to embrace a positive outlook. I began to wonder how he'd deal with a dose of his own medicine. Would he get the hint and stop? Would he realise it was out of place to be so bloody awful? Would he stop talking for five minutes and let me speak? How would he react to some friendly fire…?

Badly it seemed.

I was gentle. I waited my moment. Having just denounced yet another person for being a bad dancer and having had an appalling dress sense, I may have offered one or two comments. I may have suggested that his withering opinion on fashion had more gravitas than most seeing as he was wearing a rancid stripy blouson that he's evidently stolen from the 1980s Miami gay scene.

I may then have drawn attention to his orange skin and fake tan. I may even have offered an unsolicited comment or two about the fact his dancing looked like he'd a plank of wood rammed up his arse, as he'd all the fluidity of a garden shed – then asked if that was the only wood he ever had up his arse…

I might have pointed out that his love handles were certainly ample for more than one person to hold on to, should he ever fancy a threesome. I may have drawn attention to the fact his smile was as yellow as his socks and that he looked like a rather camp holiday park entertainer.

Like I said, I was gentle. I knew it would probably end things, but my word it felt good. Suffice to say, as I got home that night there was a message on the answer phone. By a strange, almost surreal quirk of fate, he had returned home to discover that his job was moving him to the South and thus he wouldn't be moving in. So yeah, didn't take the ribbing well, so to speak.

I sat on the sofa and sighed. I wasn't too unhappy but

ponderous. Did I try and advertise again? Did I just place an ad in the local paper and see what happened? I leafed through the remaining replies. There wasn't anyone who stood out as a maybe, let alone a yes. Come to that, there wasn't anyone who stood out as sane. I didn't mind someone moving in who had an active kink, but the thought of men coming and going every hour was not something that appealed. I did want some privacy and quiet. So, reluctantly, I decided to offer my abode to the mass audience, irrespective of their sexuality and their boundless social groups. I placed an ad in the local paper. In no time at all a straight guy came to see and then immediately took the room. It wasn't what I had wanted but I had bills to pay and the guy seemed nice enough.

He worked in hospitality so I assumed that he inevitably knew gay people. Maybe I would get to know people through him. Maybe all was not lost? Maybe this cloud could have a silver lining after all… Then I discovered that not only did he work shifts, he just needed a place to store his stuff. I was, therefore, a storage depot. In the six months he 'lived' with me, he spent two nights in his bed. He was never there. He said that he slept at his girlfriends and at work. This may very well be true, but why was he paying a city centre rent for a room to store his clothes?

Consequently, my desire to let my room to get a friend – or at least a social life – was an unmitigated failure. Week after week I would kind of hope he'd walk in and we could just chat, or go to the pub, but no. I saw him the night he moved in and then day he moved out.

This left a curious void and my mother immediately smelled a rat… Or rather, she smelled a man. We weren't talking about the big pink elephant in the room still, we talked around things like that. Yet here I was 'living with a man' who was never there. Somewhat like a lover I was trying to keep secret. Was that the case?

"Of course not!" I'd say in mortified disgust. "He's got a girlfriend and stays with her." It was true! Yet it sounded like I was trying to heap more deception onto of the obvious omission of truth that was going on.

"Why are you being so defensive?" she'd ask.

"I'm not, I'm just saying he's a nice guy who lives here, that's all. When I lived with that woman you didn't think I was in a relationship with her did you?"

The silence that followed was exceedingly awkward. Of course she didn't. I wonder why? I did think (however bizarre it was) that so long as I didn't own up to doing gay things to her, I was still technically straight. Akin to being innocent until proven guilty, I was straight until she could prove otherwise.

Consequently she went through my apartment like a gay truffle hound. More worrying for me was why a man would basically just use the apartment as a place to store his clothes. I began to wonder. I began to worry. Maybe he was a terrorist? Would I end up on the TV, saying all those things people say when they realise their neighbour is a mass murderer? "Well I didn't really know him that well. He kept himself pretty much to himself." Would the TV journalist say, "Well, yes but why did he have a toothbrush at yours if you didn't know him that well? Why were his clothes in a wardrobe in an apartment you were illegally subletting?" I didn't like the way it could pan out. I began to fret that I may indeed be sub-letting to a terrorist.

My mother wasn't interested in the terrorist theory. She thought this was just a deliberate and cunning ruse to hide the obvious. "If I was in a relationship with him," I'd protest, "Why would I leave his stuff out? I'm not exactly hiding him am I?"

"Double bluff," she'd say with a steely stare.

To her, the story sounded improbable (which, in fairness, it did). I told her that if I had been trying to hide things from her, I was fairly sure that I would be more effective than leaving a toothbrush and shower gel in plain sight. She never said, but the subtext was clear – you have lied to me about other things so why should I take you on face value about this?

One time when she was visiting I came out from the kitchen to see her in my flat mate's room. "What are you doing?" I blurted out, as she was looking through his wardrobe.

"There's one shirt and one jacket in here." She said. I was unaware of this fact, as I genuinely never snooped.

"You can't go through that!" I'd protest. Only for her to look me up and down as if to suggest that I was sticking up for a lover, rather than the fact she was simply invading another's human's privacy.

Once, when colleagues from work had actually spent the night at mine, she'd visited and noted the smell of more than one deodorant in the air. Why would there be another deodorant if I lived alone (as I did then)? I explained it was friends from work that had been, but she'd look at me with a face that said, 'We didn't believe you had friends when you called to say you weren't coming home, so let's not try that old chestnut.'

If I did protest, she'd say "So why haven't I met these friends?"

I didn't know what to say. She just hadn't. Which grown man introduces his friends to his mother? If I told her this she'd turn, looking hurt. "I am sorry I cause you so much shame. I didn't know you were embarrassed about me." And the cycle of emotional blackmail would start.

Therefore there was only one valid suggestion, I was in a relationship with a man who I was passing off as a flat mate but keeping hidden. Even when I asked why, if I was in a relationship, we'd need the second bedroom she'd smile and say, "You're thorough, I'll give you that."

On the very last day in that apartment my father came over to help me move out. My flat mate turned up with his girlfriend to discuss closing off bills. After we shook hands I spun on my heel, and with a half pirouette, looked at my father before saying, "Seeeeee!" At which point, I probably just confirmed everything he was thinking. Whatever that was.

So there I was, sitting alone and bored in my apartment. It had a rather wonderful view of the city's ever changing skyline. I loved that view. I particularly loved it at night when all of the lights were on. I used to spend hours just looking at those lights twinkling. I'd wonder who was behind each light and what they were doing. So many people, so many stories. Maybe someone was looking out of their window equally bored and lonely.

After a few weeks of this tedium, I decided to try another avenue and join a gym. If nothing else it would help me get fit. It was a well-known fact that gays loved to keep themselves buff in gyms. So maybe if I joined a gym I would get to meet people there too. It was worth a shot. It may seem incredible now, but back in the mid 1990s, Manchester had two gyms! There were about ten advertising themselves in the newspaper, but most of those were actually brothels. So I had a choice of two: the YMCA gym and a rather plush hangover from the yuppie excesses of the 1980s.

I started with the yuppie place because it was closer to work (and I am a bit of a snob). However, you immediately know what kind of gym you're in when they lead with, "and this is the juice bar…" In my experience anyone who actually wants to work out doesn't give two figs about a juice bar. They want to know what the weights and cardio equipment is actually like. After I was shown where they kept the complimentary fluffy towels and shown the walnut hard wood lockers, the fresh flower arrangements etc. we sat down to discuss terms.

This was also a time when you were expected to pay a one-off membership fee. Said fee for this place was £600! (£1050/$1650/€1460 in today's prices). After which it was £60 a month thereafter. As they had zero competition they could (and did) charge what they liked. Gym membership was a status symbol back then. If you went to a gym that gave you freshly laundered towels from a bespoke towel warmer – you were going places. It was complete and utter bollocks, not to mention daylight robbery.

I sat down for an interview to see if I was, "the sort of person" they wanted in their exclusive tiled money pit. They wanted to see whether I could pay – which is why gyms asked you to fill in such details as your salary and career details. This place went even further and asked what my earning capacity would be like in five and ten years… When I entered my modest salary of £16,500, I was told that I would be allowed within the hallowed fitness emporium, "but only just." They also made clear that they would expect to see my salary progress "dramatically," at our review in a year. (Yes, they were going to review my ongoing membership…) They wanted to see evidence that my career and me were going places. That's the kind of people that they wanted in their club. They couldn't have a pauper walking the same halls. Heavens! What would that look like?

Well fuck you, with aching glutes on.

Seemingly my earning potential pleased them more than my earnings. Had I been poorer I would have been shown the door and charged for my mineral water. We sat in this little office discussing whether I was up to the challenge of proving myself. Reluctantly, but because she "had faith" in me, the woman handed me a membership form and a pen. Having been offered the luxurious opportunity of joining this gym, I sat and looked at the form. I was trying to think of nice ways of telling her to spread her Rectus Femoris and insert her head where the sun failed to shine – when she sensed my hesitation. She decided now was a good opportunity to sum up my options. It is fair to say that the Y wasn't as posh. It didn't give you towels and their lockers were just hooks on a wall. There was no juice bar and it had a slightly municipal feeling to it. Membership there would naturally horrify anyone who sought the dubious luxury of the tiled, carpeted juice palace.

"Well, as you may know," she said. "We are not the only gym in town. There is also the Y." She stopped and smiled sardonically. "I don't know if you have been there," she continued, "It's very…" a pause for effect, "very adventurous. Very bold." She meant it was a common shit hole compared to her gaff.

"I haven't been," I answered honestly. It looked austere from the outside. It was considerably cheaper, but surely no gay would go there? Surely they'd all be here with their fluffy towels in the juice bar and cavorting in the steamy sauna.

She smiled at me. She was happy I hadn't been. Maybe I was worth the gamble, despite my piteous salary. "Well, I think you are wise not to go." She said, leaning in. "I know I shouldn't say this but the place isn't – well – it isn't as upmarket as here. I've also heard that the place is overrun with 'the gays', you know. Our gym would be a much better fit for you."

I sat and smiled. "Overrun you say?" I asked in shock.

"That's what I hear. Crawling." She added.

I was horrified by her conversation. Did she think I was gay and was tipping me the wink? Was she being genuine? Was she really warning me? I nodded sagely as if digesting the valuable information she'd shared with me.

We concluded our bottled water and our chat and I said I'd be in touch. Her insincere smile indicated that she was already spending my bloated membership fee. I walked out into a dark, cold evening. It had been raining and the streets shone their reflective brilliance. As I stepped out into the night, drawing my collar up, I set a course straight for the 'Y' gym. Within minutes of arriving I had joined.

It wasn't long before I made my way to the gym, ready to be crawled on. It was a Friday night after the usual post-work work out. The place should be over run, teeming, oozing gayness. I went through every piece of equipment. Glanced furtively in every mirror. Nothing. I looked around at the guys. They were almost all in groups. Then they all went off to play some team sport in the sports hall. Maybe Friday night wasn't our night.

I was back on Saturday.

Then Sunday.

Then Monday.

Then Tuesday.

By Wednesday the receptionist commended my dedication. I went every night and saw nothing crawling around the gym except very well toned people ignoring the desperate and tubby homosexual straining and sweating under the free weights.

It wasn't long before I realised that the 'Y' was as gay as a born again Christian blessing. I had been given duff gen. This wasn't gay. It was nowhere near bloody gay.

That weekend, having capitulated and fled to the village for some company, I got chatting to a guy. He mentioned his gym and how all the guys he met there. "The Y?" I asked in desperation, thinking of the full year's membership I had taken out.

"No," he said like I was an idiot. "That's where the straights go. No we go to the posh one, do you know it?"

I sat and pursed my lips.

"I know it," I muttered irritably.

"You wanna join there, its crawling with totty," he added as if to add insult to injury.

To this day I don't know what she was up to. Did they want to attract straights? Did they want to weed out the gays? Was she just passing on what she'd heard? As a result, I was chained into a 12-month contract to a place known for its fluorescent strip lights and creative use of plywood. As an added indignity, I had to walk past the fancy fitness palace jam-packed with muscled totty on my way to the down-at-heel Y. I used to watch the men walk in through the large ornate door and pick up their fluffy towels. I knew then. I just knew. I would shudder, grizzle and shake my head as I headed off to my gym. A city centre gym where people went just to get fit – what use was that? Gyms were for hooking up first and fitness second. This was a cruel joke and one I have never forgiven that orange plastic woman for.

As a result, I was still alone, poor and not that much fitter.

It always amazed me when I met a gay man who hadn't had a one-night stand. I thought one-night stands were obligatory. An inevitable and sad fact of single life.

Not that this bothered me greatly. The variety of totty on offer was always very appealing. Come the end of the week you would look forward to the prospect of some naughty fun over the weekend. You'd spend the week thinking it would be perfect coming together of testosterone, torsos and sweat. The prospect would be delicious, the thought of it intoxicating. All week you'd feel expectation building. By the end of the weekend, however, it was like you'd had a very bad BBQ. You looked forward to enjoying the flaming hot meat with its intoxicating spiciness, but when it came, it was never hot enough, often too sticky and sometimes left you feeling queasy.

For me, one-night stands were simply all there was. Not that I lived for them, it was just I didn't think I would ever experience anything beyond them. I looked around the gay scene and I saw very few couples. I can think of two. Even when I told myself that they were all at home making organic pasta with their new pasta machines bought by supportive Guardian reading friends, I didn't really believe it. All the faces in the bars and clubs were the same week-to-week, month-to-month and year-to-year. This was the treadmill we were all on. It struck me that any gay man in a relationship was merely having a string of consecutive one-night stands with the same person. Significant, honest, soul mates were just for straight people. I was totally sure that a meaningful relationship was impossible. Long-standing couples were rarer than rocking horse shit.

Couples declared their love one weekend and were spewing bile about the other the following weekend. Nothing seemed permanent. It seemed that we lived in a youth oriented culture where sleeping around was the only meaningful currency. And hey, so long as you were getting it – what was the problem? You were getting sex every week (or a few times per week) and wasn't that what every man wanted? Why did you want all that slushy shit?

As a result I assumed that this was the way things were and would always be. Love was a myth. You might feel a sense of closeness after some poppers as you light headedly surrendered to yet another meaningless one-nighter, but love in any true sense didn't exist. I saw one-night stands as the only opportunity to experience intimacy. The upshot was, I attempted to illicit tenderness through these fleeting lustful acts. Unsurprisingly it never worked.

I would often suggest that we 'just talked' or 'just watched TV' before the inevitable bedroom antics and was almost always met with total incredulity. At this stage we were all currency traders. The good looking had the most to trade with. The canny trader would use what they had wisely and those at the bottom end of the scale had to hope they could even get in the market. I tried to be canny. I tried to use the only currency I had to buy as much as I could, but sadly, it so often meant overplaying my hand.

Frequently I'd elevate these one-night stands to something meaningful and worthwhile. I told myself that they weren't soulless and emotion-stripping vacuums of hope. This was the life we had to live, so if I changed my perspective on one-night stands, surely I would find them more meaningful and thus be happier. That seemed like the secret to surviving gay life. It failed. Any attempt to get someone to be honest, open, maybe even vulnerable with me, was doomed to fail. I didn't have enough currency to buy that. Few of the men wanted anything other than the express checkout physical exchange. They weren't interested in the mechanics, just the rapid oil change. It was emotionally draining.

I tried to convince myself that whatever momentary intimacy I got was the gold standard. Something was better than nothing, after all. That I was lucky to still be in the game. Some of the older guys were left alone week after week. It reminded me that this was all there was, so I should make the most out of it and try and enjoy it. It wasn't perfect, but I had to make the most of what was on offer. This was gay reality, so I should just suck it up and take whatever I could from it, like everyone else did. As you can imagine, I rarely enjoyed it. What an ethos for happiness! Take what you can and be grateful… Is it any wonder I was miserable?

As time moved onwards I began to find one-night stands less and less appealing. If this was intimacy then I'd rather be alone. At least it had dignity. It is emotionally debilitating to go through so much shit just to feel the warmth of another human next to you. Sometimes after the deed was done the guy would make some excuse and just leave. Work early in the morning. Get home before roommate. Flight to Mexico left early in the morning. Looking after neighbour's feral cat which needed feeding at first light…

I began to feel used. (Yeah, it took that long for the obvious to sink in). I was just giving it away free. I wasn't trading in currencies; I was trying to bribe men to spend time with me so that I could feel fleeting intimacy. Well, I was…

The price? Whatever they wanted. That was the cost for not feeling alone, even for an hour or so. As I was desperate for any hint of intimacy, of 'normality', I did the only thing I could – I gave it away for free. I was a definite sure thing. I would offer it up cheaply in exchange for the possibility that something long term may develop with them.

It never occurred to me that I would never enter into a relationship with someone who was behaving like me. I would never go out with someone who evidently thought so little of themselves that they'd give their body cheaply for passing moments of warmth. Why not? Well, because that person obviously had issues. They didn't respect themselves. If I didn't respect myself, how could any bloke I picked up at a bar? I was stuck in a torturous cycle. Desperate to be with someone, afraid to be with someone, drunkenly giving it away in the hope I would find meaning, clarity or compassion. What a fool. Meaningful long-term relationships weren't born from insecurity and charity. That's all I was presenting as qualities I had to offer. Surely I was more than that? It meant becoming bolder. It meant being a stable gay. Yet terror would soon return and I would turn yet again to my fractured emotional state and the cycle of depression.

Sometimes people would come home with me, ask for what they wanted, and if I felt comfortable with it I would do it. Almost always they were in no mood to reciprocate and would just leave. Okay, so sometimes it was nice to get up in the morning and treat the previous evening's trouser athletics as a kind of horny dream, but increasingly they were just dispiriting. Waking alone, knowing that some man had treated me more evasively than a ship in the night, began to drag me down. Why did no one want to be with me? Why was it always limited to a 24hr cycle and no more?

That's not to say that they were all like that. Obviously they weren't! Sometimes people were nice – otherwise I would have lost faith much sooner. Despite this, the nice ones seemed to thin out and the predictable ones took their place. As time went on, I began to think that I wasn't just a sure thing, I was a bit of a whore – which is fine. If that's what you want. Yet, I would give it up for most people, most of the time. Simply put, I gave away sex in exchange for a cuddle.

I lost count of the times that I was in a bar or club and was told that they were sick of the scene, of the meaningless one-night stands and so on… it sounded like music to my ears. Then a few hours later, I realised it was just a line. Maybe they were as confused and tortured as me. Maybe they meant it when they said it. Maybe they just knew what to say to get what they wanted. Once, I met someone for a date and told him explicitly that under no circumstances would I have any sex. It was time to get to know one another and then maybe, in time… We went out for a drink, which was fine, then he invited me to his apartment for food. I went under the strict understanding it was food and only food.

Once there he made us cheese sandwiches and explained that gay men didn't do what straight couples did. Gay men had sex first and THEN got to know one another. So why didn't I just finish my sandwich and he'd give me a BJ. It felt like he was saying he'd rather get the boring sex stuff out of the way so that we could get to know one another.

I explained that he was missing the point, but he kept on about it. As we sat there discussing his career aspirations (bafflingly unattainable) I realised that we'd no future together. Maybe we could be friends, but I couldn't see him as partner material. So I finished my sandwich, did what came naturally to gay people apparently and then left feeling like I'd let myself down. As I walked home and I wondered if he was right. Was this how it was done? Sex then relationship?

A few days later I was out again. I was beginning to stay sober and get bored earlier. On this occasion I went to a nightclub as I needed of cheering up and the music was always jolly. As ever, I kept a keen eye out for my pensioner. I knew his 'told you so look' would be too much to bear. I stood, propped up against one of the pillars that dotted the basement club. Cheesy tunes played as the place filled slowly. After a while a guy came up to me and started chatting. I actually turned around to see if he was talking to someone behind me as I was fairly sure someone that amazing couldn't be talking to me. He was stunning. Such perfection. Normal too. No weird behaviour or seeming personality traits. I was sure the small print in my new 'get to know each other before having sex' policy had specific leverage for temporary suspensions...

He was a clear ten and no way was I letting him go if I could. Remember, he'd come up to me. I looked around, did he have other options? Yes. How about better looking ones? He did, plenty. Yet here he was still talking to me! Blimey... Maybe my time at the gym was paying off.

The night progressed fairly uneventfully until we started talking about relationships. He talked about how bored he was of the scene. How he wanted a relationship that would mean he'd never have to go out hunting again. He said he found the place noisy and wanted to go home, did I want to come too? DID I?

We made our way swiftly from the club and into a cab. We drove the fair distance back to his apartment and in the cab he held my hand. That simple dumb thing felt like the raciest, most daring thing that I had ever done. EVER. It felt bold, courageous and unreal. Holding hands... Sex was meaningless and disposable, but handholding was actually intimate.

We got to his apartment and he made us both drinks. We sat and chatted until he asked if we could go to bed but not do anything?

YES!

YES!

YES!

This was perfect. A clear ten that was saying everything I had ever wanted to hear. Frankly, I was already shopping for new curtains. There was no way they were staying once I'd moved in.

We went to the bedroom and I began to wonder whether this was all just a line. He brushed his teeth, put on some pyjamas and got into bed. PYJAMAS. This one was a keeper. I got in alongside him and we cuddled for a bit before he said 'goodnight' and turned the light off. He lay there. I lay there. We lay there.

I mean yes I was happy to sleep, but you know…

Then he started moving. Oddly. Mysteriously pressing himself up against me suggestively. I lay there wondering if this was a cue to take things further. So I did, but he said no. Okay… So I lay there still. The rubbing up against me began again, but I wasn't sure what to do. In the end I simply turned over and fell asleep. Yes this was more meaningful, but did meaningful also have to mean odd?

At 5am I woke up with a start and saw him staring at me. "Morning," I mumbled, still blurred.

"Morning," he said. There was that smile. I could forgive him last night. Maybe he was struggling too. I understood that. "I am afraid you are going to have to leave," he said finally, looking away guiltily.

I looked at his alarm clock. "It's five," I said. "The trains won't be on, I'll never get a cab and the buses aren't even running yet."

He looked uncomfortable. "I am sorry but my best man is due here any time now."

We both stared at each other in silence. Best. Man. What?

"What?" I managed to blurt out whilst sitting up.

"I am getting married today." He said shiftily.

We both sat in silence again. I was trying to process what was happening. I was barely awake. I tried to digest and comprehend his thunderbolt. Last night I was picking up curtains, this morning I was being taken out with the trash.

Were there any normal people left on this bloody friggin planet? Why couldn't I meet a guy that was normal? Couldn't I be part of a relationship where the highlight of our mutual dysfunction was arguing in the supermarket car park about who forgot to buy the tomatoes?

"Excuse me?" I said finally. "So what was…"

"That was my stag do," he offered, limply. "I just, well I can't upset my parents. I've known her for years. My parents love her and her parents love me so…"

I was dumbfounded. "You can't marry someone to keep your parents sweet. You have a right to be happy," I countered.

"You don't understand," he said standing up. He paced the bedroom and I got to see his magnificent body. "My parents bought me this flat. If I dumped her and went gay they'd disown me. I'd lose everything." He looked at the floor mournfully. "I'll just try and be happy," he added.

I was torn. I was angry… actually I was furious, but for him. Where was his spine? Fuck the family. You have to live for yourself. I knew that no matter what, if ever pushed into a corner I'd come out fighting. I may have been nervously crouching in the corner of the closet but no one would dictate my life like that.

"Sorry," he said with raw emotion. "You have to go."

With that, I dressed in awkward silence. He stood and watched. As I got ready to leave, I went up to him. "I think you're a fool, but I hope you find happiness."

"Sorry," he said again. "That's why I couldn't do anything last night. I just can't. I'm getting married today."

I looked at him and felt a mixture of pity and anger.

I sighed. "I think you're an idiot. I think you won't find happiness until you are the person you need to be. It's taken me fifteen years to realise that so don't throw away the best years of your life waiting to find that out. You also owe her much more than you are offering her too. Your marriage is a lie. She deserves better – so do you."

With that I turned to leave. He walked behind me and touched my back. I turned to look at him. "See you around," he mumbled.

"I doubt it," I replied. With that, my night with a ten ended and my eight-mile walk home began.

Imagine going out to meet someone for a date. Imagine all that tension, those butterflies and the wild expectation. You swing between excitement and panic. What if?

What if this is the one? What if this is the person you've been waiting for all of your life? You get dressed, taking an age to select the correct clothes. Does that make you look fat? Does this make you look needy? Does that make you look desperate? Ugly? Friend zone? 'Oh God, this is a nightmare.' Finally, you get all of the clothes together, brush your teeth, ensure there's an industrial level of deodorant applied to ensure no unsightly stains and you are almost good to go.

Clothes, check.

Teeth, checked and check.

Money, check.

Confidence – AWOL.

Hope – hanging in there!

Note to housemates in case you get murdered…

Gay bashing was so prevalent that meeting a guy for a date – whether serious or for a one night encounter – could easily be your last date on this planet. Even if it wasn't your last you could find yourself waking up in a hospital bed rather than his. Stories of men who were hospitalised by attackers who had lured them out on a date and then into a trap, were widespread. It was an unfortunate and terrifying aspect of everyday life and one you had to accept.

When I worked at the charity there was a man who lived in the city. He lived in one of the glorious red brick mill-to-apartment conversions that were highly sought after. It was dead central and easy for him to get from A – B or from A to A Bed. Like me, he'd just moved to the city and was finding his way around. He was tall, good looking and although uncertain of his future path in life, he always hoped to find peace.

One day he didn't show for our regular envelope stuffing. As this was a voluntary job, we didn't read too much into it. It was odd as he was a keen visitor. As we were supposed to be anonymous when we turned up, there were no contact details held. Then, the next week – still nothing. It was at this point that we started to make enquiries. Where was he? Had he just had enough? Finally one of the guys (the one who said he wasn't a rent boy) used his contacts to track him down.

He was in a coma.

He'd gone on a date. His date suggested they go back to our friend's apartment, which they duly did. His date said he was going to call home and say he'd be late. Instead he called his mates and told them the address of our friend. The door was opened by the date and the men came piling in and beat him up so badly he was left for dead. The walls were covered in his blood. It was only because a friend called around and found him that he was saved. Had he not, he'd have duly died of his injuries. It is my understanding he did eventually get better, but can any of us say his life would carry on as normal?

This story was truly atrocious and we were all horrified.

Horrified, but not shocked. The compounding indignity of being an outcast and looking for love meant that even if you did meet someone, you weren't sure if they were the 'one' or the 'one who'd end your life.' A broken heart seemed like small change by comparison. Week after week another story would emerge of someone in hospital or suffering a near miss. It may seem ridiculous now, but it was a reality.

As a result, going out to meet someone meant you had to take precautions. If you were out, then it was easy, you could simply tell someone where you were going. Back then, CCTV cameras were nowhere near the gay bars. CCTV cameras operated by the police within gay areas were like putting a wolf in charge of the sheep pen. It was viewed as intrusion and possible entrapment by those who, historically, had been as bad as the gay bashers despite being paid to protect us. Local councils argued that the freedom of people to come and go would be severely restricted if they felt like they were being spied upon. It was a powerful argument and one that almost everyone signed up to. As such CCTV was kept out of bars and away from the surrounding areas. The drawback, however, was the opportunity it created for bigoted thugs. In the blind spot of surveillance they could have a field day. It is not an exaggeration to say that police tape, splatters of blood and ambulances were not uncommon.

It felt as if the enemy had infiltrated us, like a sleeper cell. It always amazed me that allegedly straight men spent their precious leisure time in gay bars, flirting with other men purely to lure them to their doom. You had to ask yourself every time you met someone – are you trying to make out with me or end my life? It was a question asked in bars up and down the land.

As such, if you hadn't come out to people, you couldn't just tell them where you were going. "I'm off to THROB, not sure what time I'll be home. If I am not back tonight I may have got lucky. If I don't come back tomorrow then call the police and start your search there."

As a result, those of us in the closet needed to take some precautionary action to let any subsequent investigators know where we'd gone. Clues, email addresses, phone numbers, photos – anything we had that could link us to our possible murderer. It was not untypical to get a post it note and stick it somewhere private, but easily found, to say where you'd gone. There'd be little point including a name of the person you were meeting as in all likelihood they wouldn't be using their real identity anyway.

I had a shag pad. It wasn't my apartment, it was a notebook from which I took pages to scribble down all and anything I knew about the guy I was going to meet. If I was just going out, I would literally write my intended itinerary. I would list the bars I planned to visit and around what time.

At the back of my pad I listed, as if for historical reference, places of cruising note in the city. The implication being, if you discover that I left the bar at x time, I may well have been at one of these places, so try there.

Newbies to the city initially felt safe. The bars and clubs were always so full of people that surely everyone could see you and know where you were going and with whom. However, as most people were in the closet and didn't trust the police, most people would deny being gay or having ever been anywhere near the scene. The very last thing anyone wanted was the police to turn up at work or home and ask if you saw a man who'd gone missing from a prominent gay bar or cruising spot. I've known of situations where men denied being at a bar or club knowing full well that they were helping the attacker – but were just so terrified of outing themselves. Trust me when I say the police at that time wouldn't ask you in private… So if you didn't want to lose your job or be kicked out of your home you'd have to bluff your way out of it. "Why would I know? I've never been there before!"

The individual stakes were so dizzyingly high that you knew you couldn't rely on anyone to help the police, you just had to look out for yourself. Accordingly I had my random jottings left by my bed for the police to find and thus use in their half-hearted search for my body.

I have already mentioned there were plenty of times when I got into a car and, trusting a hunch, assumed the guy was no threat to me. Every time I closed the car or apartment door I was entrusting my life to them. I've been driven across moors, fields, back roads and down country lanes – all of which would have provided an optimum setting for meeting his gay-bashing mates to duly dispatch yet another bummer. There were times when, as the dark night sped by the car window, I would wonder if I'd see the sun again. Such was the fear and reality of meeting men.

As gay men were still scared of coming out, they hid. They hid in the shadows and in the margins of life. As anyone who understands bacteria will tell you, if you lurk around in the dark long enough, parasitic bacteria will emerge and attempt to infect and destroy what it finds. So it was. Gay men were brilliant targets. They were highly unlikely to report their crime to the police as the police would either add their own kicks and punches or they wouldn't take such a crime seriously. Gay men were easy to target, easy to attack and the crime was easy to get away with. As I've said previously, I still can't fathom why 'straight' men would spend their leisure time in parks and behind bushes just waiting for gay men. That begs questions – doth the bigot protest too much?

Naturally having a bit of slap and tickle in the bushes of the local rec centre was a criminal offence. As such, the police would patrol parks to keep everyone safe. Or, as it was historically, they'd arrest the trouser set, shame them in the local media and assist the gay bashers. That's all changed now, but it was a fact of life when I was growing up.

I always remember when I was an older teen walking through a park – quite innocently I should add – when a man walking past me said, "watch out, they're everywhere tonight." I stopped dead and wondered what he was talking about. I was on my way home and always cut through the park. I looked around nervously. As I left the park I saw the police vans. "Good!" I thought, the police will catch whoever "they" are. Little did I realise that the police were the 'they' he was talking about.

It also struck me as odd that such sting operations got so much publicity. The minute a story appeared in the paper that men were found loitering in the rose garden looking for some fun, it merely advertised that the rose garden was the place to be. Surely that initiative was counter productive? I was advised by my parents to avoid that park at night, as said activity was known to go on there. It just made me walk through it all the more often and considerably slower than normal. I wouldn't have done anything, but it was all very exciting. As soon as a rhododendron bush quivered I'd look over expectantly only to see a squirrel clamber out. Bloody squirrels. Yet back then, if the police did catch you at something, they would eagerly release the details of your attack/arrest to the press. Everyone would soon know that you'd been skulking around the bushes where gays hang out as soon as it hit the local newsagents. Your work and social life would be terminated as fast as you could say hand job.

As such, said activities carried a significant risk. You never knew whether you would get arrested, beaten up, hospitalised murdered or lucky. All such encounters carried a potential risk. You just had to try and take necessary steps to ensure the culprits may be caught by leaving clues as to your whereabouts.

I recall thinking that any note listing the places I'd visited would be a painful and haunting epitaph. What a way for my parents to find out about me. Can you imagine how that would feel? That was all they would have to link me to my demise. They would feel isolated and pushed out of a life they knew nothing of. It would create so many unanswerable questions. I did consider writing a letter to be opened in the event something did go massively wrong, but felt unable to do so. What could I put in that? 'If you're reading this then my quest to be loved hasn't gone to plan.' It seemed like an emotionally charged injustice that we even had to consider this kind of thing before going out. Where was my carefree youth?

In the end, I just carried on and hoped that I would be one of the luckier ones.

In a nutshell this isn't a happy story. It's true, sadly, but it's not great. Well, not for me anyway…

It's about the night some tried to rape me. As you can imagine I've told few people this story and writing it won't be easy. Actually, re-writing it won't be easy as I have written this a few times and then decided I'd made it seem too jovial. So I am re-doing it – re-living the night in question.

For those of you who fast forward to the end of a movie or read the last page of a book to make sure everyone makes it through okay, then worry not, I'm still here and well thank you for asking. This isn't a comment on rape or on the world of single life and pick-ups. It's not a comment on anything or anybody (well, maybe me and him). This is just something that happened to me. This is a matter-of-fact recollection of something unpleasant that happened to me. It is not social commentary. I don't even know if there's any moral to this story – I certainly don't include it to shock or anything, but perhaps rather show what can happen when you have such low self esteem. What situations you can find yourself in when you are not at peace with yourself.

My 'mentor' at the gay charity I worked at once said to me that when you don't like yourself, you don't care about your safety – your mental or physical wellbeing. If you feel that your life isn't worth much, then why not take risks? It is suggested that is why a lot of gay men drink, smoke and have unsafe sex – because why not? Their life isn't worth much so get your fun where and when you can. What do you have to lose? I made some decisions that, looking back, were mad (utterly mad), but decisions that perhaps say a lot about where I was at that stage in my life. Seemingly, I thought very little of myself.

If you hook up with someone at a club or bar and go back to theirs you are always, to some degree, putting your life in their hands. They could be a murderer or a nut job. The chances are rare, but it's possible. As such, a degree of caution needs to be used when going into someone's house. Usually when you get there you can tell if they are sane or not. A nice tidy house with a dog or cat bed is usually reassurance enough that they aren't fruit loops. So when I decided to go into a run down house in one of the city's most notoriously dangerous estates, perhaps I was playing with fire.

Fundamentally I believed people were basically good. That no matter what may be thought, people were decent, honest and good. Up and until that point nothing bad had happened to me other than being messed about and lied to. I was pretty lucky with all of the encounters – in so far as, some were funny, few were sweet, even fewer were good looking and the rest were 'we close in ten minutes' last stop on the line.

The routine of one-night stands had become a tedious ritual. It was happening less and less as I grew disheartened with the formula: Hope. Depression. Alcohol. Hope. One-night stand. Loneliness. Self-loathing. Fear. Depression. Hope. Depression. Alcohol....

The prize so highly sought after, that intimacy I craved, lured me back time and time again. However, the resulting feelings, the treatment, the price I had to pay in my quest to find that intimacy seemed harder and harder to justify. All of the tension, the passion, the bare naked lust driving me to that one moment of release seemed to be over far faster than the pain, loneliness and the sickened self judgment that followed.

I always vowed never to do it again. I would stay away from the soulless scene, never to return. Yet, of course, return I always did. I'd stand in bars, in clubs and pubs hoping that this time it would be different. The cycle of going out, getting drunk, going home with someone and waking to a reality where I felt rotten, shameful, hung-over and furious that I'd fallen yet again was draining. The cycle was always the bloody same. The only difference now was that rather than a few times a week it was now a few times a month. It was the same turgid merry go round of hope and despair. On and on it went. Repeat to fade. It was doing my head in. Surely happiness was out there somewhere?

On this night in question I'd worked late and decided on a night out. As I was late joining the fray I'd only had a few drinks when, to my complete shock, I met a guy and found myself getting on really well with him. He was well built, tall, had dark wispy hair and quite mischievous eyes. He had an imposing persona and took up a sizeable chunk of space between the rest of the room and myself. Despite this, he looked uncomfortable. He kept looking around the bar, seemingly ill at ease. Mind you, given the number of drunken lushes and queens tottering around, he could also be forgiven. It wasn't everyone's cup of tea.

He seemed different. Different from the rest of the people in there. I took a long hard steely look at him, was my wait over? Could this be a chance at happiness? Is this what it felt to be with a guy and feel normal? I was sober and chatting away merrily without ulterior motive or shame. I was also so desperate for stability that I thought everyone who spoke to me (and was sane) was 'the one' in the making.

Talking to him was genuinely refreshing. I was also taken with the fact he seemed happy to chat, not just ask a series of questions that tried to find out where I lived and what I was up for sexually. Sometimes I thought it would be easier to have a menu of likes and dislikes printed on my shirt. It would save a lot of time. Standing in front of me was a normal good-looking guy who was talking to me as a human. With respect. With dignity. This was amazing!

It wasn't long before he suggested we go back to his. That the bar wasn't his scene, it was too loud, too overcrowded and he wanted to leave. He didn't do the scene. I was only happy to oblige. It was beginning to get tacky and all you'd see were the same sad faces week in and week out – of which mine was one. I remember as we left together, some of the regular bar flies looked sickened. They knew what the evening had in store for them and they knew what I had in store for me! No wonder they were all looking at me like that.

I wasn't up for a big, late night out anyway. I was at the end of a long draining week at work and was more than happy to hit the hay, after an appropriate roll in it. We both stepped outside onto the cobbled street with its circus of neon, people and noise. The energy was infectious and we both smiled at one another. Hailing a cab, we bundled into the back like naughty schoolboys doing a bunk. Was he as exhausted of the scene as I was? Did he want to just break away from the nonsense?

I didn't catch where he said he lived, a usual rule of mine, but as he seemed so nice I didn't mind. I was sure he'd be fine. As we slumped into the deep black leather seats of the taxi, we just looked at each other.

COULD THIS BE IT?

Could he be the one? Was there any such thing as 'a one'?

I didn't feel nervous, I didn't feel dirty and for once, I was feeling quite good about myself. It was the dangerously alluring flashes of being gay and normal that enticed and frightened me. What if they were just fake? Teasing glimpses of a life never on offer. What if these sirens of the night were luring me to the rocks with promises of normality only to lie in weight to destroy me? As we raced the city streets I didn't much care. This felt good. I was actually approaching something people often spoke of. It was called happy. As we sped through the drunken wintery city streets, as street lamps flew by above us and buildings blurred into one, I was almost there. As we twisted and turned our way through suburban streets, he raised his fingers and touched my nose. "There's one thing you should know," he said. "The house is going to be freezing cold because the gas is off."

Err, okay. Odd thing to point out. It was already freezing outside, so being cold inside wasn't exactly heart-warming. Still...

"I'm sure we can keep ourselves warm," I said as the taxi drew to a stop. Disembarking from the cab I looked around and knew instantly I was in one of the most treacherous districts of the city. As a teenager I had been through it many times. The bullet holes in the windows, the sound of vicious dogs and the sea of litter were not exactly a fluffy welcome mat. This is not what I had expected.

"Come on," he said and walked towards one of the ugliest council dwellings I had seen in many a year. Maybe the bullets were an attempt to shoot the architect. He put his key in a small lock that hid within a solid, reinforced door. It opened to darkened, but fairly spacious two-story house. The moon and streetlights crashed into this darkened house like unwanted guests. In so doing they shone a beacon over the state of the property. It was empty; there was no furniture at all. Nothing anywhere.

"Let me turn a light on," I said. I wanted to make sure there was nothing more that I couldn't see. Nothing to concern me.

"Power's off too," he said bluntly. "Come on up," he whispered and started up a narrow flight of wooden stairs towards a small uncovered window above. A light at the end of a tunnel.

"Erm," my hesitation was palpable. Yes he was nice, he was good looking and seemed intelligent, but this wasn't how I imagined it would turn out. But for his key, this was a squat. The man who was tired of the scene had brought me back to a cold, empty and decaying house in a rough and violent area of town. I could be forgiven for having reservations...

"Oh," he said and hung his head. "I know how it looks."

Did he? Because he'd have given me more warning if he did – surely?

I glanced around at the piles of telephone directories, pizza menus and unopened mail. There was an ancient, musty carpet on the hall floor and barely anything on the windows. The solid thump from each stair echoed in the silence of this hollow home until they made good their escape.

"I can't afford all of that." He said looking mournful, or what I thought was mournful in the poor light. "I live with my parents, they don't know. In fact they're massive homophobes, very religious. I needed to get out, so I applied for a house and they offered me this. I took it. Then, dad got sick and the money I had for myself went to help them both out. I'm not proud of this," he snorted. "I know it looks bloody awful, but I am just about paying the rent. I needed somewhere to go, to get away from them to get away from that. Do you have any idea how that feels? Do you know what it's like to feel trapped – where you'll do anything, even this, to be alone with yourself?"

We stood together in the dank hallway, him a few steps up, both cold and lonely. Yes I did know. Yes I did understand… What had been a dingy little hovel that inspired nothing other than fear became a rose amongst thorns. This was the sad and sorry state of gay acceptance at the time. Here was a man forced into hiding, into a dark, cold, unloved space just so that he could love. A man who had to finance the very people who (knowingly or not) had driven him into such a state of desperation. This was the UK. This was here and now. This wasn't a historical piece or a war torn dictatorial country. This was a modern progressive Western country – yet look at us. Forced into the shady shadows by those who didn't understand. This was our life and it was very far from glamourous. He was shivering. I felt an overwhelming desire to protect or help. He may have been considerably bigger than me, but he seemed so very small. So vulnerable.

I started up the stairs, passing him as I did and trailing a hand behind me. He took it and we walked up the hollow steps together. "Left" he whispered, as I entered a large room. A threadbare, disintegrating net was slung unconvincingly across the window. It's odd but that was what made me have doubts. It was too lazy. Too dodgy. Surely a lonely dejected soul would have made more effort? It was eerie. The room was genuinely freezing, plumes of breath exploding in front of us with every word uttered. There, as if shaking in fear like an imprisoned refugee, was a mattress huddled apologetically in the corner of the room. It lay flat on the floor and was draped with the thinnest sheet I had ever seen. It lay crumpled in a ball as if slung there in a hurry. Both looked damp.

I looked at him in disbelief. Even if I did have my own secret shag pad, I would have made it moderately comfortable. "All the money I've spare goes on the rent," he said unprompted. "I've nothing left. This is my only hope." I wondered how many men stayed and how many fled. How much good will was there in the world? Surely even he could do something better? This looked like a junkie's hang out. It didn't inspire warmth, even if his story had. I contemplated leaving. Yes he was lonely, yes I was lonely, but I was moving away from such sacrifices. Happiness was never coming to my rescue dressed like this squalid squat.

My sympathy was beginning to wane. Not only could he not

make the place even marginally habitable, which ruled out any long term future for us, but if he could pay rent… Why keep it on in such a dismal state? Why not request a flat or somewhere smaller and cheaper? Why keep such a large place on just to keep it empty and uninhabitable? It also irritated me to see this man abusing the system. People needed homes and he was hogging this one. However, I wasn't there to discuss politics. He turned me around and we kissed. At first I was unsure, worried, cornered. Soon, the concerns were gone, if only to be replaced by a bone chilling cold. We slowly made our way to the 'bed' as the night began to unfold, in some ways, at least how I had expected. Before long, the cold was diminished (if not banished) and we began to enjoy one another. Our two bodies, desperately seeking the gentle touch of one another. Two people, one forced to hide behind a threadbare curtain and another behind a threadbare lie.

Two people, wanting, needing and craving each other. There was something so symbolic in this. Something so fundamental. He seemed to enjoy proceedings and took a more dominant stance. Experience taught me to keep that in check, but not stop the flow. Some got carried away, others not.

"Let's fuck," he said whispering into my ear as we contorted together.

"You have any condoms?" I asked. I had no intention of shagging, but this question always taught you a lot about the other person.

"Don't need any," he answered and started to remove my underwear. His breath became more marked and faster. I could see why he needed a clandestine spot to bring his conquests to, but as previously thought; I wondered how often that happened. He certainly was keen – was he just lonely?

In a fleeting moment I felt very sad for him. I shared his quest for normality and acceptance. I was also equally as turned on, by that and by him. The connection was thus both physical as it was emotional. I understood where he was at and where he was coming from, so to speak. It seemed genuine.

"Let's fuck," he said again.

"No," I replied, "Not now." Maybe at some point, but not tonight. I wanted tonight to represent everything that we both felt and shared. After so many meaningless one-night stands, how could this be anything like that?

Despite what I might have said or even thought, what I really wanted was love. Surely someone so frightened felt the same? If they weren't after love then simple intimacy? In that damp cold hole of a house I finally knew what I wanted. The quest for fleeting intimacy was over. The one-night stands could carry on but for the right reasons – for fun, not for some sense of fulfillment.

Seemingly, someone so frightened didn't share my feelings. "Come on," he said, his large hand snaking across my body and pushing expectantly where he wanted to go.

We were now lying on the cold, damp icky mattress. He was using his hands less to caress and more to restrain. I am all for a bit of kink, but this had the hallmark of something else, something sinister. He was holding one of my hands tightly and trying to hold it down. Every time I tried to withdraw my hand, his hand swarmed over it and attempted to bury it into this makeshift bed. Never sure if this was all part of a game, a bit of fun, I didn't express immediate concern but it seemed that our movements were becoming less erotic and more combative. He was quite a bit bigger than me and seemed to want to lie on top of me. In a flurry of physicality, like a deft wrestling move, he spun me over and pinned my legs and hands down as he did. It was quite a feat.

At first, although immediately suspicious and acutely aware of what might be happening, I was also questioning my own senses. Maybe he just liked it a bit rough. Fair enough… but…. As the wriggling and hand grasping continued, I decided to test the waters. Was this what I thought it might be? Surely to God not? Really? Was this happening?

He had a knee on each of my legs and his hands were pushing my hands down, with his body keeping my torso flat. It was an uncomfortable position and I didn't like how things were shaping up. Things were moving very quickly too. Intimacy was long gone.

I told him clearly to stop – more than once. That my wrist had been hurt. In truth it hadn't but anyone just up for a bit of fun would have stopped there and then. Anyone decent would have recoiled and perhaps even apologised. Anyone who didn't show concern had no concern. At this point, we were beginning to start a bizarre wrestling bout. After much gyrating and noises akin to a playground brawl than a bedroom ball, he set about kicking my legs apart. He pulled one of my hands back behind my head and pushed my face down into the stinky, musty mattress.

This was not good. "Stop wriggling," he said as if I was just

224

trying to get comfortable. "You'll enjoy it more if you just stay still." At that point I heard him generate a generous mouthful of saliva in his mouth. Once, then again and again. As I started to fear what was actually happening, he was gathering as much moisture and make-do lubricant as he could. Whilst I appreciate that this sounds like it happened over a week with breaks for sandwiches, it actually happened so very fast. I was trying to process my thoughts, to try and get to grips with what was happening. Surely it wasn't. Was it? It was… Knowing there and then that the inevitable was imminent, I channeled all of my energy to one side of my body and shaped myself accordingly. Then on cue, he removed my neck from his vice like grasp and cupped his spare hand to spit into. He began to draw himself up slowly, so that he had the optimum angle for an aggressive and determined shot at goal. At that moment, knowing he'd be off balance, I pushed up as hard and as fast as I could.

Taken by surprise, I was able to shake him off and send him crashing to the floor. He landed with a thud, his hand expectantly still cupped in expectation that he still might have use for the contents. I jumped up as fast as I could. He looked surprised, as if I was being unreasonable. What was my problem?

"What the fuck do you think you're doing?" I yelled. I was fairly sure his neighbours had heard worse.

"Shut the fuck up," he said standing up. Like a snake disseminating its venom, he lunged forward swiftly and grabbed my arm. His grip was not playful and took me by surprise.

"I AM going to fuck you," he said matter of fact. "Get down!"

His face was cold and full of menace. He kicked very forcibly at my legs and I hit the mattress and the floor hard. He spun me round and began pinning me down. This time he was more determined to go straight for goal. He was using his fist and fingers with exceptional force to prepare his target – which was extremely painful. I presume his hope was, so long as he could start the process I would either relent or be in no position to fight back. He was pushing me down with so much force my body ached all over. I could feel the floorboards beneath the thin mattress. The chill in the air banished as adrenaline rushed in. Fighting for survival now, I waited for him to transfer his attention from pinning me down to my arse. As he did, I managed to spin around with surprising swiftness. He kept pushing me down, but when that failed, he started punching me, trying to get me to lie down. We began fighting.

We were up, we were down.

He tried to hit me again, to get me face down again. It was a clumsy attempt and had left him off balance. At that point I gathered together my fist into a ball of hatred and fear and threw a punch at his head as hard as I could. He stumbled backwards, clutching his face in shock. He stared at me in disbelief as if I was in the wrong and came at me again. This time I was up and able to render a brief but decisive kick, which sent back in pain. I bent down to pick up the pile of clothes as fast as I possibly could. He was shaken but still determined and came at me again with pure unadulterated aggression. I knew that if I didn't manage to get out, I was going down, he was going in or worse. Where did we go from here if I didn't get out? How many others had suffered in this dank place on this sodden mattress?

I held some of my clothes in front of me to mask my hands and as he neared, I swung again, this time connecting to him with every ounce of force I could muster. He took some steps back and slipped on the sheet on the floor. In the ensuing confusion, I grabbed every item of clothing I could see and bolted for the door. As I ran, stumbling and fumbling down those echoing stairs, I was shaking and terrified. I heard things drop around me as I ran to the foot of the stairs. I dared not look back or stop for a second in case it slowed me down. Genuinely afraid, I bunched the clothes to my chest and felt for a door lock. I could hear footsteps and swearing from upstairs. He was getting nearer and I knew that if I didn't get out, I might never get out. The door opened and I jumped out into the icy blast of fresh air and welcome freedom. I was naked, petrified and desperate to get away. I slammed the door behind me and ran down the street, still clutching the clothes like a streaker at a football match. I hid behind a privet bush in someone's small front garden and prayed I wouldn't be spotted – by anyone. Forgetting him, this area was so violent that a naked man in a bush was a sitting duck. I glanced at my watch, it was 2am. I tried to hold my breath, then breathe slowly into the clothes, so that my breath wasn't visible to anyone walking past. The streets were quiet but for the odd bus, car and taxi taking early Christmas revellers home.

I heard a door open, some grunting, exceptionally loud expletives and violent outbursts. When I had to draw breath, I tried my hardest to breath into the clothes, so as not to give away my location. As I breathed into the amorphous pile of clothes, however, I could smell him. In my panic I'd picked up his clothes as well as mine. It made me feel physically sick.

I remained crouched in a ball, but looking up. I could just see him through the hedge that shielded me. He was naked but for a pair of boxers. He threw something across the road and it stotted off a parked car. He was kicking and punching the wall by his front door and I could see his fist slathered in blood. He came out from his house and began to pace the street. He walked towards me, and as he did, I genuinely feared for my life. I stayed as still and small as I could. He was a few feet from me and closing in when suddenly his door slammed shut. He turned in panic and fled back to his house to get back in – which he did. He stood at the door for what seemed like a lifetime, shouting and punching. Finally, a door slammed shut with great ferocity.

I stayed behind the bush in silence for what felt like an eternity. The cold was horrific and my whole body stung – bruised from him and raw from the cold. I was cut, bleeding and in shock. I sifted through the clothes and, whilst trying not to move, got dressed as fast as I could. It was absurd. It was a freezing cold night and I was in a small front garden, covered in soil and trying to dress without standing or breathing.

The inhumane chill of the night was wrapping itself around me as fast as he had tried to. I had managed to gather my clothes together, as well as his. The only snag being, I only had one shoe, but mercifully, I had my wallet. Seemingly, my shoe was now lying on a car opposite his house. I could try and get it, but it seemed like too much of a risk to take. I spotted an available cab coming towards me and with a burst of energy, I ran down the street hailing it silently. In my panic, I blurted out my place of work. I knew I had a key on me that would get me indoors and keep me warm – and safe. I couldn't go home. Even though he was without clothes and had absolutely no idea where I lived, I was scared. My apartment was on the ground floor, which always gave it a sense of vulnerability. I had once caught someone climbing in through the kitchen window to burgle or attack me. I managed to chase them away, but it left me feeling like a soft target. At that moment in my life I couldn't deal with feeling so exposed. In the office there were several doors with security codes between him and me. I knew I'd feel safer several locked floors up.

Reporting such a crime to the police was a no-no too. If I had reported it then there would be some unavoidable questions:

Why were you in a gay bar?

Why did you go back to a man's place?

Why were you naked with a man?

Why did you go to that area of the city?

Why are you scared of reporting it, what have you got to hide?

Not to mention the police didn't have the best reputation for being gay friendly or even mildly sympathetic. Some questions can't be dodged, so it's best to avoid the circumstances in which they are asked. The taxi driver stopped at my office and I slowly got out of the cab. I ached. It was about 3am and freezing cold.

"You alright mate?" he asked, looking concerned.

"Yes thanks," I said flippantly. "You know the score, we had a row!" I added holding up the clothes.

"Night in the office?"

"You mean the dog house!" I said, attempting a smile.

"Sleep well," he said before speeding off. I stood on the pavement in shock. The wind churned its icy embrace around my vulnerable frame. I looked at the taxi as it vanished. Why had I just protected a rapist?

I dumped every item of the bastard's clothes into a bin outside of the office and hobbled across the car park to the front door. Walking with only one shoe on gives one a pronounced limp, which, after everything that had happened felt like it was visible from space. I let myself in to the building and slumped against the wall of the sterile, shiny steel elevator. It felt clinically bright after the darkness of the previous hours. Typing in innumerable security codes with scratched, shaking fingers; I made my way into the tropical warmth of the office. I crashed into my desk chair and stared into the distance, the adrenaline that had kept me going and kept me alive, began to ebb away. I sat, shaking, cold and alone. I didn't even put the lights on. It felt as if I was still hiding.

I took little pleasure from the fact he'd be stuck in his house naked, hopefully unable to leave. I knew I had to get some new clothes… and some new shoes. It was the weekend, so I was hopeful no one would come into work – but what if they did? Weekend working was quite common. I decided I'd leave the office after first light to avoid any early birds and sit it out at my gym until the shops opened. I was sure I could stay warm and safe there until a shop opened. I could also shower and clean myself up too. I just hoped they wouldn't ask why I only had one shoe on… I wanted to return to my house feeling human and fully clothed, not scratched, scarred and hopping.

Until first light, I just needed to rest and recover. I leaned back into my office chair and waited for sleep to wash over me and take me to the safety of slumber. The clock ticked, the drinks machine buzzed and the photocopier kept waking before snoozing again.

I sat, eyes wide open, unable to sleep. I ran over the events and tried to think if there'd been any obvious signs. There hadn't – his dank house and sob story aside. He'd do it to others I was sure. I was terrified for them and for myself. I sat there and looked out over the city landscape, a carpet of brightly lit orange dots randomised against a black backdrop that sprawled out towards the house in question. I knew that whatever happened, gay or straight, I didn't just need new clothes and new shoes but a totally new outlook. I don't know his name but I imagine he's out there, even now.

Today if you live in the western world and have HIV, you are usually offered a series of treatments that – by and large – enable you to live your life pretty much as normal. In fact, I was told the other day that people who have HIV had better life expectancies than people without because they look after their health better. Crikey. How things have changed. These days we are told that having HIV is no different than having diabetes, say. There are even medications available that one can take to stop you catching it. The maker assures us it is 99.3% effective (which begs a question about the 0.7%). Suffice to say that HIV is something people live with. However, there was a time when having HIV meant you were going to die. As one sexual health professional once told me, "We can try and make you comfortable but then it's just easing the pain until you fade away."

Cheers for that pal.

He always struck me as odd though. He was really interested in checking me for testicular cancer – I mean REALLY keen. Repeatedly he asked to examine my balls. I assured him they were getting a ton of attention as it was and I didn't feel the need to have him rummage around looking for something hard. I hadn't gone in there for that, I had gone in there to discuss HIV, but time and again it was back to balls. I thought that peculiar. When we finally did get on topic to chat about HIV, he just wanted to emphasise the immediate and inexorable decline to death. HIV led to AIDS, then about the same time it took you to suggestively eat a banana, you went from your diagnosis to your funeral. Or so this morbid sexual health worker (and the media) would have you believe.

HIV was not something to be messed with or taken lightly. You had at least to be aware of it, how you might get it and what it would do to your immune system. It stalked the gay scene more than most, as there was still a tag of 'gay plague' about it. Working in the gay health charity stuffing cardboard envelopes with condoms and lube, I was more aware than most about HIV. Sadly, I was so aware that I was paranoid. There I was working alongside people who had HIV and didn't bat an eye, yet if anyone showed their cock to me in bed I was in the clinic for a test before you could say viral load. I was illogically paranoid and overreacted on a regular basis.

HIV tests at special GUM clinics had to be anonymous. Just having a test could increase your insurance premiums in later life or even mean you could get turned down for jobs, insurance, services and support. It was felt that if you had a test then you were obviously a high-risk lifestyle person. If you were a safe pair of hands with a suburban house, a dog and a nice car you wouldn't be messing about with infected deviant strangers. HIV could also be caught by intravenous drug use, so either way; insurance companies and employers (who could access your medical data) wouldn't want anything to do with you. You were obviously a high-risk person, a gamble, a threat and worth avoiding. It seems medieval now, but there was always something very cloak and dagger about getting tested. Given the need for anonymity and my propensity for getting tested, I made sure I went to a different clinic each time. It resulted in me having to travel 30 miles just to find a clinic I was not already known at…

The faces of those in the clinics ranged from terrified looking teenagers with nervous but supportive parents, businessmen who did their utmost not to be seen, jack-the-lads who tried to look cool and then little old ladies who you looked at and thought, 'dirty, lucky cow.' Then all of a sudden, amongst the people with smiles and a spring in their step came someone sobbing uncontrollably. Men, women, children, it didn't discriminate. Maybe they'd just stubbed their toe, perhaps they'd got a paper cut or heard that they had a mild dose of crabs, but we all assumed they had been given their death sentence. This led to a sombre, dark and brooding environment. Waiting rooms in these clinics were thus only places to sit in silence and stare at the floor praying for deliverance.

As the test became more efficient, the results came quite quickly. Sometimes the next day (I think it's within the hour now). The first time I ever had a test, you had to wait TWO WEEKS. Two long, agonising weeks. Before the Internet came along if you wanted to know where to have an HIV test, you had to ask someone. Try as you might there was never any real anonymity. Accordingly, I went into see my doctor. The receptionist panicked when I mentioned HIV. I was never sure whether she thought I was about to start slobbering over everyone and infect half the town (such was the fear) or whether she knew that doing so through my Dr. would hamper my chances in later life. Accordingly I was re-directed to the local hospital. I remember making an appointment. To protect my identity they gave me a number. A long number! Although practical, it brought to mind the branding of Jews in concentration camps. I was, hereafter, only to be known by this serial number. It made the waiting room a curious place. All of these nervous faces with no names, just numbers.

Today a blood test is little more than a small syringe. Back then they took more than a pint. I've no idea why. The nurses all put huge gloves on and as I lay on the crisp white bed I felt extraordinarily dirty, infected and wrong. I watched as my crimson blood gradually filled the bag. I can clearly recall that feeling – seeing my blood in such quantities for the first time. There was such a wonderful beautiful liquid, rich in colour, swirling within a translucent medical bag. There, draining from my arm, a miracle of creation and something that could kill me. I transfixed on the blood as if trying to spot the virus itself. I felt acutely alone. Again. I know it sounds melodramatic but it felt as if I were sharing a room with death itself. As if it sat on the bed next to mine.

I told no one of my trip. I did everything alone. I imagine if my parents had known what I was going through they'd have been mad and have told me that I shouldn't have endured everything without support. However, given how my gentile mother is a menorah away from being a hysterical Jewish mother, I doubt a trouble shared would have been a trouble halved. I fear that it would have made everything far worse, albeit in a well-meaning way. I would have had to worry about her as well as myself. I didn't have the energy back then to do that, so I had to cut myself off. It was a cruel side effect of not being out.

The treatment was professional and efficient.

Back then you had to have counselling before you had a test too. The government were worried that if you found out you were positive that you'd go out and throw yourself from the top of a tall building. As a result we all had to chat through our feelings before a test. We had to say what we would do if we found out we were positive. It was usually all a bit pointless. What were you supposed to say? "Well frankly if I *am* positive I'll make a bee line for the nearest bridge and take a header off the top?" You knew only too well that your cards would be marked and there was no chance of a test. Accordingly, you had to react in a very British way. Your reaction to the news of your impending death had to be akin to hearing poor cricket results. "Well naturally I would be disappointed, but you know, it's only a game. Life goes on." You had to sound earnest and smile whilst nodding and maintaining eye contact to suggest you weren't off your rocker. That would re-assure them you weren't a flight risk and in the needle would go.

The feeling was, however, that life might not go on. It was a frightening scenario. So I waited. Two agonising weeks. I was told that I would be able to call for the results two weeks after the test – except that fell on a national holiday. So it was two weeks and one extra long, dark scary and lonely day. That last day was horrific. All day I kept thinking, 'tomorrow may be my last.' Obviously it wouldn't, but the fervour was such that you could easily think so.

When the time finally came I went and found a public phone box (no trace) and called. They took some time to find the results, which was agonising and irritating as I only had so much change! I was clear. I thanked them and hung up. I stood in the call box just staring into the distance. I thought I would feel elated. I didn't. Yes I was glad, delighted, but I felt sad at the same time. I thought about all those people, all the faces, and those long numbers. Were they all okay too? It was an odd feeling.

Since that first time I'd had quite a few tests. Some people may think I was responsible, but others would say it was just paranoia. That was probably true. If a tip of a penis came within 3ft of my exposed skin that was enough to send me scurrying in. I knew I was being silly, but in my gut I feared that I was one of the 0.7% to whom life wasn't kind.

It felt like being fast-tracked in counselling, as I knew exactly what to say. Before they'd start I'd tell them I wasn't going to commit suicide if I was positive (not strictly true) and that if they didn't offer it to me I'd go elsewhere. I suspect fear made me bolshie and I probably wasn't that pleasant. I remember one guy just looking at me flatly when I said I'd have the test one way or another and saying, "fine, let's see if you are going to live or die," before the needle went in.

With my visit after the attack, however, I had a reason to be there. Sure, there had been no 'high-risk' activity between us, but until I had the all clear I couldn't turn that page and finish that nasty chapter. I felt curiously defiant walking in. I wasn't there to feel timid, scared or shamed. Oddly, the clinic was near his house.

Getting a bus to the drop-in centre was quite unnerving; as it was the first time I had been back to that area since that night. We went past his house, that front door, that bedroom window and that privet which had shielded me in my getaway.

Was he in? What would happen if I knocked on the door? There was a misguided notion back then that if you did the shagging you wouldn't catch it. He was probably sufficiently arrogant to think he was immune. I walked in to the clinic with my head held high. What if he was there though? Would he look away ashamed? Would we end up brawling?

It was three months after the event. You had to wait three months for the antibodies to show up. Which always meant that if you ever thought you might have been vulnerable to infection you had three months of agony waiting just to find out. So it was. The man who seemed so obsessed with my balls was on duty. His eyes lit up when I went in. "What can we do for you today?" he asked gently.

"I'd like an HIV test please." I replied.

"And why do you think you need one?" He was obliged to ask.

"Well." I said. "Someone tried to rape me. There was no penetration but I kind of want to know for sure so that I can move on." I paused, then looking up at his gaunt face added, "and my balls are fine. I checked them for lumps before I came here."

His face was a picture. He asked about my well-being and whether I had reported it. We talked about life. It became more of a heart to heart than anything, but I got the test and the negative result I craved. Even though I knew I would be fine, it was always a rather unsettling experience. A sleepless night (or fourteen) and then a slightly altered version of normality.

Not that HIV was the only sexually transmitted infection I ever worried about. I worried about a great many, but thankfully however, they came to nothing… well, except one.

I had been putting it about a bit, but had decided I needed a break from all of that. One day at work I simply couldn't get comfortable and went to the toilet to rearrange myself. It was whilst in the toilet that I spotted what looked like black spots in my pubes. I picked and picked at one that simply refused to come off. After some sharp nail digging it finally sat on my fingertip and I was able to draw it up close to see what it was. There, on the tip of my finger, was a translucent creature that was on its back and wriggling its legs in the air. I can still remember the icy cold chill of that deathly dawning realisation, which cascaded down my toilet squat frame. That wasn't a spot! Wide eyed and horrified, I knew I had crabs. I had never had anything like this before. What the hell did I do? I was dirty. Unclean.

Do I shave my pubes off? Did I get a shampoo?

In my blind panic I called my mother. I did. I actually called my mother and told her I needed her to go to the chemist and get some shampoo for crabs. So not only had I made my poor mother go and get pubic lice shampoo, I also basically told her I had crabs. I got home and my mother handed me a plain brown plastic bag in which contained a large tube of lice killing liquid. I was urged to go upstairs and wash. I did. Unbeknown to me my mother then gathered all of my clothes together, put them in a bucket and covered the lot in bleach. In so doing she may have killed the lice but she also destroyed a perfectly good new shirt. I was surprised she didn't drop a match into the bucket where my clothes were rotting, just to be sure. The stuff stunk. Yes I was happy I was about to rid myself of the critters, but I reeked. I explained to her that I must have caught them off a gym towel, as I hadn't been up to anything naughty. She seemed to buy the story. After all, it may well have been true…

I gave a good deal of thought to the possible culprit. All I could think of was a teacher who I had experienced a dalliance with. It must have been him. Later that month he bumped into me and was chatty and polite and seemed pleased to see me. This was a new experience. When I did see people again they usually looked straight through me. Despite this, I was in no mood for small talk.

"You gave me crabs!" I announced in that deftly subtle style that had endeared me to so many over the years.

"I fucking did not," he said looking genuinely aghast. "It must have been someone else."

"You're only guy I've been with," I spat back.

This conversation spiralled out of control and he stormed off. It wasn't long before he was back, clutching at my arm with some force. "If you don't let go I will notify security of this attack," I said as if I were writing a letter to The Times.

He threatened to have me beaten up and pointed to a group of friends who would silence me if I went round saying such evil things. I laughed at his threat and invited him and his mates to do their best. This infuriated him and he marched off to join them again. I was determined to stay long enough to show defiance, but not so long that I couldn't make a speedy getaway. I made sure I was standing near the door at all times. Then after a good hour or so, I left. Turning out of the club I jumped into a taxi and sped off to safety. Luckily, I had gone back to his, so he had no idea where I lived and couldn't trace me.

As the anonymous black cab bumped through the city streets I reflected on the night and on his gross over reaction. Surely primary school teachers got crabs too? Yet, as I sat and thought, it suddenly occurred to me that the night after I had met him, I also met another guy. A rather scruffy unkempt guy. Someone whose house I then remembered as being rather filthy. "Oh yes," I thought as we drew up to my door. "It wasn't the teacher was it? It was that scruffy bloke."

I still feel guilty for accusing him.

A BOMB GOES OFF

It is no exaggeration to say that I know EXACTLY where I was on Saturday 15th June 1996 at 11.17am. I was on the toilet. I had been out the night before and had, as was the way, consumed far too much alcohol.

Despite trying to stay away from the scene, I was slipping back into my very tried (and not to be trusted) cycle of going out, getting depressed, drinking to overcome the gloom, drinking a bit more and then BOOM, experiencing the tidal wave of drunkenness that knocked me flat. Sure I wasn't so nervous any more, in fact, rather foolishly, I thought I was courageous. Whilst my attitude was less about desperation and a little more defiance, ultimately it was the still the same old routine. No matter what the motivation, the facts remained – the more I drank, the lower the bar was set. With each pint consumed, the more my poor taste and worse judgment was let loose. I probably wasn't alone in that.

To guard against falling to the mistakes I had made so many times in the past, I developed a failsafe against this. It was brilliant. Simply put, as soon as I arrived, as sober as a judge, I would award people points. A ten was obviously a complete gilt-edged sublime specimen that was almost certainly out of my reach. A zero was a smelly troll with flies buzzing around him. These points were awarded and would be stuck to no matter what. I had to be ruthless. The system could never be compromised. These ratings were never up for change once allocated.

NEVER.

EVER.

I would remind myself, quite robustly, that no matter how much the alcohol took effect that a seven wasn't a zone that encompassed the numbers five through to eight. Nor was a four really a seven in poor lighting. These rules were set in stone, never to change.

As the evening wore on and the beer worked its magic, I'd stand there pondering, "Well, you know… a two isn't exactly bad. Who said twos were bad anyway? A two is just a four without the right moisturiser. And a four in poor light is easily a seven. And hey, a five could be a ten if he joined a gym." It wasn't long before I realised that this failsafe was as susceptible to the effects of alcohol as my taste. I tried to kid myself for sometime that my system was genius and ensured the bar was perpetually raised, when in reality it was a large dam with numerous holes in it. No dyke with a thirsty finger was stopping this torrent.

The bar I usually went to was very much a come-as-you-are place where everyone seemed welcome. The place was a large split-level pub with seating at the top for those few people there to socialise and a dance floor on the lower level. It was largely open plan with a large bar on each floor. Men used to stand around the perimeter of the lower, darker room as if forming a human chain around the dance floor. Despite being almost surgically attached to one another – nobody spoke. The idea was to look casually around the room as if you popped in for a quick pint before heading home to the wife. If you caught someone's eye, or they caught yours, that might be the start of something. Catch it once and maybe you were in. Catch it twice and that was the green light to try and catch it a third time. Catch it a third time and then you had to stare for at least five seconds to show intent. Eyes locked across a smoky room. The music thumped, the bodies writhed, the base rattled your ribs, the carpet stuck to your shoes and your head felt as though it was filled with cotton wool. You stared. You stared. You stared. You Stared and You Stared. Five seconds.

If a series of fleeting looks took place and were returned, it could feel like you glancing with Morse code.

Do. You. Want. A. Shag. STOP

Maybe. Not. Decided. If. I. Could. Do. Better. STOP

Then a few minutes later.

Okay. Go. On. Then. STOP. You'll. Have. To. Do. STOP

Then a man whom you never knew prior to locking eyes would come to you (or you to him – or even half way) and start talking. Rarely did anyone tell you their name. Rarely did you ask. You would spend enough time chatting (1min – 1hr) to try and rule out any notion he may be a serial killer. At some point after this was established one of you would ask where the other lived. This was just a casual request, as if you were asking about the price of soap. With a foggy head and eager pants, it would usually be agreed that whoever lived nearest to the bar would host the evening's event. That was unless something meant that you had to divert it – living at home, visiting relatives, religious fundamentalist flat mate who owned a gun, lecherous landlord that wanted to join in etc.

There is nothing more brutal and humbling than standing in a bar as men silently bid on your attractiveness and shagability. Like being picked last for football, standing alone on the line begging to be noticed. Those left beyond 11pm were the ones who were the social misfits, the uglies and the rejects. If you were still standing, it was because the survival of the fittest had played out before your very eyes. The fit had copped off with the fit and the bottom of the gene pool had been left to mate amongst themselves – and you were there. How do I know? Well, I think you know.

You'd stand, as if in a shit beauty parade, trying to look composed. All the time looking around as the fit gradually left with the fit. Were you that bad? Surely it wasn't just about youth, was it? Your options were constantly being re-assessed as people left. There'd be a few you'd pray were left. Just someone ordinary, someone who didn't make you wretch and who, importantly, wanted you too. It rarely happened. Typically, as the night snaked forwards and every pint was downed, so the bar was lowered a point. Whereas seven was the minimum you'd accept, now it was six, or a very good five…

That guy who was ignoring you before and wouldn't give you the time of day was now looking at you constantly. That meant when he was sober he'd decided that you were maybe a four or a five (or less!), but as his choices diminished, he was settling. His bar was being lowered too. Deep down you both knew that if you were sober you would neither have picked the other. You knew that whatever you had together was a by-product of necessity rather than attraction. It was very depressing and did nothing to enhance self-esteem. Yet, when a guy looked back and you knew for sure that a deal had been done, (or even better when a few eyes were attempting to open negotiations) you could dance gently on the spot. You knew you had (at least) one in the bag so could play hard to get. The process was always a bidding game. Could you do better? Could you get more elsewhere? Could they? What was your worth? It wasn't empowering at all. It was just sterile and cold. Almost always the resulting encounter was conducted on a business-like understanding. It was a trade. You do that for me and I will do that for you. There was no emotion, rarely any feeling.

I felt compelled, as if by forces beyond my control, to do this. Week after week. Month after month. Around 80% of the men who I slept with left after the deed, or depending on the time it happened, as the sun rose. Almost all promised to call – leaving as they did without a number. Some stayed and were polite. Often we shook hands on the doorstep. "Thank you for last night, it was lovely," one would say, now sober. A passer by would be forgiven for thinking we'd been to the theatre, rather than getting naked together under the sheets.

Very, very occasionally there was one who wanted to see you again. Tragically, they were usually the guys for whom you had lowered your bar and therefore the prospect duly horrified. I knew the pain I had felt when someone said they'd call but didn't. I didn't want to give false hope to anyone. I tried to be as nice as I could be, but they knew. They always knew. Just as I had. There was no getting around the fact they knew it was them and not me.

This period of my life, liberated after coming out at work, was meant to be an explosive chorus of sexual and emotional freedom. In reality it was just an endless dirge of meaningless encounters and depressed weekends. Every Friday as work ended the prospect of an exciting fun-filled weekend beckoned. In reality, it was the same pattern:

Out. Drink. Drunk. Bad Sex. Regret. Guilt. Self Loathing. Work. Work. Gym. Work. Work. Gym. Work. Repeat.

On Friday 14th June, there I was standing shoulder to shoulder with many other men who wanted the same thing. The clock ticked down. The silent horse-trading began.

This night was different though. I wasn't feeling too good about the process. I was getting bored of the repetition. The way I sold myself short in pursuit of intimacy, validation, hope, faith, love and yes to get my rocks off. I stood as if by default. I stared ahead, not at anyone, just into the distance. An older man started chatting to me. I wasn't bothered and I wasn't interested. Chat away old man. I decided I would leave; I really wasn't in the mood. My pint was low and so was I. He offered to buy me a drink. That was sweet. People rarely did that. I wasn't in the mood but I saw loneliness in his eyes that I knew all too well. I accepted his offer having made my intentions crystal clear. We sat down at a table – a table with chairs! I had never sat down at that pub, ever! We just chatted. This was unchartered territory, sitting down, in front of people and talking. They could see us. We were in the bit with proper lights and chairs. It was very bold.

I watched and saw all those familiar faces that joined me on the perimeter of the dance floor every night looking at me in disbelief. Given that they knew the kind of guy I usually had to settle for, they knew this one wasn't my type. They looked at me as if to say 'Is that your dad?' 'Is that a friend?' Unlike my dear old 70-year old, this guy did look his age.

Instead it was just an older guy who was lonely. He kept plying me with drinks, which I presume he hoped would change my mind. Maybe they would have done, but I had plans for the weekend. It was Father's Day on the Sunday and I had to go shopping before travelling to my parents for the weekend. I knew this guy wasn't an up and leave at dawn merchant, but I declined his advances. I had done my shift with OAPs. I was polite but sure of my decision. I stumbled to my feet and left – alone.

I walked home. It was a beautiful warm night and I really loved the city at night. Once home, I soon crashed into bed. I knew that it was an early start and then a train to see my parents.

Suffice to say I woke with a banging headache and a strange feeling. This was new, different. I wasn't sure what it was but decided it must be what relief felt like. I had dodged the bullet. Rather than get drunk and waking God knows where with someone old enough to have false teeth, I was in bed alone. Hung-over – yes, but without regret. In fact, this sensation of not feeling regret was empowering. Where had that been all my life?

I called my parents to say I was running late and set about

getting myself washed and ready to go out. I tottered into the bathroom and was sitting on the toilet, slumped forwards in the international symbol of post alcohol hung-over distress. At that moment I was blown across the bathroom.

I was startled and sat bolt upright on the floor. What did I eat last night? There I was on the slumped by the bath and all I could think of was – was that the curry I had for dinner? It was then I heard various car alarms going off outside the apartment.

I opened the window and looked out.

I looked one way and saw nothing. The sky was full of helicopters. They were shouting at people to evacuate the city. What chilies did they put in that Jalfrezi, if it resulted in calling up the emergency services to evacuate a city?

I turned the other way to see a cloud of smoke billowing into the sky some 1000 feet in the air. It was then I realised what had happened. It transpired that the IRA had detonated the largest ever bomb in UK peacetime history in the heart of the city. It had wiped out the commercial centre. As it happened, it also gutted the shop I had planned to visit. I was meant to have been in there shopping, but for my hangover.

Glass lay everywhere, sirens wailed, people screamed and smoke filled the streets. Thankfully no one was killed. Many hundreds were injured and I know people who suffered mental health problems for years afterwards. Had there been no warning, however, the death toll would surely have been in the thousands. There were 80,000 people evacuated before the blast occurred. It was a miracle no one died.

Despite the sirens, the cordons and the smoke, there was a calm. Walking the city streets blissfully ignorant to follow up blasts people were determined to show that life went on. Restaurant chalkboards across the city were used for slogans and messages of hope. 'Manchester United,' was a popular one, along with a few less polite ones about the perpetrators. The bombed city was now all cordoned off like a war zone. Whole buildings jumped into the air. Shopping centres collapsed. An entire city centre had been decimated. Yet, around the cordons and tapes, life continued. There was unbelievable defiance. Tables and chairs appeared on pavements, happy hours were extended, people came out – life in Manchester was going to go on and no terrorists were putting a stop to that. It was bloody marvellous.

The chaos meant I had to stay in the city. I hadn't planned to be in the city that night, but there I was. So… I headed off to the bar. Would it even be open?

Wandering the streets, with its dazed residents, diners and drinkers, it felt as if another bomb had gone off. I got to the bar (the long way around the cordon) and found it half full. I stood, this time contemplative. I wasn't interested in the eyes. I just stood. I needed a few weeks away from the scene. I needed some space. So after one drink, I left and made my way home. I felt as empty as the city's retail centre. Ripped out. Exposed.

Ironically, I can also remember where I was on 27th July that same year, when a bomb detonated at the Atlanta Olympics. I was watching it on the television. It was the first week that I had returned to the scene after my break. It was the first time I had ventured back into the city at night. I had hoped that I would feel different, but found the bar to be exactly the same as when I had left. It was as if I'd popped out for 10 minutes, not six weeks. The faces were the same, the sights, the sounds, the smells; it was all the same as ever. 'Twas ever thus. Yet, something felt different. Was it the bomb? Was it me? I wasn't sure, but something was.

So there I was that Saturday night, slightly fresher and more positive, standing in the same room, in the same place, looking at the same faces.

A rather pleasant guy was looking at me.

Stare.

Stare.

Stare and hold. Five.

He came over to chat. He was visiting the city from out of the area (a usual line if they didn't want you to go home and see their wife). His story seemed to stack up, however, as he actually had a room in the hotel with his friend. They had come to the city to have a night on the tiles but his friend had pulled and left him alone.

This was a rare event. He was high up my scale and I wasn't drunk. Not only that, but I wasn't going to be left alone at the end of the night. I felt like one of the fit copping off with another fit person. Was this what being a fit person felt like? It was intoxicating. I could see why they were all arrogant twats.

We were chatting and getting along quite well when he suddenly asked me back to his bedroom. He was staying in the rooms that resided above the bar we were in. It was beginning to feel like quite the triumphant return! First week back, the night yet young and here we go. We finished our drinks, my head wasn't THAT wooly and off we went. Up the stairs and into the hotel we went where a member of staff greeted us.

Had we been shown around? We hadn't, said my new companion. So we were. The hotel employee had seen that there was two people booked in the room and assumed we were the two. He didn't realise that my companion's friend had pulled many hours ago and was now humping in some leafy suburb of Manchester.

He mentioned checking our details. It was at that point my companion, quite innocently, mentioned that we'd just met. The man's face changed. It went sour. He grabbed me by the arm and literally escorted me off the premises. The hotel had some very strict rules about guests. No paying guest could accommodate anyone they had just met. I was duly frog-marched down the stairs like a common criminal, as my companion protested, "but he's nice!"

As I was being man handled towards the exit our genial host explained why I was being given the boot. It was, he said, because things could turn nasty and the police would be called. He also stated that getting blood off the walls was "a bitch."

The odd rent boy posing as a genuine cruiser would get a guy back to the room and then demand money. The hotel guest would refuse and would thus be attacked for the cash. A fight would break out and so the blood would be spilled. As I turned the heavily clad carpeted corridors, still being man handled, I protested my innocence, "Yes, but I'm not a bloody rent boy," I declared. It would have taken someone with an exceptional sense of imagination to think that!

It was a rather grim reality. You planned a weekend in the city, you booked a hotel room above a gay bar and hoped for some pitching or catching. Then the weekend ends with you in hospital and everyone knowing why. It was a rather unpleasant and grim undercurrent that ran below the gay scene at the time and maybe still does.

Suffice to say that guests weren't allowed to bring trade back to their rooms. Any paying guests had to either smuggle their new friends upstairs or hope the other guy lived locally. I was thrown into the street as the hitherto delightful host said, "AND DON'T COME BACK!" This seemed like an odd thing to say to a very loyal customer.

My new companion could be heard arguing with the man behind the door. "Well can I at least say goodnight?" I heard him say, as I stood in a side street, looking at a closed fire door. The door creaked open and my companion said in a loud voice, "Sorry it didn't work out." He leant into me and kissed me on the cheek. As he did he thrust a key into my shirt pocket and whispered, "give it 30 minutes."

I nodded and walked away dejected.

"Sorry lads," said the man. "Rules are rules."

I walked off and headed to another bar for a pint. I waited my 30 minutes and returned. The key didn't work. He'd given me his room key, not the front door key. I set about looking around for gravel, twigs or any discarded debris and started throwing things at the guy's window. This was in full view of several revellers and made me feel quite peculiar.

Finally, after I considered whether it would be too extreme to throw a litterbin to get his attention, he opened the window. He'd been in the shower. He crept down, opened the door and the two of us crept back to his room like something from Tom and Jerry.

We jumped into the room and he locked the door.

"Do you want a drink?" said my companion.

"Yes please!" I said, enthusiastically. I had been standing outside for an age. It was then he turned to boil the kettle. Oh.

"Look," he said slowly.

Oh here we go, I thought. One coffee then I'm gone. Man handled like a rent boy and now rejected. I couldn't go back downstairs – everyone would know I was rejected or think I was a ten-minute merchant. Either that or they would think I was actually a bloody rent boy. Bugger.

"I don't know about you," he continued, "but I am sick and tired of the scene. The one-night stands. I am sick of the meaningless encounters. Can we just, you know, sit and watch the TV?"

I didn't know what to think. All of that prowling around outside in the lane just to watch Saturday night TV. Was this what my new life was like? Hold on though – wasn't this what I had actually craved? Was this the tomato in the car park moment? Surely this was the mundane experience I had wished for.

I stood staring at him as he sat in his hotel dressing gown.

254

"Okay," I said with more resignation that anything else.

So with our cups of hotel coffee we sat on the bed and watched the TV like a couple. Then the bomb went off (again). We watched in horror and chatted about the bombs going off. After a while we went to bed and together, side-by-side, we slept. That was it.

It felt as natural as putting on a jumper on a cold day. In the morning over coffee he explained that he lived far away and we both agreed that long-term relationships rarely worked so we should see that night for it was. A nice night together. Something we both enjoyed, a night we both needed, but that was all. We had another coffee and talked about our lives as if we were old friends. We sat in comfortable silence and, after the drink was finished, I left.

I walked through the empty early morning bombed-out streets and wondered what had happened. What was that? What had happened? What was different about that? By the time I was back at my apartment the penny had dropped. I realised what it was. I slumped down onto the sofa in my lounge and sat in silence. My flat mate was, as ever, nowhere to be seen. The cold light of a Sunday morning percolated through the window and tried in vain to warm me up. I couldn't shake the feeling, couldn't escape the inevitable. All those attempts, the years, the women, the stupid dates, they all flashed through my mind. Finally I knew what was happening.

"I'm gay and I want to be in a relationship," I said out loud, after a few heavy breaths. This time I was sober. No one was around to hear my declaration, but then there was only one person who needed to hear it. "I'm a gay man." I declared, as if to clarify.

It wasn't the first time I had admitted it sincerely. I hadn't said it by mistake or in a guilty whisper. It was as matter of fact as you like. No guilt. No shame. No anxiety. Peace.

It had taken a glimpse of the mundane reality I was so desperately (and bizarrely) seeking. That night just watching TV had been my wake up call. Up until then, every time I imagined being in relationship, being happy, I would try and imagine myself with a man, but would have him supplanted by a faceless female form. She'd push him out. My subconscious mind continued to remind me that only men and women could be happy. Only they could be couples. I desperately wanted to be 'normal,' yet I was always made to feel that was incompatible with being in a relationship with a man. Like I said, relationships were for straights and one night stands were for gays. Yet this unassuming night, this rather workaday unremarkable evening watching TV and drinking coffee, had changed that. For the first time in my life, ever, I could glimpse the future I wanted. I could see a future for myself as a gay man. It was possible to be in a relationship with another man and doing such giddy things as watching TV and drinking hot beverages. This was an actual revelation. As I sat there working out why I had been wrong for so long, I also knew in one heart stopping moment, that no matter what tomorrow held in store, I needed to be a stable gay.

I wasn't outing myself anymore, it wasn't enough to admit to being gay, I had come to terms with what that meant. I had to embrace it and change my outlook on life and myself. I wouldn't find a stable gay who wanted a relationship by hanging around the perimeter of a pick up joint. I had to change. Everything had to change. The realisation I was gay may have taken over a decade to sink in, but I had to be sure that the next phase of my life wasn't going to take that long. The evidence I was gay was overwhelming, I had to accept it. The greater challenge, however, was becoming comfortable with this reality or, heaven forbid, actually liking it. I now had to live within this new skin. It was no longer diseased. I no longer needed to feel shame. Is this what they meant when they talked of pride? It was time to stand up, be counted and embrace it. I had to be sufficiently confident to tell a total stranger I was gay and do so without recoiling. I had to be proud. That was genuinely terrifying. I had to tell my parents. This had to become official.

The long struggle for normality was coming to a climax.

It was now clear that the carousel of one-night stands and dangerous liaisons weren't working for me anymore. I was quickly coming to terms with the fact I was gay and a gay person who could be happy. I wanted something more meaningful than one night stands. That meant, of course, that I needed to stop hanging around gay bars! I needed to change my approach. So, when I saw an ad for a 'gay church' I thought it might just be what the pastor ordered.

This would surely be the polar opposite of the seedy, one-night stand environment that I had come to know and loathe. This was as wholesome as organic whole-wheat pasta. One Saturday afternoon I found myself in a chapel on the fringes of Salford city centre. Tentatively, I walked in and looked around. It was a beautiful building that had evidently seen many better days. A large space, vast ceilings with the plaster and paint peeling away. That eerily lit and cold/warm that you get with large stone buildings. The lobby had a plethora of wilting posters offering everything from salvation to support. It was, as these places always are, dusty. There were some imposing solid wood doors ahead, which seemed to grow out of the ground itself. Hesitantly, I pushed one aside and walked into the chapel. There was a fairly standard church setting and standing around it were men of many ages, about twenty or so in number.

I stood there like a lemon until someone came over and

introduced themselves. They were exceptionally friendly. I think –
without sounding too biblical – they could spot a lost sheep. I did
contemplate telling them I was looking for a good flock… but
refrained. With little fuss and nonsense we went straight into the
service, which was perfectly charming. There was a moment during
the service when we had to turn to the person sitting next to us and
basically say hello. I had done this before at a service where we all
had to shake hands. On this occasion however, they turned and
hugged me. I nearly screamed in fright. It took me by surprise. We
were British after all, we didn't hug strangers.

So we sat and sang. We prayed. We listened. I felt calm, which
was nice. I sat and watched the events unfold and as I did I looked
around at the congregation. They were mostly older gents. Older
couples. They had kind faces and troubled smiles.

Given that we were still meeting in relative secrecy on the
outer fringes of church approval, I didn't feel like joining in with
the hallelujahs. This wasn't inclusion. Looking around I could see
the pain etched on their faces. They had known far greater ill than
me. It made me feel slightly fraudulent. I sat and wondered
whether I was actually lucky. Lucky to live relatively 'out' and
moderately untroubled. As I sat and took in the sight before me I
didn't feel like I was living in a golden era of openness, it just made
me angry. It made me angry that these lovely people were being
treated like second-class citizens. I was angry at the organised
religions that made these good people meet in the shadows and
turned a blind eye to them, rather than outstretching a hand of
peace. I was angry that we needed a separate service in the first

bloody place. Why did we? What was so bad about us joining everyone else? Did they think we'd taint them? What would Jesus think of that?

After the service we all gathered for refreshments. I hadn't expected that. So we stood around and drank tea and coffee and ate biscuits and fruit tarts that members had brought in. Being British I felt guilty about arriving empty handed but was told not to worry. We stood around and chatted. It was polite. It was jolly. We spoke about the strawberries that had been baked into the tarts. We discussed which shops sold the freshest and the juiciest. We chatted about baking and smiled at one another when silence fell over the group.

I can genuinely say, that as I stood there I could feel the pain and suffering each one felt. I looked up at that crucifix and at those gathered at his feet. I grew angrier that these were people being persecuted in his name. Whether you elect to believe in God or not, that is not what Jesus stands for. Not then, not now, not ever.

Tell me it's imagined, pattern matching, projecting – whatever, but the pain was palpable. I felt a fire, an energy that I hadn't felt for years. Yes, I was angry, but I was feeling motivated too. These people wanted to worship and were being made to feel that they couldn't. The Jesus I was taught about, my Jesus, would never ever discriminate, yet a bunch of old men in fluffy frocks thought it was okay to turn their back on these genuine believers.

That made me fizz with rage. It still does.

I saw their pain and their desire to live in peace and be accepted. I knew that feeling. I was feeling that too. I saw the love and purity in their eyes. It made me want to cry. I wanted to shout. How dare these people be made to feel less than everyone else. I had gone looking for peace, for answers, for possible friends and maybe even that illusion of love. What I found was overwhelming warmth from the people but an icy cold embrace from the reality that drew them all together. I hated that, I resented how it made me feel. I resented how I think they were made to feel.

Oddly, as I stood there in silence clutching my teacup, I began to rage. The reality dawned like a blinding beacon. The longer I slept around, drank to distraction and reflected on my own boring problems, the more I was betraying every gay person who had ever gone before me. I felt like I was insulting everyone who had never had a chance to know love. I know that may sound melodramatic, but it felt like it wasn't just about my personal journey, but that my journey was a small tile in the greater mosaic for equality. Having bars and places to meet, drink and fuck isn't equality – it's quarantine. I wanted to walk hand in hand with someone I loved. I wanted to walk into a church, a hotel, a garage, a bar, a shop, a government building, a supermarket – you name it and be treated as an equal – both as an individual and as part of a couple.

I knew that I had to throw off the shackles of self-doubt and move forward with biblical determination. Yes, I had to come out. I had to be bold, to be defiant and to tell people to go fuck themselves if they had a problem with my sexuality. I wasn't going to live through that pain and anguish these kindly souls had. I left later that afternoon giving them all a warm hug. I knew I'd never be back. I couldn't. Why on earth would I go somewhere that made me feel like I was a second-class citizen? Why should I have to be demoted for feeling love and wanting to be loved?

Who says that? Jesus? God? I don't think so. I think its head-up-their-arse elitist organisations that seek their own survival through self-importance. I know why people went to that church but I refused to validate the status quo of prejudice. Anyone who turns away a soul from love is no Christian. That was a lovely church, filled with lovely people – yet it was just a huge neon sign that said 'never equal.' Right there and then, I knew. This time it couldn't mutate into self-pity or 'things will never change,' but rather a 'things must change, starting with me. Starting now!' That's when I knew my life was about to change once and for all.

Maybe God does move in mysterious ways.

Within a few months of my visit to the church I had moved cities, houses, jobs – the lot. I left Manchester behind. I had loved the city but sadly it had not been kind to me. It was time to move on. I needed a fresh life somewhere else. I needed to get away from the same faces, the same places and the same outcomes. All change comes from within and I had to embark upon a new part of my journey and my life. I still think about my time there and the city. I still miss it. I even visit every now and again but there and then I had to leave.

My new city wasn't a million miles away from my last and I still popped back on the train every once in a while. I knew that I wanted this to be different. I wanted to make a fresh start and be more upfront and out there.

We weren't living in entirely enlightened times so you didn't go around telling all and sundry you were gay, but I knew that I wasn't going to hide away from it any more. Now was the time. This was different. So, rather than repeat what I did in Manchester and get a house and try and get someone to move in, I would move straight into a shared house. That way I could try and develop a social network. It was certainly worth a shot.

I sat in a bar one day and by candle light (annoyingly the bar had no windows) I fingered the classified section. I looked through the accommodation adverts that said they were hunting for 'young professionals.' These young professionals would share a house with other young professionals and have the kind of ecstatic communal fun that would rival a sitcom. Maybe we too would have our own sofa in a coffee shop. The reality, however, meant you stood more chance of sharing a bathroom with a bitter divorcee or bewildered single dad. There'd be less partying and more being kept awake at night with crying, attempts to get you drunk (and bitter) and their endless apologies for breaking the communal whisk.

I answered a few ads and popped over to various houses. One, which had made a virtue of the satellite sports TV they had, was full of blokes. As soon as I got there I knew that I wasn't staying. Having decided they needed another lad in their image, they asked questions that ranged from my favourite football team to my favourite super model. I kept up as long as I could but they'd weeded me out when I had to say whom I would invite over to a dinner party in an ideal world. Seemingly Boy George, Alan Turing and Oscar Wilde weren't blokey enough for them. One of the others was occupied by two women and (if I moved in) two men. The men had the upstairs and the women the downstairs. Facilities were shared. There was a mini kitchen upstairs and a shower room, whilst the lounge, main kitchen and bathroom were downstairs.

The day I moved in the guy on my floor was out, so I decided to pop down to the shared lounge and say hello. I stuck my head around the door. "Hello, just wanted to say hi as I've just moved in upstairs."

Both women sat on the sofa staring at me. Their boyfriends sat beside them waiting for the girls to say something. No one said a word.

"I thought I'd pop down and say hello. I am just on my way out, but I didn't want to go out without saying hello."

Silence. More blank looks.

"So, urm, anyway, if you see me around and in the kitchen you'll know who I am."

More silence, more staring. I thought about saying that I had deviant sexual practices, which may or may not take place in the shared shower, but I just smiled.

"Yeah, so anyway, this is me. I'll no doubt see you around." I stared at them long enough for them to say something or for simply acute embarrassment to take over. Nothing.

I walked backwards out of the room and closed the door. There was silence for a few second and then the sound of their TV programme again. My presence in their room was erased like a bad smell being cleansed by a swirl of air freshener.

I walked off into the town centre utterly bemused by my fellow housemates. I made my way to the town's gay bar. I thought it quaint that it had only one, having been used to a collection of them. If you wanted a gay club you had to wait until every third Saturday or every other Thursday. It felt as if the town's folk had said, 'we're fine with you being gay – now, let's see when we can fit your lot in…'

Popping into the delightfully quaint bar I popped myself up onto at bar stool and stared at the rather bizarre television show that was on. I looked around, no one was watching it.

"Excuse me?" I said chirpily.

The bar man came over. "Yes mate."

"The TV," I said pointing at it like he didn't know what I was on about. "Since no one is watching it, can I turn over to the football?"

He stared at me for some time in disbelief.

"The football?" he asked quizzically.

"Yeah," I nodded. "European championship."

You could see him thinking A) Was I straight? B) Did I know this was a gay bar? C) Why wasn't I watching it at a straight bar? And D) Why did I want to watch football at all?

"Urm, err, well…" He said looking around the bar for anyone paying the TV attention. "Yeah, erm, sure," he said and turned it over. The second the cheers from the crowd on that TV filled the bar room, the entire clientele turned to the TV screen, staring in wide-eyed disbelief. Having seen the TV was showing a fiesta of heterosexuality, they all looked at me. Someone shouted out. "Why'd you put this shit on?" Whereupon the barman sidled over to him and told him I had asked for it.

In time, someone came over to me. "So you like football?" I nodded without looking at them as we were through on goal. "What is it you like then?" He asked.

I never knew what to say about that. I almost wanted to say, 'Well I like the cross stitch on those delightful little outfits,' or 'the sound of men running on grass.' I just stared at him, bewildered.

"I like their legs," he said as if to offer me some help. "I love their big masculine legs."

I turned to look at the screen. I had never really looked at a footballer's legs. It wasn't something that had occurred to me.

"Oh yes?" I said in faux interest.

"What's his name?" said the man pointing at a player. I told him who it was. "He has lovely legs doesn't he?"

I looked. I didn't think so especially. In fact I thought them a little spindly.

"Well, not really. Not for me, but hey each to their own."

He stared at me. This was new territory. Was I simply lost? I could see him trying to work me out. I could sense tension in the bar was rising. The bar had been attacked before and thugs had come in and hit the customers, so it wasn't without precedent. There was a moment in that awkward silence when I could sense they were all thinking of a polite way to find out whether I was friendly.

"I'm gay." I said without looking up. "Stop worrying."

As if by magic, the room lightened, the mood lifted and laughter returned.

"And you're telling me you don't like their legs?" the guy said again in shock.

I turned to look at him. "No, really, I don't."

"Wow," he said to me. "You're odd."

I smiled.

Yes I was. Equally so were my housemates. They refused to speak to you in the hallway, in THEIR kitchen or anywhere. So rude were they, that I didn't know their names. As a result I simply called them 'A' and 'B'.

Although the facilities were shared they made it clear that the downstairs was theirs and theirs alone. That meant we had to make do with a shitty little kitchenette upstairs. The shower upstairs, however, was rather oddly a shared facility. Not only shared but predominantly theirs. They filled it with every kind of cosmetic known to humanity. Bottles upon bottles lined the cubicle. The turning circle was minimal as a result. I decided I needed to leave. I hadn't escaped the city and the loneliness only to be ignored. One month after moving in, I moved out. They were abusive to my floor mate and I simply wasn't putting up with that shit, so I left.

After leaving, I used to meet up with my former floor mate and we'd discuss developments in the girls' behaviour. One-night, having had a few Sherries, I confessed something to him. It irritated me no end that they treated us both so badly and yet dominated that shower like we weren't worthy to even share their air. All of those bottles. All of that shampoo and conditioner left unprotected… Mistake. I told him that for the last few weeks of my stay there I'd leave a little liquid gift in their shampoo. If ever I were feeling frisky, I would ensure that any result was deposited in the bottles. It took some target practice. That's what you get for calling me a faggot, I thought as I aimed for the bull's-eye!

My former floor mate was shocked. "You didn't!" he said, horrified.

I nodded with an evil grin. "Oh come on," I protested. "It's not like they weren't evil to us!"

He smiled. "It's not that," he said looking earnest. "I used to wank in their conditioner too." With that we realised that A and B had experienced a joyous protein-rich scalp treatment.

Having moved out I found myself living in a rather splendid

house that, true to form, was full of young professionals. It was more like a party house filled with people with shared interests. Although I had the smallest, pokiest room right next to the boiler, which meant I was always searingly hot, it was fantastic. They were great and friendly and I was beginning to feel happy. In fact, this is what I had wanted university to feel like some ten years previously. Had it been that long?

The people in that house changed everything for me. Having some people that I grew to call friends, having chances to meet new people and an actual real social life. I dread to think what my life would have been without them – poorer, that's for sure. They are still my friends today. It was a golden period in a slate black era and I remember it very fondly.

At the time and despite everything, however, I had yet to come out to these new people. I didn't think it was relevant. This time it wasn't a shame-based reason, just circumstantial. Despite years of angst I had come to a peaceful truce within myself. My sexuality wasn't an issue. If I was in a relationship then yes it would be relevant but until it was what was there to say? After all, people didn't go around telling everyone that they were straight. It was not an issue. If they'd asked I'd have told them, no big deal.

Another week brought another party. This time a biggie. I would get to meet even more people. Things were getting better and better. The party was a fantastic buzzing affair. It ended in the wee small hours with all the survivors in the kitchen. There were still twenty or so people. We were talking about things we'd done, confessions we'd like to make. I was about to tell them something from my large collection of stories. We stood in a circle like some kid of cult.

"I've something to tell you!" I offered breezily. My story was a doozy.

"We know," shouted one of the more inebriated guests, exasperated. "You're bent. We get it."

A massive, shocked silence fell across the room. I stood silent, cold and freshly sober. I knew in that spine tingling minute this was what being bold meant. This was not the time to go scurrying away back into the closet. If I had meant what I felt in the church then I should just embrace his drunken comment.

"How very perceptive," I said. It was all I could think of, which is odd. I stood for a few seconds but found the silence suffocating. I turned and left the room. One of my housemates was coming back from the loo. I felt she had the same rights to know as everyone else.

"I've got something to tell you," I said, as she passed me.

She looked at me with some surprise. "Yes, I know, you're gay!" It was so matter of fact, as if she'd just asked me to get some milk, whilst I was out. Why she thought I was going to tell her that I was gay I never knew, but that's what she said.

"Err, yes," I said nodding like a bizarre toy dog on a back car window.

She smiled and hugged me and we walked off in separate directions. As I headed off for some air in the garden, I had the dawning realisation that my journey from A to B was finally arriving at its destination.

Coming out, accepting that I was gay and also being accepted by others, was happening now. It wasn't anywhere as scary as I had imagined.

I sat on the front garden wall and looked up and down the empty terraced street. I thought back over the previous decade. From university to this point. Ten years of what? Pain, confusion, stupidity, fear, sex, anxiety, panic – the list goes on.

I knew that after all of those years, the genie was out of the bottle and so was I. There was no turning back now.

My new job was all very exciting and as most new starters I was very keen, conscientious and hardworking. The toilets for our office were shared with other companies within the same building. The loos weren't entirely salubrious but hey, they did their job. (Actually they were disgusting. Always smelly!) Someone had once written 'this place sucks' in excrement across the whitewashed breezeblock wall. I presume it was their own – unless they were skilled opportunists. We were told it was an aggrieved ex-client of the gym at the basement of the building. Perhaps he was told he wasn't earning enough money…

The toilets were housed in a large bright room. There was a row of cubicles that ran down one side of the room and then a row that ran down another, at right angles to one another. This meant that the corner cubicle was larger than the rest and also benefitted from its own window. As a result it was the most popular.

I headed, as most men do, for the cubicle at the furthest end of the room. I wanted to be as far away from the sound and smell of other men bidding a torturous farewell to the previous evening's curry as I could. There, in one of the many cubicles, I could relax and take stock of how my new life was shaping up. It was early days in my new life and I was already out!

A door would be heard to open, followed by footsteps. At that point, one could easily calculate where the person was heading by the velocity of their stride. I would stop all thoughts, clench and pause until I knew that they were happily busying themselves elsewhere. The unwritten rule was simple. If you are at one end of a row of cubicles, then the next man in has to go at the furthest point from you, so that there is as much socially acceptable space between two naked men as humanely possible. If a third man comes to the toilet, he must locate the cubicle in the middle. If another enters then either: one leaves, he goes and comes back or ONLY IF HE IS DESPERATE, he goes into one of the remaining cubicles and is as fast as possible. There is no talking, no sound and oddly enough, rarely any farting.

It didn't take me long to realise that these toilets were not the calm temples of bowel evacuation one would hope for. The door opened and in came a man. I stopped, clenched and listened. Surely I should have heard a door lock by now? Suddenly a shadow outside my door.

OCCUPIED! OCCUPIED! OCCUPIED!

He paused and then, as my heart beat louder, he went into the cubicle *next* to me. That simply didn't happen. Either he had OCD and had to go there or more worryingly, he was up for some trouser based action. I was in panic. 'Oh, no. Not now. Not here.' It was like being haunted by a particularly mischievous gay ghost. 'This is my new job, this is my first few months, please leave me alone.' He sat down and as he did I was acutely aware that I hadn't heard any trousers dropping. That wasn't good. It was then I noticed his foot slide under the cubicle wall towards me. What was it doing there? Why did the guy in the next cubicle feel the need to straddle the bowl so aggressively? Was he about to pass an unfeasibly large motion? Would I need to reinforce the cubicle walls as he forced it out? Was this to have structural complications?

I sat, transfixed. I stared at the shoe. Then, all of a sudden the shoe began tapping. I couldn't take my eyes off it. Was he listening to music? It seemed like an impatient rhythm. The shoe, (I can still see it now) was a flat, tattered white leather training shoe. I stared at the shoe still wondering why on earth it had strayed into my private space. The shoe would go still, tap, up, down, still and tap.

Suddenly I jumped back like a Labrador seeing a snake – as the shoe pushed even further into my cubicle. This was getting strange. Either he was giving birth in there or he wanted my attention.

It was then it struck me. This wasn't accidental, this was communication. As I stared, I became distressingly aware that this foot was appearing under the cubicle to tap out an invitation. I wasn't sure what to do. I remained static. Rigidly leaning forward staring. Then, with a sudden jolt, this foot was withdrawn, the door opened and the occupant left the room. I fell back and wondered what on earth had just happened. I waited long enough to make sure the coast was clear and beat a hasty exit.

I wasn't entirely a stranger to toilet-based action. Curiously, my first encounter with this was as a teenager on one of my first ever forays into the city centre alone. It happened within the first five seconds of arriving at Manchester Piccadilly train station when I'd moved there. Needing the toilet I headed down straight for the WC.

They were a magnificent example of Victorian conveniences. Tucked underground down a large flight of sweeping stairs, they spread out before you like a festival of Victorian manhood. They offered a large, central porcelain island, which featured urinals on both sides. A horny gay man couldn't have designed it better. Unusually the urinals were literally opposite one another. This design meant that you were pointing Percy at the porcelain whilst looking directly at a man opposite you. (Or trying your hardest not to look…) If you both looked up at the same time you could quite merrily have a chat and a slash. Maybe the Victorian's weren't as prudish as history would have us believe. Perhaps that was the idea. 'Gentlemen can discuss the latest news from their mills whilst relieving themselves…'

As a result, the toilets were a place of excruciating embarrassment for most straight men. Most men, all things considered, didn't want to look up at a gruff railway worker whilst cradling their cock in their hand. The result of this meant that you often saw two lines of men, all of whom were looking at their feet. It was in, out, shake it about and go. No one stayed there for a second longer than necessary.

Naturally, this created the ideal environment for the opportunistic homosexual. Any man that dared to look up, by definition, must be a bummer. After all, who else would look at another man whilst stroking his todger? I, on the other hand, have the social awareness of a car alarm. So when, scurrying down to the toilets, unzipping my trousers and then letting out a sigh of relief I did what I always do – I looked up as normal. There, I saw a man smiling at me.

'Ah,' I thought, there stands another fellow who knows the

sublime joy of releasing a stream of pent up pee. As courtesy dictated, I returned his smile with a whimsical nod. I was new in town and was sure that I'd love it here if everyone were this friendly! I noticed that amongst the few men in there we were the only ones looking up. I looked down the line. This was odd. Not only that, but the ones who weren't looking up seemed tense all of a sudden.

I looked back at my pissing buddy. It was then he upped the game with a wink. That wasn't entirely what I was expecting, but then everyone said that people in Manchester were friendly. I looked down at the floor and slowly began to wonder why, when every urinal on the opposite side of this magnificent porcelain island of piss was free, he'd elected to stand exactly opposite me. That *was* odd. I mean, you wouldn't, would you? I paused my stream long enough to move down one – the plan was simple. Would he move too?

He did.

So I moved one again.

He followed.

I realised that I would quickly run out of urinals to stand at. It also dawned on me that I was, in effect, making step-by-step come hithers towards a cubicle, which lay at the end of the urinals. One cubicle that had, by pure fluke, its door wide open.

I stopped and considered my options. Just keep looking down? Hope that he'd realise I was just in for a wee? I mean, what did he want? What did he think would happen? It was a major train station. People came and went, surely they'd see two men slink into a cubicle together. SURELY. I stood still feeling relief that I was nearing my mission's end. It was at this point that, as bold as brass, he walked around the island and then came and stood to my right, slap bang next to me at the urinals.

I froze. What was happening? I could feel him drawing closer to my cold, frigid, fearful torso as he made a pointed effort to look at whatever was being held in my now sweaty fingers. I felt the gaze of a man assessing my wares. As I stood, as he looked, I became aware of his surprise: OH MY GOD, I WAS ACTUALLY TAKING A PISS. He wasn't expecting that. Who knew that men came in for a wee?

I moved to the urinal to my left in sheer panic.

He moved down one too.

I moved down one more, trying to stop and start my flow as I did.

He followed.

I moved down two, this time sending my urine cascading across each urinal as I did.

He kept pace.

At that moment, I was – in public convenience terms – skittishly playing hard to get. I knew that I could move to the other side of this island and he'd follow. We were playing a very adult gay version of musical chairs; except it wasn't a chair he wanted me to sit on. I rapidly zipped myself up, but not before a warm pool had dispersed across my trousers. Despite that, I made a hasty dash towards the exit.

The stairs that led from the toilets were tall and very steep. I was half way up, having jumped three to four steps at a time, when I stopped and looked back. I had to see, I had to know. Maybe I'd turn into a pillar of salt. Maybe I'd flee in screaming hab dabs. I just had to turn.

There he stood, staring and smiling at me.

There was a surreal moment of calm, of cosmic peace where we both stood looking at one another. Two strangers in a train station. The romantic notion of steam trains and Brief Encounter punctured somewhat by the knowledge that he wanted anonymous cubicle sex. As we stood, no one came in, nothing seemed to move, until he gestured for me to return. At that point, I turned to flee.

For some unknown Victorian notion, the toilets also housed a barber's shop. The idea being that once you had relieved yourself you could partake of a short back and sides. At that very moment two men left the small hair salon and stared at me in some surprise. There I was, a bloke standing marooned on the stairs of a train station toilet, his trousers soaking wet. I stared back at them, not sure what was happening. They looked down at the toilets and again at me. My suitor had vanished into a cubicle at this point. The two men continued their look of bemusement.

"Never mind mate," said one finally. "We've all done it." They smiled and walked off, chuckling.

I turned to the toilets once more to see a cubicle door open enough for a finger of invitation to beckon me forwards as I finally turned and sped away…

That was enough for one lifetime, so I hoped that the shoe was just 'one of those things'. I was in a new city and a new job. I was trying to leave all that behind. I wanted a new start. I didn't need to hide in toilets – people knew about me this time.

Over the coming days, when I was in the toilets I wasn't exactly tense, but as a precaution I elected not to sit in the honey trap cubicle where fancy footwork took on an entirely different meaning. I sat in the roomier corner plot with its natural light, bordered by two cubicles. I was sure this sent out a clear 'don't go anywhere near me' message. I hoped this would do the trick. I was thus amazed and appalled when the door opened and a man walked in and beat a path straight for the cubicle next to mine.

Surely not? Were they lying in wait?

I sat there, pensive. The room was utterly silent. He was listening for me and I was listening for him. Was he listening for me to see whether I was being political i.e. passing a motion? Or more ominously, was he hoping that I was sitting in bored silence awaiting the sight of a shoe? Maybe he was listening to see if I was listening to him? Was he listening to me, listening to him, listening to me? Was he desperate for the toilet but scared of my shoe? Was it shoe or poo?

If that was the case, why go in that cubicle next to me? We both sat in silence, listening to one another. Was that a breath? Did I hear a strain? I haven't heard any tinkling yet… Sooner or later one of us had to do something. We both couldn't hold it in indefinitely – whatever 'it' was.

As I ran through the options of what was going on, there was a ruffling sound. I was tense and fearful. Would there be a foot?

Would there be something else? Or was he just dropping his pants readying to engage the enemy? I nearly shouted 'THE SHOE!' when I saw a tattered white leather shoe slither expectantly under the partition. This was getting ridiculous. Did he lie in wait for me or was it pure coincidence? Would anyone do or was this a targeted campaign?

I was transfixed at this seemingly meaningful offering. Yet this time, before I could say anything or do anything, a piece of paper torn from a journalist's notebook was rolled under the partition. It had writing on it.

I stared at it in disbelief. I was motionless – in every sense of the word. I was acutely aware of the painful silence of the room. I was even more aware that I sat, vulnerable, with my pants around my ankles. As I did, I was still staring at a tatty piece of paper with writing on it.

I had to pick it up, I had to know.

Nervously, I bent down and with great trepidation picked the paper up and unfolded it.

'What you looking for?' It said.

I sat there holding a piece of paper that asked me what I was looking for – I was in a toilet. What did he think? I was tempted to reply 'peace and quiet' but assumed it was not an option.

It took a moment or two for me to digest exactly what was happening. This chap certainly had a unique and oddly British way of trying to solicit slap and tickle. It was then I realised there was a distinct flaw in his plan. How could I respond? I rarely came to the toilet expecting to engage in correspondence, so had arrived without stationery. At that moment, to my complete incredulity, a chewed blue plastic pen was rolled expectantly towards my feet.

I know I used to have pen pals, but I had never before been invited to join in a correspondence with a man in a neighbouring toilet cubicle. Was this now a thing? Was this a forerunner to instant messaging? I sat there, my hand trembling, my trousers resting just above my shoes and wondering what I should do. I picked the pen up and wrote, "I'm looking to have a shit!"

I then threw the paper and pen back under the cubicle and set about getting ready to leave. I thought the door would open and the white leather shoe would walk out of the room in muted shame. Alas, not this shoe.

I was therefore utterly astonished when the paper was returned again – along with the pen. I knew that whatever he'd written he was expecting a reply. I also knew I was going to double wash my hands after this rather curious incident.

'OK,' He had written, 'At your house or mine?'

I was genuinely shocked. What did he think we were playing? This had to end. The room remained silent and in amongst that studious silence of a shared toilet, two men were writing notes to each other about where one wanted to take a dump. There was something ludicrously fascinating about this rigmarole. I should have just walked away or knocked on the door and had it out with him, but I am British and so I am genetically coded to be terribly polite.

"Neither," I wrote politely. "Have a nice day."

HAVE A NICE DAY? He hadn't just bought a pound of

plums. I threw the paper and pen under the cubicle wall again and paused to see if I could hear anything. The paper was picked up but I was aware that no reply was forthcoming. It was then that I had a very strange and strong sensation that I was being watched.

Crouched like a vulnerable woodland animal, I began to tilt my head upwards. There – leaning over the cubicle wall – was a blond haired man in a plain white T-shirt. His foppish hair dangled down over the wall as he stared at me. This head belonged to the body that wore that white shoe.

"Hello," he said brightly.

OH. MY. GOD.

I assumed the teasingly coquettish correspondence we'd been enjoying had now elapsed and we had moved onto an actual date. This in the space of about five minutes. I stared back at him, wide eyed, mouth open, pants precariously perched on my knees.

"Nice cock." He said as I scrambled for my trousers to cover my humiliation.

Did I say thank you? Would it be rude to just ignore him? I mean – on the one hand he was kind of stalking me and on the other he was paying me a compliment. I received few of those in my life, so even though it was from a man who spent his leisure time spying on other men taking a shit in shared office toilets, it was nice to hear.

I remained silent and hastily stood up, trying to dress in haste. I opened the cubicle door to leave. As I did he was already there, standing between the door and me. I glanced at the sinks, noting that whatever happened, I needed to wash my hands.

"So then," he said cheerily putting a finger between the buttons on my work shirt. "Fancy some fun?"

It's in moments like this that you realise your capacity as a communicator can fail you at any minute.

"I, I, err, I," I mumbled, simultaneously conscious that my job was in fact in the art of clear communication. I was flummoxed. What on earth did I say? I brushed his hand away. Then, taking a breath and mustering as much Victorian moral outrage I could I said, "What? In a public toilet?"

He moved towards me, which made me take a step back and stumble into my cubicle and against the jumbo municipal toilet roll dispenser that was large enough to satisfy the sanitary needs of an elephant. I yelped in shock.

"Okay, so where do you want to go?" he asked matter of fact.

We were standing as close to each other as you can without needing to be naked – or on public transport in rush hour.

"Nowhere," I said. "I don't want any fun. Just leave me alone please." There was timidity in my outrage and as a result my command remained unconvincing. After all, had I been truly offended I'd have walked off or punched him. Instead, I had engaged him and given him some form of encouragement. Straight men wouldn't have responded. So, you know, maybe he had a point. He looked me up and down and smiled mischievously.

"Another time," he said with a grin and a wink. With that he turned and left the room with a nonchalance I could never have dreamt of having.

As he left someone else walked in. Afraid that whomever it

was coming in would put two and two together and get a sordid four, I quickly closed the cubicle door and sat down. I'd wait until he was committed to his task and then flee – shaking and confused. I closed the toilet lid and plonked myself down. What had just happened? Was this for real? Did that actually just happen? Had I encouraged it? Was I to blame? Why did these things happen to me?

I listened. Was the coast clear? Had the guy got on with his business? Could I leave now? At that very moment a black leather shoe slid under the cubicle from the other direction and immediately touched my shoe. I hadn't expected that and shot up in shock. This time I decided I wasn't going to engage and so opened the door to leave as fast as I could. At that point a man in a suit, stood alongside me.

"You live locally?" he asked.

Not sure why this was relevant, I nodded, nervously. "About ten minutes away why?"

"Ten minutes," he repeated. "Haven't got that long, it'll have to be here," he added walking back into his cubicle.

I realised there and then that we had touched shoes (albeit by mistake) and he thought we were on. Whatever 'on' meant.

"Erm, can you wait a minute?" I asked. He looked at me quizzically. "I need to check to see if the coast is clear." He gave me a half smile and nodded.

I walked to the door and opened it as if to check outside. I have no idea at what point he realised that I had made one of the fastest, most breathless runs of my life down that adjoining corridor and into the relative safety of our stationary cupboard. I sat there, clutching supplies and listening for footsteps. It was only when a startled colleague opened the door to see me hugging a ream of paper that I felt safe enough to leave.

"What you doing there?" She said incredulously.

"Hiding" I said simply. "There're too many scary people out there."

She just rolled her eyes and walked away. "You'll be late if you don't get a move on," she said walking away.

I pushed the door open and looked either way. My office was far enough away from the toilets for me to feel relatively safe. I knew one thing; I was never going back there. I'd find other toilets. Standing up, I left the warmth of that idyllic cabin of pens and pencils and headed off to a meeting.

"Ah, Jack," said the receptionist as I passed.

"What, what, what do you want?" I blurted out guiltily.

"Nothing," she said bemused. "Just to let you know that the coffee and biscuits are in the room for you – that's all." I nodded furiously and thanked her. "Your meeting is good to go, they're in there now." she added looking curiously at me.

I sighed, sweated and thanked her and set off for the safety and secrecy of the meeting room. I opened the door. "Sorry to keep you waiting," I offered to the rep selling me goodness knows what. The man turned and smiled. I yelped, audibly. It was the man in the suit. I stood staring at him in shock as his colleague looked at me like I was a weirdo.

"Shall we get down to business?" He asked with a wink.

I would imagine that most gay men have, at some point in their lives, gone for a walk (or a drive) looking for a dose of intimate attention. And by intimate attention, I naturally mean trouser action.

I rarely did it…

No listen, wait, what I mean is I rarely did it *outdoors*.

The idea of making out with someone whilst standing behind a bush alongside a canal, in the rain, held little allure. You'd really need to be desperately horny/lonely to contemplate that. Not only that, but it was usually overweight, insecure, middle-aged closeted sales reps that would be found fumbling amongst the foliage… I'm told…

I remember once walking through an underpass and overheard a man telling a woman, "be careful, this is where the trouser set meet." I was intrigued. Out of purely sociological research I returned night after night only to discover this man had lied to his lady. I was disappointed. I rather liked the idea of being part of a set. If women had beavers could I be a badger? A distant relative of the trouser set. Although, if given the choice, I'd be an otter. A collection of otters is known as a romp. Now that's a set I would like a membership card to. Yet, despite the excitement of being a badger or otter, I rarely did it outdoors as it wasn't my cup of tea.

Curiously, I nearly always stumbled into these places for horny souls by mistake. As I've surely established beyond doubt, I am surprisingly dim. Years previously whilst living in London I went out with friends. It wasn't long before I was caught up by my usual and rather tedious morose fixation with my dismal future. As was the way, I had excused myself from the pub and gone for yet another frigging walk. I had just moved there so I didn't know where I was. I also didn't know where I was walking. I just walked. I saw a gate and walked through it. That led to a park, some grass and more trees until I realised the lamps had long since vanished and it was pitch black. In London, pitch bloody black. How? Where was the light pollution everyone was banging on about? I stopped, turned and looked. All I could see was grass and greenery. Well I imagined it was green, it looked like a dark grey carpet. Aside from the occasional tree, this carpet seemed to stretch for miles. How was this possible in such a vast city?

I was genuinely lost. No park could be that big. I decided that if I just walked forwards I would eventually come to a gate. I had tried to retrace my steps but as I had left paths and crossed fields so many times there was no point. At least I was on a path. So I walked. And walked. And walked. It was then I had a brainwave. All being well and normal, any such dark park at night would, typically, have the odd gent looking for fun. I had to go and find them. I had to seek out the trouser set. I had to go into the bushes, the trees and the dark foreboding foliage. Activate gaydar…

In so doing, I was sure it would become one of the strangest moments in cruising history. The only thing I needed from those sexually aroused men were directions. I didn't want anything else but for the way out of this infernal infinity of greenery. I stopped, I sighed and then walked purposefully towards a bank of trees that rustled in the wind. Was I an idiot to go into a wood enveloped in darkness only to confess that I was lost? Did I expect to find two men, one on his knees, unable to speak whilst the other, leaning against a tree, saying, "Yeah mate, just turn left at the band stand, and…"

I was lost. Plain and simple lost.

I wandered nervously into the darkness. In the far distance I thought I saw the outline of a man walk off. I sped towards him. By the time I reached where I thought I saw him, he'd gone. I continued walking hopeful that I'd find someone who'd point me in the right direction. I was cold and tired and all I wanted was my bed. To be alone in my bed. Asleep. I walked, I stumbled, I stood, I held my breath, I jogged, I flinched, I walked, I stopped, I stared, I hid, I crouched – I was a lunatic loose in the dark. The night grew colder and I shivered, my nose ran but still I walked. I had set out at 11pm at night. It was now 5am and I hadn't seen one horny fucker all frigging night. Where were they? Where was I? After the sun came up and I was able to see my way more clearly, looking like any other clubber who was returning from a night on the tiles, I was finally able to find a gate and make my way home. Where was this place I had been lost in? A sign at the gate told me everything I needed to know. 'Welcome to Hampstead Heath,' it said.

720 empty acres of bloody inner city parkland and surely a new world record. I must be the only gay man to have wandered around Hampstead Heath and left without seeing any action, despite spending the entire night looking for men – if only to ask for

directions. Not only that but I then had a five-mile walk home again.

Bastards.

Put simply, I was too much of comfort queen to have sex outdoors. That was on a par with going camping. Why would anyone want to sleep under canvas? If I don't have easy access to private, spotless bathroom facilities and a soft bed with fluffy pillows then count me out.

That said, like most people, I was usually more open to the prospect of a bit of outdoor intimacy after a few Sherries. Moreover, if I did ever meet anyone out and about I always insisted on going back to theirs or mine. Outdoors after the pub with a feint whiff of kebab special sauce wafting through the air definitely doesn't do it for me. On those rare occasions that I did solicit some furry familiarity, I saw the location as a mere facilitator. Meet there before going back to somewhere that had the capacity for heating and warmth. These were spaces to meet, rather than indulge. Cold, often dank, places to meet.

Back in Manchester it was by a canal, under a bridge. It was barely lit and about as appetising as a fungal infection. If you were there either A) You had just arrived late for fun or B) You had failed to get any action in any bars or clubs. It was a great leveller. No one could claim to be better than anyone else down there as everyone was equal in the shadows. The point system was suspended, as everyone was a loser. Water dripped onto dank moist moss, feeding and enabling it to prosper in the dark. City lights flickered and the sound of zips opening and men coughing echoed across the eerie damp silence that covered the canal basin. This was definitely the last chance saloon.

In my new city, however, it was well known that all of the trouser based action happened down by the historic city walls. All furtive liaisons were through the walls, beside the canal, up a small hillock and roughly beyond the picnic tables. Should you be there on a Friday or Saturday night it was not uncommon to spot one or two fellows noshing on the odd sausage or gnawing on an egg across said picnic tables.

Now, this place was totally off the radar to me. Everyone knew about 'the walls,' but as they ringed an entire city for several miles there was no one place that would instantly spring to mind about where this alfresco slap and tickle was going on. I was rather oblivious to the fact there was an area of gentlemen's pleasure and hadn't gone looking for it until I was actually accused of cruising there by the police.

I know. Me?! ME!

It was quite surreal. I was walking home from the train station along the canal (as normal) when a gaggle of thugs were heading straight towards me along the canal path. I knew the area had a reputation for violence. Everyone knew that gay men out walking along the canal got attacked. The canal was massive so I was never sure where exactly they meant, but I couldn't take any chances. It was dark, it was late and I was tired.

Seemingly, large feral gangs of heterosexual men didn't like the idea that gay men had been alienated and excluded by society to such a degree that a small part of the bushes in the rain was all they had left to find some happiness. Accordingly, gay men were routinely attacked. Knowing this and seeing this drunken, marauding, loud collective of Britain's finest coming towards me, I decided I needed to take action and get out of their way. Accordingly I climbed the small but steep hillock and sat on an empty picnic table waiting for them to pass. Having done so, I set about my way home again. I was only a few steps forward when I was blinded by a torchlight that was being brandished in my eyes.

I brought my hand up to block the glare and stopped dead.

"What are you doing then?" said a Special Constable.

Special Constables are part time police officers. Essentially they volunteer to do it. Some will tell you that they are an indispensable part of the nation's police and bolster the full time officers. Others will tell you that they are plastic policemen who are jumped up on the uniform and a sense of power. Not having had the extensive training that ordinary Bobbies have they can, therefore, let the side down somewhat. That said, they have all the same powers and largely can be relied upon to do a good job.

"Walking home," I answered perfectly honestly. I was. I'd also had a pretty bad day so was in no mood for silliness.

"Expect me to believe that do you?" He replied.

It's hard to know what to say in these circumstances. It invites sarcasm, which is maybe what they want.

"Well, yes," I replied somewhat incredulously, "It's true. I've just got off the train and I am on my way home – would you like to see my train ticket?"

I thought this would be fairly conclusive. Whatever he thought

I was doing, surely a valid train ticket that proved I had just alighted from a train would quell any suspicions.

Sadly, however, I was in the company of a power hungry Special who couldn't quite get into the real police. I literally sighed. "As I was walking along here I saw some drunken youths…" I was hoping he'd spotted them too, or at the very least heard them. "Not wanting to encounter them I stopped up on the bank for them to pass me. As soon as they did I set off again and that's when you arrived."

I couldn't have been more comprehensive if I had tried. Other than GPS data or CCTV imagery, what would it take?

"So then, why were you loitering in the bushes?" He probed.

I turned to look at the clearing on which sat a few picnic tables. The exact spot where I'd sat down.

"What bushes?" I asked innocently.

He looked irritated by the fact that he was accusing me of hanging around bushes only to discover that, well, there weren't any. What WAS I up to? Had I eaten the bushes? Had I burnt them? Had I shagged them?

"Think that's clever do you?" He asked stupidly.

I was perplexed. Was this police harassment? It was one thing for him to stop me if I had been up to some level of sauciness in the bushes but sitting on a picnic bench?

"No, I am just asking you to show me the bushes you think I was loitering in? Point at them." I said pointedly.

He stared around desperate to see appropriate foliage but couldn't. That was plenty around the corner from where I had been sitting. You could see some branches creeping around the corner, but that was about it.

"Okay," he said. "Wait there," and off he went. He walked around the area, shining his torch on the floor. What was he looking for? Needles? Condoms? Chocolate wrappers? Was he going to have me for being lewd or littering? Was he hoping I'd run? He marched back towards me. As he did I chuckled. Here was a black officer harassing me. Was this a racist event? Was it homophobic? He stood in front of me again looking rather irritated. I told myself no matter what happened I must remain calm, however bad my day.

"Take your clothes off," he said matter of fact.

"Excuse me?" I blurted out, looking rather horrified. If he'd handcuffs I was game, but not on a canal toll path…

"Your jacket, your sweater – off," he said.

I was tempted to say, "What? Before you buy me dinner," but assumed I would just conform to his bigoted view anyway. So, I put my bag on the path and began the ungainly process of undressing. With my jacket and jumper off I stood there looking at him dispassionately. I was aware that he was trying to get me to react, but I wasn't going to fall for that. So I just stood there. He padded me down so thoroughly I was worried I'd react to the frisking. He was that thorough I thought I'd ask how my colon was doing. I stood, my arms out, presumably being stopped and searched. He found nothing, obviously. I was tempted to add, "and if you feel anything hard it's not a gun, I'm just pleased to see you," but thought better of it.

Having padded me down, as passers by looked me up and down in disgust, he seemed even more annoyed that I wasn't concealing any weapons. He looked stumped.

"Can I put my clothes back on now?" I asked.

He grunted.

"What's your name, address, date of birth…?" He began firing off questions, which I answered with disdain. He said he was going to do a Police Check on me. See if I was wanted for anything. Again, I stood silently as he read my personal information into his walkie-talkie. He wasn't quiet and was more than happy for those around us to see him do this and hear my personal information. At this point I was beginning to get a bit ticked off. Having loudly read my information into his device, we both stood and waited to see whether I was a wanted man. Maybe they would see that I had once failed to pay a full tip in a restaurant. Maybe they'd realise that I forgotten to pay a library fine when I was a child.

The device crackled back into action and to my special officer's evident disgust, I was perfectly innocent. He glared at me. "I never forget a face and I know yours," he said finally.

"Do you?" I asked coquettishly.

I was fairly sure he'd seen my photo in the local paper – but that was promoting an event with work, not because I was a fugitive. I did think of pointing this out, but I wanted to make this harder for him… so to speak. He stared at me and desperately tried to think of something else. You could see him thinking – 'bushes, check. Face, check. PNC check, check.'

"Can I go now please?' I asked.

He leaned in to my face and said, "I never want to see you here again." I could feel his breath on my face.

"I walk this way to work every day," I said. "So you might."

"You know what I mean," he said.

I didn't. "No, I don't," I replied honestly.

"Here, at night, again." He looked up beyond where I'd been sitting. The historic walls of the city curved around the picnic area. There, just around the corner were the trees and bushes. I looked back at him.

"Why?" I asked matter of fact. I looked back at the bushes that were now shrouded in darkness. "Why would I want to go there at night?" I added incredulously.

It may sound odd, but sometimes I really am that stupid.

"You know why." He replied again, tartly.

I sighed. I didn't know, but okay, I'd not go there at night. No skin off my nose.

"I've no idea what you mean, but whatever." I said rather petulantly. I was tired and wanted my bed.

"I'll be watching," he said staring at me.

"Good," I uttered, before adding rather playfully "Sleep well!"

As I walked home it occurred to me that I hadn't seen him when I was sitting down on the bench. Where had he been? It dawned on me that he was actually lying in wait, hoping to catch some bush-based cock fondlers in action. It was, ironically, him that had been lying in wait in the bushes. Sick bastard.

The next day, as luck would have it, I had a meeting with a very senior police officer. I had met him a few times and had got on very well. He was running late and by means of apology, he explained that he'd just been given the unenviable task of managing the special constables across the force.

Had he now....

"Well..." I started, as I made the coffee, "I've a story to tell you..." and tell it I did. The guy's number, name – everything. The senior officer sighed. He shook his head. "Leave him to me," he said. Something I was happy to do. My officer friend was high ranking and very old school fierce.

As our meeting ended and he reassured me he'd deal with it, I asked, "what exactly did he mean, he didn't want to see me there again? Why not?"

The senior officer laughed. "Well you know what goes on there don't you?"

I shook my head, my eyes open with vacuous naivety.

He chuckled and said "It's a cruising area for local homosexuals."

Given that everyone at my new place of employment knew about my sexuality, although being British never talked about it, it didn't occur to me that he was laughing because he was giving me cruising information. Here was a senior police officer giving a known homo the keys to the cruising area. He could have said it was a drugs area or where teens meet, but he told me the truth.

"Is it?" I said slowly and with a mischievous drawl.

He nodded towards me and wandered off chuckling as he did. 'So then, that's where they meet is it?' I thought to myself. 'In that case, I will most certainly be going back at night...'

I was in a beautiful, blissful, sleepy nirvana. The darkness of the night exquisitely comforting as I lay. I luxuriated in a profoundly deep and restorative sleep. My dreams took me to the ocean, to the river, to a crystal clear blue pool as I cut through the pristine ripples. I sat under waves of cascading water, replenishing, invigorating – I was being soaked.

Then, getting bored and impatient that the message wasn't getting through, my subconscious gave up on metaphors and screamed to my conscious mind, 'you're dehydrated, you need to drink some water. Now!' I began to stir and wake to a different hell, far away from the cool, calm, balmy bliss of a refreshing infinity pool.

My eyes, seemingly stuck together by a mischievous imp, slowly prized themselves apart. The dry crust of a night's sleep fell thoughtlessly to the pillow. My vision stirred, against the backdrop of a throbbing headache and sense of disquiet. The ripples of imaginary water were crudely usurped by waves of exhaustion and nausea.

An evil, throbbing, pulsating force started work behind my eyes. It was as if someone was repeatedly trying to inflate a balloon in my head, pulling my temples painfully together at each attempt. The repetitive strain brutally continued without mercy. What was this hell?

With my head seemingly too heavy to lift from the pillow, I

started to wake and slowly take in the room. I focused on the curtains. Two massive, long thick blackout drapes that enrobed the room with the solitude of darkness. I stared at their lush red velveteen faux luxury. This wasn't my bedroom.

I began to become aware of the unsatisfactorily uneven lumpiness of the bed beneath me. My sensitive and tender frame, seemingly aware of every small deviation in comfort, stirred.

WHERE THE HELL WAS I?

I was aware of body heat before I turned to look. Who was that? I glanced at the lone chair with clothes slumped on and littered around. That makeshift clothes rail was a poor substitute for the real thing, but when you're in the mood and good to go, you don't think about where to hang clothes. You just wonder why you still have them on.

I glanced around at the room, the headache no less severe, and my vision no more clear. Visions, memories of the night started flooding into my head – as if ready for a punch up with my hangover. As I lay, inquisitive, unsure, there was movement and a low groan. I stared straight ahead and cast my mind back as far as I could. I tried to piece together the mental jigsaw of broken, drunken memories. When? Where? Who?

Without moving, I scanned the clothes piled in a mixed heap on the chair. In the murky shadows of the early morning, with light attempting to breach the perimeters of the drapes, I tried to make out what was mine and look for clues as to their identity. Did I remember last night? Did I want to? The best course of action was to get dressed and leave. Quietly, quickly… queasily.

The only obstacle to surmount was my lack of vision. Having felt my contact lenses dry my eyes (and make me sleepy) in the club the previous evening, I had surreptitiously binned them. I had felt sure that I didn't need to see as I had already pulled. Without the lenses, however, I was prone to bumping into things – especially when the room was bathed in the somber dusk of morning after regret. I always tried to keep my lenses in, but when they looked like they were going to make me nod off before the party started, they soon got flung into a bin.

I scanned the room, trying to distinguish one grey item of clothing from another. Were they my pants? Was that his shirt? Was it? Really? It was awful. I looked around for my socks and shoes. I made as much of a strategic map of things that vaguely resembled my clothes and plotted my departure. As he was sleeping peacefully, there was no need to wake him. At that point, a large, hairy arm snaked around my body and clamped my frame further to the bed. Still my head pounded.

"Morning," I heard somewhat tenderly behind me.

"Morning," I replied tentatively, giving up any pretence of sleep.

"Thanks for last night." The voice said.

"You're welcome." I replied. We were now conducting the mandatory business part of our morning. Last night, naked and entwined we were ardent beasts of passion. The morning after we offered one another stilted speeches applauding our respective efforts.

"It was great, but… I'm afraid you're going to have to leave. I start work in twenty minutes and I really need to get ready." The voice said.

BONJOUR!

I masked my happiness. This was ideal. "Oh, I see. Okay." I said mournfully. Didn't want to over do it though. I wanted to ensure he knew that I wasn't that kind of man. I slid out of the bed and without looking at him, I made my way to the chair. Once there, it was as if I was sorting through volumes of donated thrift store clothes, as I tried to find things that looked like mine. 'Were they my pants? Oh God, we've got the same socks! Is that my belt?'

Getting ready, whilst not looking down at him under the ruffled bedclothes, I tried to remember why we ended up there. The cold light of day seemed only to shrug its shoulders.

It was extremely frustrating that the clarity that alcohol always brought never survived the night. Damn alcohol for its piss-poor staying power. If I were still drunk now then I would totally understand!

He got up and started to dress in front of me. It was like I had just seen him for the first time – like a naked man just jumped out in front of me. Accordingly, I was struck that we were two men, naked in each other's company. This wasn't a gym, a locker room, a clubhouse – this was a bedroom and we were alone, naked and together. Albeit fleetingly. I was still struggling to come to terms with this part of my life.

I stared at him and took him in. He was very good-looking, younger than me, very fit and very attractive. I could see why we'd come back to his but I had no idea why I had been allowed to do so. Surely he could have done better. I stared at him and just enjoyed the view.

Gathering together what I could find of my clothes and getting dressed, with him doing the same, I ogled him in silence. It was then that I was able to take the room in a bit more. It had an en-suite. It was a large room but struck me as being quite old fashioned and musty. It didn't seem like the kind of room a man like that would have. Were we at his parent's house? That would be mortifying…

We both finished changing, him into shorts and a T-shirt, me into last night's clubbing clothes that had the unmistakable stench of smoke and stale alcohol. The walk of shame was about to begin.

"Let me show you out," he offered. "I think you'll be okay."

I was unsure of what to expect. Who was beyond the door? Was it an angry Catholic family? A lover? Why would I be okay?

"See you around," he said and kissed me. As he did I had flashbacks to the previous evening. I was immediately aware that his lips lacked any of the warmth or the intensity of the previous night. They were cold, sterile and it made me feel very uncomfortable. A man had just kissed me. I should feel something. Then again, of course, it wasn't intense, it was a bloody Sunday morning at God-knows what time! What was I expecting? Sometimes I exasperated myself. He smiled a grateful smile and accompanied it with a short appreciative nod of the head.

We knew we'd never see each other again and as we exchanged glances, we both communicated our loneliness. I saw it in him and he in me. We knew we were pathetic plasters, covering each other's wounds. We knew the journey was going to continue as it had so many other times. After our Sunday morning pause for reflection, we made our way out.

The large door opened and we were, much to my total surprise, in a hotel corridor. We got a room? Did I pay for it? As we walked I tried to remember checking in. There was nothing worse than waking up with a hangover and a hotel bill. But wait! He had toiletries in the room so it was obviously his. Was he visiting? If so why the rush? Why was he off to work if he was a tourist?

As I walked, I soon realised that my poor vision was to be my saviour. As he led me down a corridor with its thick, plush red carpet with gold crown motifs, he set me free to make good my escape through the lobby. It was a long, tall, ornate galleried room, with reception desks down one side. A huge, high atrium set off the copious gold leaf everywhere. A large chandelier dangled in the tiered space and sparkled in the early morning sun.

I glanced at an ornamental clock. It was just 6am on a Sunday morning. The lobby was empty but for receptionists, cleaners, the night porter and the like. A vacuum cleaner broke the reverential Sunday silence. I heard sniggering and looked up. There, in front of me, I saw every member of staff watching my long walk of shame through the lobby in last night's clubbing attire. All ages of people, all cultures and beliefs. All standing, smiles on their faces, watching as I made my way slowly to the gauche gold revolving door.

"Bye!' He shouted at me across the lobby. It echoed. It

reverberated. The vacuum was turned off. I turned to wave, whilst trying my hardest not to look up and see anyone. Not having my contacts in was a blessing.

He vanished and I was left alone in the vast lobby. I stood out like a dog shit on a wedding cake. Although my eyesight wasn't tiptop, I could see in the various gilt edged mirrors everywhere that there were rows of staff members staring and sniggering. It was then that it struck me that he wasn't a guest, he was a staff member. They were staff quarters. I had just been another dish of the day by the resident kitchen guy.

I pushed the door – nothing. I pushed again – nothing. I could feel the heat from everyone watching me, dissecting me, picking up pointers to taunt the kitchen guy with. To my dismay, the door was locked. Slowly and shamefully I approached the reception desk. "Can you let me out please?" I mumbled, trying everything I could not to make eye contact.

A concierge grinning broadly nodded and made his way to the door. "Have you got everything from Ben's room?" he bellowed, as the sniggering grew – clearly audible now. "Socks, pants, shoes… thong, accessories…?"

I nodded sheepishly, eyes fixed to the floor. I stood, just waiting for the door to open so that I could be set free. "Can we get you a map of the city?" he said quite unnecessarily and with a hint of delighted evil.

"No thanks!" I said firmly.

"Dinner reservations, theatre tickets…" he added with relish.

I looked up and finally gave him a cold hard stare. He smiled, nodded and set about walking towards the door. Despite this, he made sure that he took his time. It seemed to take an age as he had the 'wrong' keys… and so it went on until my embarrassment was at maximum velocity. Finally, the door opened and I tore into the sunny street with its icy cold morning air.

The concierge stood at the door. "Thank you for staying with us sir, we hope to see you again."

With that I turned a corner, and not for the first time in my life, I fled.

BLIND DATES

I don't want you to think that all I ever did is feel self-pity and have tediously regrettable one-night stands. I concede that did consume most of my time, but when I decided to get off that particularly enthralling roller coaster, I did date. I went on a ton of blind dates. I was now more of less out of the closet so it was my moral obligation to find someone to love. Besides, I needed that in my life.

I'd grabbed a copy of The Pink Paper from one of the bars in Manchester before I left. I needed to know where I could get the paper in my new town. It was available from a little shop hidden away in the corner of a courtyard. When I travelled to the bookshop, I had expected to see a pile of them popped by the doorway – as in the bar. Alas no. The paper was considered so inflammatory and bad for business that it was kept in a box, hidden from the public behind a thick floral curtain that ran across a shelf unit.

As gay people were still very much a thing for discussion (and usually repulsion) any business that stocked such an item would get a 'reputation.' It would soon go out of business as no one would want to use it for fear of being labelled an AIDS strewn faggot. Even a rainbow flag on a window or till would cause uproar. They were duly hidden away and only available slyly, when the shop was empty, upon request or if the owner knew and trusted you. It felt like we were exchanging secrets in the Second World War with the

Nazis patrolling outside as they sneered at the old bookseller knowing that all academics were in it together. The bookshop owner was a kindly gent who just wanted to help the gay community. He wasn't gay himself, which made this all the more remarkable.

The first time I went in, I wandered around silently browsing. After an age he came over and asked if I needed any help. "Do you stock… *magazines?*" I asked with emphasis.

He immediately looked at a middle-aged woman flicking herself through the romance section. He nodded sheepishly and with the wave of his hand drew back the curtain to reveal the box of magazines and papers. The curtain was released and hidden again.

"Perhaps you'd like to look through our non-fiction section before you leave," he added nodding towards the woman.

I smiled and carried on looking. When the coast was clear he came back and drew back the curtain. I bent down and grabbed a copy, sneaking it into my bag as fast as possible. Given that the publications were free and he was running a business I felt as if I was taking advantage of him. There were no books I wanted at that point, so I thanked him and left. Week in, week out I would do that. It was one of my few lifelines to the outside world – to the possibility that gay people existed and that I wasn't alone. Moreover, there were scores of lonely men all looking for love.

As these guys had placed a paid-for advert, I reasoned that they must be serious. These weren't bar flies. They too were looking for love. Sadly 99% of them were in places I didn't live. As and when a candidate appeared within 20 miles of my home I would reply. I suspect it was like pigeons swarming onto one discarded piece of bread.

This resulted in a handful of dates. The adverts would follow the usual lines. 'Gay man seeking similar for fun times' – again that meant sex. They wanted someone with a good sense of humour – duh. They wanted good times – really? Please…

Crucially, however, they wanted a relationship – now that was the clincher. That was what had been missing from the scene. To prove they were serious few would agree to a date without seeing a picture first. This was such a nerve-racking moment. What would they think of my badly taken holiday snaps? There was always a glorious undertone of buyer beware: the responder wanted to ensure that the product (i.e. me) wouldn't be defective or unsuitable to his needs. My over zealous attempts to find love and stability meant that it wasn't long before I didn't have a picture of me left in my photo album. They were all sent off to PO Box numbers in hope rather than expectation. Replies were forthcoming in plain brown envelopes. It was like being in the secret service. All of this in the hunt for love. All of this clandestine activity to live a mundane life. It's rather pathetic isn't it?

Some didn't reply. Some didn't send the pictures back as promised. Sadly most of my favourite pictures of that stage in my life were sent and never seen again. This was well before digital photos and if you didn't have the negative, you couldn't reproduce the pictures. My photo albums have gaps like missing teeth in a broad smile. A huge portion of my young adult life wiped out looking for love. I rarely look at those albums, but when I do each gap reminds me what it was like and how far we've come…

So the photos and letters went out. I had a few replies. Some of the most notable ones, but by no means an exhaustive list, include… One guy set about discussing, with earnest determination, the new Millennium Dome on the Thames. He thought it should be a sporting venue. I said I thought it might end up as a concert venue. He stood up and looking me up and down said, "Well if that's your position on it, I don't see how we can have a future." He then grabbed his coat and to my complete astonishment walked out of the bar. We'd been sitting in a window seat and he walked past me without even a backwards glance. I sat there on a bar stool clutching my pint, his drink still half full and wondering what the hell had just happened. I often smile when I see the Dome now. Given that it did end up as a concert venue I wonder how he coped with his life. I knew the place was controversial, but that was weird. That was the extent of that date.

One guy turned up and looked me up and down. I suspected he was my date. He'd seen my picture in advance but I hadn't seen his. As I went to say hello he walked away. You had to be careful not to approach total strangers in case they turned nasty. It wasn't necessarily going to be a case of humorous mistaken identity, you could end up in hospital. So you had to assume that most people were violent homophobes, rather than your blind date. He then re-approached and again looked me up and down. I stared back, quizzically. We both stood there on the pavement outside a cafe and an electrical shop as people walked between and around us.

After a few minutes of this surreal stand off I said his name. He walked towards me and without blinking or changing his facial expression sighed.

"This isn't going to work," he said matter of fact.

"Why not?" I just about managed as he started to walk off.

His hand gestured towards me, up and down, before he raised his eyebrows as if to say, 'need you ask?'

I was baffled. He'd seen my picture. It's not like I was sending pictures out of some muscled hunk only turn up as a rather nasty shock. I stood there on the busy city street and felt pretty irritated. I wasn't offended so much, I was just annoyed. Who did he think he was? "What did you expect?" I said. "You do have my picture I trust? Can I have it back please?"

Again, he looked at me without emotion. As if I had broken a contract and cost him so much money he could barely speak.

"I wasn't expecting this," he said. "And no, I don't have your picture" he added, before walking off and leaving me on the pavement, wondering what on earth I was doing. No sorry, no feeling, no photo.

I then went out with a guy who loved sports, loved politics and theoretically was pretty perfect. When we met, however, I knew immediately he wasn't my type. Personality wise he was perfect but in the flesh he was very far from it. If you were to design the very antithesis to what turns me on, it was him. He was lovely, but I knew we had no future. I felt bad and shallow, but it just wasn't to be.

We met outside a record shop and went on for a few drinks. I knew that I had to put aside all personal feelings and just see how things went. Maybe I would find myself attracted to his personality so much that I could overlook all of the other things that made me feel queasy. We had a good night out and I wondered if we could at least be friends. Chances were, however, that it wasn't going to happen. "Can we just be friends?" is almost as bad as saying – I think you're as ugly as fuck.

We did go back to mine as I was determined to give this guy a fair shake… I just couldn't end it like that. It seemed so unfair. So we went back for coffee. It was as we sat down chatting on the sofa that he turned to me and said, "Can I confess something?" It was always a rather uneasy question. What did he want to confess?

"Err, yeah," I said with trepidation.

"It's embarrassing," he started off, moving forward on the sofa so that he could look me more squarely in the eye. "It's just that…" He paused and looked to the floor.

I stared at him intently. What was next in the rather curious cavalcade of confessions?

"The thing is, you see… I can only get going, you know, get aroused – if we rub noses for 30mins or so, I can't get it up without the nose thing."

I sat transfixed and motionless. His head started to rise so that he could look at my expressionless 'WTF' face. What do you say to that? It may have been fine, even a novelty for a bit. What happened after 10, 20, 30 years together? You'd be there feeling frisky at the end of a long week and he'd say, "Let's just get the nose thing done and I'll be ready." Surely it would be, "Oh for fuck's sake Brian, do we have to do this Eskimo shit again? Don't bother I'll finish myself off."

I sat still, staring.

"Does that put you off?" he asked quite legitimately. I was aware that he'd shared something personal. I didn't want to be a tosser and hurt his feelings but you know, yes it did put me off. That and his body was covered, quite literally, in hair. His neck looked like it was wearing a scarf of human hair. It was hot and I could see pearls of sweat cling to his hairy neck.

"Well, I'm not sure, I haven't really had chance to process it," I answered softly and honestly.

He smiled. Presumably that wasn't the type of direct rejection he was used to. This must have translated as a come on as he lurched towards me with his tongue out, like a lizard spotting a fly.

"Shall we see?" he asked. I will admit that I wanted to see just how hairy he was. Surely it couldn't be all over? It just couldn't, so I agreed.

To my surprise, yes, he was matted in hair. His entire body was like a wet rug. When he stood up he looked like a modestly shaved Wookiee. It wasn't a case of sack, back and crack; it was an all over coating of werewolf. He lay there dripping. When we embraced I was saturated. So there we were. Sweaty and wet (not in a good way) and rubbing noses as he tried to get the tent pole up. Suffice to say 30 minutes nose clashing is a bloody turn off. I kept looking at my watch and acting like a kid on car journey. "Are we there yet?"

He asked me if I'd call. I said I would and I didn't. I did feel

like a shit, but it seemed kinder than explaining why I wasn't going
to call.

I met one guy who was rather well turned out and very well
spoken. He was a bit older than me. We went out for dinner and a
few drinks and that was that. The next date was dinner at his. It
was all very proper. As I sat and ate the meal I was struck by the
darkness of his apartment. Curtains remained closed and a lot of
porn was scattered everywhere. I was beginning to wonder what
was hidden behind the various closed doors off the main corridor.
After a while, out of nowhere he said, "Tomorrow night we are
going to the cinema." At first I thought I'd misheard.

"Are we?" I said as a point of clarification.

"Yes we are." He said to confirm my suspicions. "We are going
to see a remake of a classic I want to see. It's on at the local
cinema."

Are we indeed?

We continued to eat and conversation continued. I was
intrigued. "You're spending the night here tonight," he said as
readily as someone asking for the butter.

"Is that the case?" I replied. I didn't know whether he was just
trying to show enthusiasm in a very cack-handed way or whether
he was a bit weird. We left the dining table and went into the
lounge that, despite the summer evening outside, felt dark and red.
He had red sheets, not curtains, just sheets across the windows. It
felt like an avant-garde Shakespeare production set in the womb.

"I'll need your home phone number too," he said not even
looking at me.

"No can do," I replied briskly.

He turned and stared at me. "Why not?" He seemed offended, betrayed by my sense of independence.

"I've just moved into my new place," I told him. "I told you earlier. We don't have a phone yet."

Both were lies, but they were a good foundation for blind dates as they provided the framework for plausibly denying that A) you knew where you were and B) that you didn't have a phone. This was before cell phones ruined that ruse.

He recalled that I had indeed told him that and that satisfied him. "We are going to bed now," he said. I smiled. Not at the thought but at the ludicrous situation. "You are going to do what you are told," he said in that matter of fact way. "You are going to do what I want."

He was smaller than me, which amused me. In fact I snorted. That didn't please the little man much and he pointed at the bedroom as if I was naughty puppy. Again I smiled and sat back.

"I'm not ready for bed," I said defiantly.

He walked over to the front door and locked it. Given what had happened previously I should have been worried, but I wasn't. I actually found it all rather entertaining. I stood up and walked up to him. He puffed his chest out. "Thanks for dinner," I offered and opening the front door again and brushing him aside, I walked out and away.

That was another one crossed off the list.

I met one guy. He said he could only meet up late as he worked shifts. Okay... I met him and we went back to his for a few drinks. We were chatting and laughing. At one point he asked me to be quiet. I looked around his roomy detached house and asked why. Was I disturbing the neighbours?

"No, it's not the neighbours," he said getting me another beer. "It's my partner. He's asleep down the corridor."

I stared at him in silent shock. "Sorry?" I asked as if I had spectacularly misheard. "Your partner?"

He nodded and handed me the beer.

"I thought this was a date." I said, as if to myself.

"It is," he said cheerily.

There was a pause as I digested what was happening. "So, you are on a date with me and your other half is asleep in the room down there?"

Again he nodded.

"So, what, is this like an open relationship?" I asked trying to comprehend.

"Well," he sighed. "Sort of. He wouldn't be surprised to find a man here, let's put it that way. He's not too happy about it, but he accepts it. He once joined in. But I like to keep this just for me if I can."

I sat on his sofa, beer in hand staring in wonderment.

"But in your ad, you said you wanted a relationship," I reminded him. He nodded. "You are already in one!" I pointed out tediously and obviously.

"Yes," he conceded finally. "Don't you feel there's something better out there? That you could do better than you have?"

Yes. Right then. At that very minute. I was astounded. He was auditioning new partners whilst his current one slept next door. How long before he was seeking something better than his next love interest?

"Have you had enough beer yet?" He asked, bizarrely.

"Why?" I replied quizzically. I was about to leave, so this struck me as an odd question.

"I just wondered if you needed the loo," he asked as if he was the perfect host.

I did. "I'll go before I leave if that's okay?" I said, bemused.

"Can I ask a favour then?" He asked, standing up.

"What…?" I replied, cautiously.

A twinkle sparkled in his eye before he asked. "When you go to the toilet – will you piss over me?"

Again we remained static.

"You want me to piss on you?" I asked, mesmerized.

He nodded with an eager smile.

"Won't it go all over the floor," I asked naively. I was more concerned about the cleaning than the implications of the request.

"I'll get in the bath."

Now I was utterly baffled. He'd been feeding me beer since I arrived just to get me to go to the toilet. Whilst simultaneously auditioning me for the role as his partner, as his current partner slept down the corridor. Oh yes, this one was a keeper. I knew how to pick them.

"I only shit on someone's face on a first date," I offered somewhat irritated. "If you want me to shit on you, I'll do that with great pleasure."

He wasn't keen, so after I purposely finished my beer I left, leaving him home and very dry.

I had a date with a spectacularly good-looking guy. He was handsome, funny, clever and generally great fun to be with. We struggled to find time to meet, so we finally agreed to a swift pint after work. I knew that he needed to get an early train home, for which he apologised profusely. He'd a family commitment that he couldn't get out of. I was okay with that. After work we met for a few pints and generally had a bloody good time.

Towards the end of the date, he leant over and asked for a kiss. I didn't usually do anything like that in public. I was always uncomfortable with public displays of affection. Yes, we were in a gay bar, but still. The scars from years in hiding didn't heal overnight. I looked around to see everyone consumed with their own activities. I hesitated, but I didn't want him to slip through my fingers. I knew his departure wasn't too far off, so I did. We both slumped back afterwards and I began to wonder whether my streak of bad luck was about to conclude with spectacular good fortune.

At that exact moment a women was going table-to-table selling various gifts to fundraise for charity.

"I'll have two of those," he said grabbing at some T-shirts. He slung them over his shoulder once he'd paid for them.

I was intrigued. "Not sure they'll fit you," I said looking at the shirts. He downed a decent mouthful of his pint. "They're not for me." He said looking at his drink.

"Who are they for?" I pressed.

"My kids," came the reply as straight as you like.

It wasn't entirely usual for gay men to have kids, but this was unexpected. Given we were on a date I would have thought he'd have mentioned he had kids.

"Oh wow," I offered. "You have kids?"

He nodded. "Two," he said smiling.

"That's great," I offered looking, and feeling, genuinely happy.

"That's why I have to dash back," he said, taking a gulp of beer. "I've to get back to read to them."

I paused momentarily. "You live with them still?"

"Yeah of course," he declared with yet another beautiful smile, but as if I'd said something stupid. He was just looking at me.

"So, who's with them now?" I asked. I was conscious that he was in a gay bar kissing me, whilst two kids were brushing their teeth, getting ready for their bedtime story from Daddy.

"My wife," he answered matter of fact.

"Your ex-wife," I tried to correct.

"No, my wife. She'll have my knackers on the block if I am not back in time for the kids bedtime stories."

I sat there confused, trying to work out what was happening. "So are you still married right now, at this minute," I queried, looking for a wedding ring.

"Oh don't be a dick," he said with a snort. "Don't be one of those guys who gets all up himself. I'm married yes. I have kids yes. So what? What we have now and what we might have in the future will just be a bit of fun. No strings, no guilt and definitely no attitude. Just between us okay?" He smiled and nodded like I was supposed to do the same.

Now, for those of you unaware of bizarre gay etiquette, let me tell you there is a very odd code of conduct on the gay scene. Everyone is welcome and supposedly no one is judged. You may be married or straight – we are supposed to welcome and accept everyone, no matter what. That's because gay men have been persecuted for so long that these bars may be their only refuge. As such, all are welcome and no one, no matter what, is judged. On this occasion, however, I wasn't feeling very welcoming. He wasn't being persecuted, he was just a prick. We sat at the furthest end of the bar from the front door. As it was a Friday night, the bar was crowded and was filling up steadily.

"No it's not okay," I said, standing up. I reached over and grabbed a generous handful of his expensive shirt, right between his shoulder blades, and grasped his belt. I then literally ran him out of the bar throwing him onto the street. "Now fuck off back to your wife you two faced prick," I shouted at him, as he stood astounded in the street. People walked past and sniggered. I walked back through the saloon doors and back to my seat. I caught glimpses of people shaking their heads and tutting. I had breached the cardinal rule of global unrelenting acceptance. I could hear the bar staff discussing whether they should ask me to leave. I finished my drink and slunk off into the night angrier than ever – and I was the bad guy?

Men!

A WEE DRAM TO KEEP OUT THE COLD

I was at a conference for work. These were exceedingly rare. The industry I was in was extremely straight-laced, conservative and exceptionally traditional. Not to mention tight. Having accidentally outed myself to almost the entire company at my previous job, I was determined to be as straight laced as possible. My colleagues knew, but that didn't mean anyone else needed to.

We were at a rather jazzy conference on a beautiful loch in Scotland. We were staying in a castle and most bedrooms had French windows out onto the Loch. It was absolutely stunning, truly picture perfect. For someone who thought getting an extra large portion of chips at the weekend was exciting, this was all rather amazing.

We were there with similar organisations from across the UK. We were introduced to each other over the coming hours and could put faces to names and voices. It was all very meaningless but jolly. The organisers explained what entertainment had been laid on and pointed out that we were all to be treated something extra special that night. A meteor shower was due to start just as the bar closed. We were all thus invited to join everyone on the loch, with our drinks, to watch this impressive cascade of fallen stars. It seemed too good to be true.

We were grouped together by regions; as such my organisation was seated for dinner with those from neighbouring Northern and North Wales regions. Thankfully conversation was free flowing and we all got on well. One of the Welsh contingent was a rather good-looking rugby player who was quite entertaining. He was fairly straightforward, probably drove a middle of the road car, had a middle of the road fiancé and ate middle of the road food. That said, he was quite cute.

In due course the men gravitated to the bar. Conversations grew louder and more boisterous as the whisky was downed. The time for the meteor shower arrived, so everyone ordered their drinks and waited. We drank, the bar closed and we were told the meteor shower was delayed (quite how, I will never know.) Lots of people headed off to bed whilst other bemoaned the lack of a bar to keep them company.

The Welsh rugby chappy whispered to me, "I know where there's more beer."

I turned and looked up at him, he'd quite the large frame, "Oh yeah, where?'

"It's in my room." He said matter of fact. "I brought quite a few cans with me."

"Excellent!" I said genuinely quite happy at the news.

"Come on then," he said and off we went.

"What about the others?" I asked sincerely.

"They'll follow along in a bit," he reassured. So, like a child being led away by an evil stranger, off I skipped.

"Your room has a view of the loch doesn't it?" he asked as we navigated the corridors. I nodded. "Mine doesn't, so how about I go and grab the cans and meet you in your room?"

That sounded reasonable, so I agreed.

Before long he was back clutching six cans of beer. I recall thinking that it wouldn't get far when everyone else arrived, but didn't give it much more thought. I opened the curtains and the doors and gazed out. We had the lights off so that we could more clearly see the display. As a result only the ambient light from several odd sources – the alarm clock, the coffee machine, the TV standby light – illuminated us.

After a while a few meteors had shot past us as we stood together watching. We watched… was that one? That was one. Oh look at that one. That one was fast. No you missed one. Look up there that's where they're happening… In due course it began to feel like whatever was to come later would merely be the same as what we'd seen so far, so we came in. I turned on a lamp and we sat – him on the bed, me in the chair.

"Final can?" he said and without waiting for an answer cracked it open handing me one. I finished my existing drink and slumped back quite contentedly into my chair. I sat and sighed a sleepy sigh. I wondered where everyone else had got to. Maybe they were outside 'oohing' and 'ahhhing' at the best meteor display ever seen in Scotland.

There was a silence, but nothing particularly odd or uncomfortable as he was lying back on the bed. Just as my thoughts turned to bed he sat up and looked over at me. Sensing he was about to speak I pulled my head up from the sumptuous wing back chair and looked at him.

"Sorry," he said hesitantly. For what? Only having six cans? I'd forgiven that… Sorry about what? I wasn't entirely sure what he was talking about. He shuffled forward and sat opposite me on the edge of the bed.

"Sorry?" I said quizzically, "for what?"

He sighed. It was a deep, heavy and contemplative sigh. I was perplexed at what he had to apologise for. He picked at the duvet cover. "I don't know," he added mystically. "This is just…" He trailed off.

Was he sorry I was missing the meteors? That he wanted to talk and keep me awake? I wasn't sure, but I was beginning to wonder what was happening.

"I'm sorry, I'm being odd aren't I?" he said finally.

I hadn't actually noticed. As far as I could see he was being the same as he'd been all night. So if this was odd, then yes he was being odd. Otherwise I thought he was behaving perfectly normally.

"It's just that…" he continued. I leaned forward expectantly, "I've never slept with a man like this before," he said and clasped my hands in a tender embrace.

I sat there unable to move.

Say what now?

Was this just a comment? Was he just telling me something like 'I've never dined in Paris by moonlight?' 'My favourite colour is blue but my favourite fruit is red.'

"Erm, what?" I asked finally. He was staring at me now with some intensity.

"This," he said looking at me and at our still clasped hands. "I've never done this before. Slept with a man that is."

I was still frozen in disbelief. What the fuck did he mean? What was THIS? I thought we were coming back to drink and watch meteors. What the hell did he think?

"This?" I said rather shocked. "What do you mean this? What THIS?"

I couldn't decide what I found more objectionable. That he thought I was gay or the fact that he knew I was gay and thought that meant I was easy. Who was he? We spent the night talking work and sports, a group of us, so how on earth would that lead him to think THIS was going to happen. He looked back at me confused.

"What do you mean 'you have never been with a man before'?" I repeated as if to make sense of it to myself. "What did you think this was?"

Now he looked shocked. This was something that I could easily make a formal complaint about. He'd be sacked before the next round of meteors had skimmed the night's sky. This was sexual harassment.

"Oh my god!" he said standing up. "I'm really, really sorry. I misjudged the moment, I thought this was something it wasn't and I'm really, truly sorry."

I stood up and found myself between him and the door, which he was eyeing up with some panic.

"Sit down!" I said firmly. He did. "Are you saying I am gay? Is that what you think? You think you can just come in here and get sex? Is that what you're saying? So, even if I was gay you think I'm easy?"

He sat, his head slumped forward into his hands, apologising over and over again looking genuinely horrified. He was obviously uncomfortable and was getting emotional. As I walked to the door he saw a chance and stood to leave and began walking quickly towards me. I turned the lock. "Well luckily for you mister…." I said walking back and taking my sweater off. "I am…"

There was a moment where I could see he wasn't sure I was being serious. However when my pants hit the floor he was up and walking towards me. Soon we were in bed and getting down to the kind of business I had never expected when I boarded the plane earlier that day. He said that he wanted to know what it was like with a man. I wasn't fooled. For a timid first timer he seemed to know where all the pipes were and what to do with the plumbing. He certainly knew how to handle a stopcock.

Afterwards, we both lay there and talked about our lives as we may have done on the conference floor after a burger. He talked about his fiancé. I asked why he was in bed with me whilst a woman he'd one day wed was at home? I asked him what he'd do after he got married?

He explained that his wife's family were very traditional and wouldn't approve. 'Well yes', I thought. Knowing that their future son-in-law was in bed with a man whilst on a business trip might disappoint some traditionalists. I was on their side on that one. He explained that he'd seek opportunities like this one after he was married. He would take his chances where he could. I asked how he could accept that part of himself, how he could live two lives? How he could betray a woman who trusted him? At that point he grew sad, so we just lay there. As if we'd been planning a three-story house but had been told by planning we could only build a bungalow.

I felt like I was betraying his fiancé too. A woman I had never met. I felt bad for her. As he lay on my chest, I also felt an odd sense of inevitability. With two-timing men aplenty, was this my future too? I came out; those around me finally accept me and I get into a relationship only to discover he's a massive twat. Was that my life?

The next morning we talked about sports again. The previous night gone. We said we'd go and watch a match together some time (and I was hoping to be his future opportunity if I am honest), but I knew in my heart of hearts that it was not to be. That would not happen.

We dressed and he stood to leave. We checked through the peephole to ensure that the corridor was empty. He turned and kissed me, thanked me and with a whoosh he was gone.
The rest of the conference it was as if we'd never met. As if we were strangers sharing a lift. However odd I felt, I knew he must have felt worse. From one gear to another. From one life to another. Some days later we were on our way home. A furtive glance towards each other minutes before we all jumped into taxis was all that was needed to say goodbye.

Curiously, a few months later I was at a music venue with friends when he and his fiancé walked in. I went cold. It felt very odd. I was tempted to go over and say hello and ask what happened to our plans for watching rugby. Then wait until his girlfriend asked where her fiancé knew me from and watch his face as I said, "well we met in Scotland on a business trip. Remember we shagged?"

I watched them laugh and joke and I felt slightly cheated, used and angry on her behalf as well as mine. In the end I just made my excuses and went for a walk...

WHEN A MAN'S GOTTA GO!

I have only been clubbing in Amsterdam a few times. I know that sounds terribly glamorous (or maybe it just appears seedy and salacious), but in reality it's neither. I visit straight friends who live in the Netherlands. They are all family orientated, 'let's play in the garden, mind those roses,' types. When I visited, however, they insisted on taking me to gay clubs to show me how wonderfully inclusive the Dutch are. I was all too aware of their alleged inclusivity and looked at every bus that passed for teenagers masturbating…

This was all fine by me as the clubs were always friendly and the music was usually all of the best songs that you had forgotten from the 1980s. It was always a fun night and being surrounded by big blond muscle guys was not to be sniffed at either. My last visit to one of the biggest clubs in Amsterdam didn't end too well, however. In fact I had to flee in red-faced embarrassment.

I was there drinking with said friends. We'd been there an hour or so. The music was good. The vibe even better. In a nutshell, it was very enjoyable. It was only when I decided that I needed the loo that things took a sinister turn.

I had already made a fool of myself earlier in the evening at another bar. In a crowded toilet I'd mistaken a free cologne dispenser for a soap dispenser. In so doing, I had nearly blinded myself trying to wash my hands. Thinking it was a soap dispenser I bent down and gave the machine two sharp hits. As soon as I did, I was assaulted by a scented mist, which was propelled with great ferocity at my head and into my eyes.

In that bar, various Dutch men laughed as I flailed around scratching my eyes and gasping for air as the latest hip scent stung my eyes. It wasn't nice having a bathroom full of Dutch men laughing at me. At least my trousers were up. I was, therefore, going to be sure that this didn't end with the same humiliation.

So I set off to find the toilets and was directed to a set of doors on the top floor of the club. The club was open plan and set across a series of balconies/floors. A huge mirror ran down a wall opposite the balconies meaning everything felt very open and you could see everything across the club no matter where you were. Accordingly, as I scaled the stairs, I could see the toilet doors – there were two sets. One to the far right of the top floor and the other to the far left. I assumed one was for women and one for men. From the top balcony you could look down across the three or four floors of the club. You could also see yourself in the mirror or see deep into the balconies below because of it. The top balcony was very crowded with men talking, standing about or looking at the festivities below. I approached one set of doors and couldn't see any signs or labels for which gender toilet they were. I walked to the other. Same again. So I asked a man who was standing alone and watching me. "Which one can I go in?" I asked.

"Either," he answered with a kind of shrug, like I was a bit stupid. "But they aren't open yet."

This seemed like an odd thing to say. Surely toilets were always open. I wasn't sure about Dutch legislation about access to toilets, but I was fairly sure they would insist that a place must offer access so long as it was open. Surely this was just a translation error. I imagined that he meant that they were occupied, rather than closed.

"You mean someone is in there right now?" I asked, for clarification.

"No," he said with a frown. His look said, 'I know how to speak English you mono language speaking buffoon.' "It isn't open yet," he said slowly like I was simpleton.

I didn't find this funny. I was getting desperate. I wasn't sure what he meant, but I knew I needed to go!

"That's ridiculous," I said. "Are there any others anywhere else?' I asked.

He shook his head.

There were two sets of toilets to service a nightclub holding a few hundred people, and like something out of the militant 1970s, they only opened for a limited period of time. This was surely a mistake or the weirdest situation known to Western Europe.

My disbelief at what I was being told seemingly made me need to toilet even more. Frankly, I wasn't far off pissing my pants. Slowly at first then in a more animated style I began that desperate side-to-side foot hop. Whatever happened, I just couldn't wet myself. "I really need to get in there," I said looking desperate. "When do they open?"

The man looked entertained and amazed. "You really want to get in there bad, don't you?"

"You have no idea," I replied. "I am desperate. Seriously, I can't wait much longer. It's been ages since the last one."

He looked at his watch. "It opens in about ten minutes."

"TEN MINUTES," I blurted out. I doubted that I could last that long. "Is that other one open yet?" I asked and set off to see. The door was shut. I grabbed the door handles and rattled them aggressively. If someone inside heard this they'd open them for me. Whoever heard of a toilet being closed?

"It's not open yet," said another voice.

"Yes, so I'm told, but I'm desperate. I really need to get in," I said and grabbed my crotch.

At this point most people from the balcony were now looking at me. Seemingly the Englishman who was running around desperate for a piss was entertaining them all. I went back to the other doors. "Is there someone I can ask to get these doors opened?"

The Dutch man who had been largely impassive to me looked concerned. "Just calm down. What's the rush? You'll be first in when they are open."

Did people not piss in the Netherlands? Did they not know what a bladder filled to the brim with Amstel felt like? There was no alternative, I had to leave the building and go elsewhere. "Do you people not go to the toilet?" I said with a degree of heightened irritation.

"Of course we do," he said with a deadpan laugh. "Why do you ask?"

At that moment it felt like he'd just farted in my face.

"WHY?" I said. "Because I need to go and if I don't I am going to do it in my pants, that's why."

He smiled. "So go to the toilet then!"

I stood transfixed. Was he trying to take the piss as I tried to go for one? "They aren't open for ten minutes apparently," I squealed like a petulant five year old. "The doors are locked, I can't get in."

He started laughing and soon everyone else on the balcony joined him.

"Zis is not a toilet! This is a dark room. Where you have the sex. This is ze place you can't wait to get in because it has been so long since your last one. You know, because you are so desperate…"

I froze. A chill and sweat passed over me in the heat of my desperation. I could hear laughter fill the balcony where I stood. Everyone was laughing at me and pointing.

"Oh," I said, dejected.

My Dutchman pointed to the stairs. "The toilets are in the basement and yes, they are open."

"I see." I said timidly. "Thank you." I then made my way through throngs or men laughing at me and made my way to the stairs. As I ran down the stairs the laughter seemed to spread like an infectious disease.

"He said he was desperate to get in," I heard one voice explain. "But he wanted a piss not to fuck, he thought they were the toilets."

I ran as fast as my bladder would allow to the basement and found the toilets and was finally able to achieve the near heavenly blissful state of bladder voiding. I sighed a heavenly sigh, which again drew curious glances. As normality returned, it dawned on me that I had been banging on the doors of a dark room, telling everyone unashamedly that I was desperate to get inside. It was to be expected that they would think I was odd. I sidled back up to my friends and glanced up to see people still pointing and staring. "Where have you been?" said my friend, "you've been gone ages." I looked around and tried to think of what to say. "Do you want a drink?" he added. "I bet you are desperate, I mean, really desperate for it, it must have been ages since your last…"

I stared up at him, sighed and made for the door. As we left, I heard more laughter. I turned and glanced back to see the large black doors open as people wandered in.

BAD GAY! NAUGHTY GAY!

"You're not a normal type of gay are you?" The question hung in the air like a fart in an elevator. An odorous silence followed, as the stench of the question slowly dissipated into a faint pong. I could quite clearly detect a degree of disdain in his question. As if somehow I had disappointed him – let him down. My gayness being below par in one-way or another.

On the one hand I was rather taken aback, shocked almost. On the other I was amazed. It wasn't so long ago that I would have a genuine fear about being bludgeoned to death for actually being gay, now I was being passive aggressively reprimanded for not being gay enough.

On the rainbow spectrum of sexuality, I was evidently languishing in the hitherto unknown grey zone, which if you are a homosexual, wasn't the done thing. Where was the chiffon? Where were the pink ribbons, the glamour and the geishas? Had someone thrown a cloth over my mirror ball?

How can you have self-respect and yet be a grey gay?

What was going on?

I had finally admitted to being gay.

I had said it out loud and in front of people. People I knew. People who knew me back. The secret was out. It was a secret no more, well, except to the family. Yes, it still felt odd but the 'problem' wasn't consuming as much time as it had or as I feared. So other then finding love (if it existed) surely I had done most of the hard work. Surely to God, my suffering ended here or hereabouts. That was it. Signed up, its official and I can get on with the rest of my gay life?

Yet, seemingly, that wasn't enough. Apparently I wasn't exhibiting the standard traits of a late twenties, single gay man. Where was my ironic, but comfy and fabulous, feather boa? Where were the bottles of vodka chinking on the floor behind the door? Where was the Eurovision bunting and flags? (Actually they were neatly stored in the cupboard. I'm not a monster for Pete's sake…). Where was the jazzy razzmatazz that the good people of this nation had come to expect from us gays?

For that matter, how could I brazenly open the door to strangers in jogging trousers and a rugby shirt? Not a styled, 'look at my abs' rugby shirt, that you see in magazines, but a real rugby shirt that had an unidentified stain on it somewhere. Where was the Prada? Where were the racks of designer lines and a bulging credit card balance? What WAS going on?

Should someone call the emergency services? Report a missing person. "One homosexual, last seen … well we don't know when he was last seen but we're sure he exists."

The good people of this nation had gone out of their way to accept my sort and yet here I was failing to uphold the small print on the tolerance contract. They had come to terms with the fact I liked sex with men (which, frankly, made their stomachs turn), but the deal was clear – in exchange for them allowing us to do things like find love, eat toast, make jam and buy houses, we had to be fabulous and entertaining. Given this, I was letting the side down. I wasn't froo-frooing it up for their delight. Think about it. What happened if all my sort did this! The average man would never be able to spot us in a crowd. What if there were more like me? Where would it all end? Is he one…? Is she? Oh my God they're everywhere… You see how scary it is?

"I mean…" he said and looked me up and down, "well, you know what I mean."

I wasn't too happy about this degree of condescending contempt. I looked myself up and down as much as I could. "What?" I answered bewildered. Oh, that's where the stain was…

"YOU know," he said knowingly.

Anyway, what did he mean normal gay? Wasn't that an oxymoron? Aren't we all to believe that being and gay and being normal are diametrically opposed points? Is it possible to be both? Is there any such thing? And what is normal? A normal gay? I was a perfectly normal gay, I liked cock – wasn't that enough? In the terms of ticking boxes on the checklist of gay male homosexuality poof queer questionnaire, I was fairly sure that would be the top answer. "Hello sir, do you like cock or fanny?"

"Cock."

"Excellent sir, that's lovely. I can confirm you are a certified homosexual. Congratulations – the panel will be in touch with a small cardboard envelope with condoms and lube."

I had been through a vigorous testing regime and could certify that I was homosexual 2000 compliant. What exactly did he want me to do to prove my point? And would I say no?

I stood staring at him as he looked at me with suspicion. Was this the face of progress? Was this the equality that the gay rights movement has been fighting for all these years? The riots, the assassinations, the marches, the parades, the ribbons, the wristbands and all the bitching – just so postmen could accuse us of not doing our bit – of not upholding our end of the bargain? He stood transfixed, my parcel in hand, looking at me with undisguised pity – at a gay man who'd evidently lost his way. A single gay man without any glitter. He surveyed me with a pity that simply said, "Tragic".

"I mean," the postman continued despite the ensuing silence and withering confusion. "What gays like rugby?"

I stared blankly. Did he want names and addresses? Was I supposed to log into the poof database and check the files for all those who registered as sports fans when they filed their gay papers?

"I dunno," I offered by means of clarification. "I do."

My postman, a not unattractive man in his early 40s, who stood at around 5ft 10, had a full head of thin mousey hair and occasionally captivating blue eyes, shrugged and pulled a face as if to display utter confusion and mystery.

"I know why!" he said pointing at me, smiling broadly. "It's all those men with big legs isn't it? That's why you like rugby?"

I wasn't going to lie and tell him that I'd kick some of them out of bed, of course I wouldn't! Who would? Heavens above, never…! With their rock solid frames and arms the size of small car tyres. My god, they could call me Dorothy and take me up the yellow brick road, as many times as they liked – but no, I happened to like rugby for the sport. I enjoyed playing it at school and enjoyed watching it. As anyone who has ever watched sport with me would also testify, I am a highly competitive, shouting, swearing nut job that thoroughly enjoys the full-blooded gladiatorial contest on the pitch. It doesn't just have to be rugby, football, athletics, tennis – you name it.

I don't watch sport because I fancy the players or just so I can comment on a player. I've never once watched it and thought about what they were wearing (!) or how big their thighs were... deary me, even writing that has made me feel queasy. I like sports. That was it. I was thus wearing the rugby top to reflect my affiliation for the sport. Not to mention the fact that before slankets, this was the best we had.

"I'm not being funny," he added...

I always loved it when people said, "I'm not being funny." It's basically just an ill-educated 'With All Due Respect.' It meant the same thing – I think you're a freak but being British I want to be polite about your mutant dysfunction. In this case, that I was a gay man that might not be detectable to the naked eye. Ironically, since coming out, I seemed less and less gay. It was the law of inverse probability. The more I tried to be out the more I vanished from the gaydar. Now I could almost get lost in a crowd of normal people... Can't have that. Can't be a normal abnormal man. My abnormality needed to be more in keeping with expectations. Not being funny though...

"No of course not," I said with a sigh. "So is that it?" I gestured down to the large parcel he was holding for me.

"Yup, fraid so," he said, having satisfactorily covered today's topics: Why do gays pretend to like sport? "Is it another one of them calendars?" he asked saucily, raising his eyebrows again and again, in a nudge, nudge manner. His stare was fixed, as was his cheeky grin.

"No," I said, matter of fact, prizing the parcel from his grasping hands.

"Shame," he responded with some mystery.

'The calendar' marked the inauguration of our conversational relationship some twelve months earlier. He was delivering a present to me from a friend (that friend being me of course). The present was of a calendar adorned throughout with near naked chiseled models. Sadly the packaging had ripped apart. Accordingly, when I went to the door that winter's morning I was assaulted with an A3 glossy picture of a muscled man. He was artistically captured, strategically covered in mud, steamy from the hot shower and resting against the tiles of the changing room. What's more, he only had a muddied rugby ball to cover his delicates. I stared down at the picture and up at the postman who was grinning a little too enthusiastically.

"Aye, aye?" He'd said.

"What's this?" I asked momentarily confused. With no packaging to speak of, I was curious why my postman, who had heretofore only ever said good morning to me, was presenting me with a Gay Gods 2000 calendar.

"The packaging's ripped but it's definitely for you," he said, dancing his eyebrows about suggestively.

"Oh," I managed. "Thank you." I took the shiny – but forever tainted – calendar from him and turned to leave, blushing.

"Don't you want to check to make sure the package is all there?" He said, sniggering like a five year old.

"I'll take your word it's complete," I said not looking at him. I began closing the door with a rather weak, "Thank you."

"July is very good," he said interrupting me. I opened the door again. "The lads in the sorting office thought you'd like him best."

The lads in the sorting office? What on earth do they know of me? And why would they think I'd like July – whoever it was?

"What? July? Why?" I managed with some exasperation.

He grinned. "Well, we reckon you'll like him because you can just see a bit of his co…" I spluttered and coughed before he could go any further.

"Thank you," I offered meekly, now keen to get indoors and gaze at July and his bit of co…

"I didn't know you were into that kind of thing," he said matter of fact, quasi hurt. Here was the opportunity to change perceptions. This was my golden get out of jail card. I could tell him that I bought it for my girlfriend or as a joke for someone in the office. Should I lie or should I just accept that it was evidently for me? Should I just take the calendar willingly and let the postman know I was a friend of Dorothy?

"Why would you?" I managed with a small degree of defiance, but without a tacit admission.

"No reason," he said nodding. "Good to know, though."

I couldn't begin to imagine why my saucy semi-naked calendar and the resultant implication of my sexuality were good to know. "Why's that?" I ventured, cautiously.

"Oh, we always get loads of stuff for your lot."

Your lot?

"Stuff that people return because they get embarrassed or whatever. Instead of binning it, I'll drop it over to you. You might as well get some fun out of it. Morning!"

With that, he was on his way. So began my roller coaster year of a fluttering letterbox activity with porn magazines, sex supplements, contact mags, fetish clothing catalogues and anything with a near naked male torso on – almost all of which ended in the bin. Some twelve months on and here we still were. I was talking to the person who represented the longest relationship I'd actually ever had with a man. The postman. A married man with three kids, one 'mad' ex wife and a curiosity for the intricacies of my life.

"Oh well," he said, "Can't stand here chatting all day." "Enjoy your new calendar," he offered cheekily. As before, it was obvious he and the lads from the sorting office had looked into the parcel to make sure it was this year's installment of hirsute hotties that would stand over my desk as we marked the march of time together.

"July isn't as good as last year's," he offered ruefully. "But November makes up for it. Don't think you'll be too disappointed. Anyway, better be off – I expect you'll want to have a wank. Cheerio." Off he went, whistling as he walked.

I glanced down at my sealed, opened and resealed parcel and sighed. He was right – I wasn't an ordinary gay. I didn't conform. I didn't fit in. I was glad he was unaware of what happened a few days earlier. I'd never hear the end of it, of that I was sure. I had been walking through a shopping mall when an attractive, chatty and persuasive woman stopped me. It was there and then she asked me if I moisturised.

I laughed. I actually laughed. Did I moisturise? Could she not see my skin? I came from a wind battered North Eastern fishing village. My skin was made of leather. If I had put any cream on my face (which hadn't been prescribed), I would have been taken out in a boat and thrown overboard. Moisturise you say?

I frowned, as if to suggest I was confused by what she'd asked. "A skin care regime," she added as if to clarify.

I appreciate that there's a growing market for men's grooming products, but I was more likely to have eaten a bucket of shellfish (to which I am allergic) than I was to have a 'skin care regime'. My skin care regime consisted of putting my skin under a shower, cleaning it and coming out from the shower. I wasn't sure whether that constituted a 'regime,' but at least I had something to discuss. Besides, does our skin actually require a regime? Weren't we toppling regimes the world over? Weren't we told they are bad things? Aren't I, therefore, a skin care revolutionary?

"I used to have a skin care regime," I said mischievously, "But it was agreed that we needed regime change, so now there's just a void." I smiled.

She looked at me perplexed, like I was a weirdo.

In truth, I did have some moisturiser at home. This was bought because my gusset rubbed in hot weather, so I needed something to tend to the red-hot chaffing. Even then it was in a white plain tub with ugly functional lettering. I purchased it from a pharmacist, not a fashion store.

She seemed a little crestfallen but evidently not surprised. Thus began the sales pitch of why this Himalayan body scrub, body butter and balm would be the answer to my prayers and my skin care problems.

I wasn't entirely aware that my skin care had problems, but hey, I was still listening. I had a demo with some elixir rubbed onto my hand. Gently she massaged the exfoliating cream into my skin. She looked deep into my eyes as she did. I was half expecting her to say, 'you will feel sleepy, you will buy my Himalayan goo.' She finished her tender touch and wiped the excess minerals sourced from the foot of the blah-de-blah mountain with it's natural river babbling over it's something or other leaving the thingy better for your what's it.

"There," she said standing back admiring her work. "How does that feel? Doesn't it feel smoother?"

'You are feeling sleepy...'

I had a prod about. As far as I could see it was no different to before except for the fact it felt a bit oily.

"Oh yes," I said faking it. "Smooth."

She set about applying another cream. One that would take away the oily one before. Same routine, into the eyes, look deep into my eyes...

Afterwards I had to remark that yes, it felt far less oily. She smiled. She was pleased that her product hadn't failed her. Sure my skin felt soft, but the thought of doing that to my face every day was utterly preposterous. Beside, my hand now felt like it had been coated in a non-stick surface. If I had that on my face and ever went to kiss someone they'd squeak to the floor with a thud as my face actively repelled them.

I smiled but knew that I was not going to be her customer today. Accordingly I thanked her for her wonderful sales pitch but that I wouldn't be partaking.

"It'll get rid of those red marks and spots," she said bluntly.

Without missing a beat, I smiled. "Yes but I like my spots and blotches," I told her. "They're what makes me, me."

Not the greatest come back, but true. I am not the kind of person to stand for hours applying various levels of cream on my face. The skin on my heels, for example, was so cracked that had any certified skin care specialist been given a glimpse, they would surely have suffered an immediate cardiac arrest. As far as I am aware, you can't polish a turd, so why bother spending hundreds of pounds on something that will just make my rather unimpressive face a bit softer?

"Nah, I'm okay thanks," I said and turned to go.

She tutted and huffed. I could tell she wasn't exactly thrilled. "You are a bad gay!" she said to my surprise. "Bad gay! Naughty gay!"

This idea thrilled me. Not only had she castigated me for being sloppy in my skin care regime, but had outed me and then judged me for being bad at being gay. All of this and I was just shopping for a frying pan! It seemed ludicrous that I could be all of these things at once. 'You have finally been admitted to the homosexual fraternity and already you are letting the side down. That three month probation you are on is looking shaky.' First the postman…

It also made me wonder whether to be a 'good gay' I had to comply with a skin care regime and live in the gym. What if I just wanted to watch TV? What if I didn't mind the odd spot? Was it so bad that I preferred a slice of cheesecake to leg day in the gym? Did she have a point? Did the postman? Maybe the reason I was languishing on the shelf was because I wasn't gay enough. It was true I had become less gay since I'd been officially gay. It was also true that most gay couples seemed gayer than me. I took a long hard look at myself. Maybe they had a point. I wasn't over weight, I did go to the gym and I ate relatively well, but I prioritised comfort over most things. I was unlikely to make it into the gym if it was raining. I would just have a sausage sandwich instead and promise to go the next day. Which obviously I wouldn't. I looked relaxed. I looked lived in, like an old battered leather sofa. Comfy but unexceptional. Maybe they were right. Maybe I needed to moisturise, camp it up a bit. Maybe I need to be gayer?

I had a weekend away with friends planned, so I decided (quite tragically) that this would be the weekend that I unleashed my inner gay. I told myself that my failed attempts in the past were simply because I hadn't done them correctly. This would be the weekend everyone would see the <u>real</u> me.

What a total wanker.

Come the weekend away and I was planning to be gayer than ever. It was a clandestine operation. Appear normal all the way there and then pow! As I had no gay friends and only ever encountered gay people who were bad and naughty gays like me, I took my inspiration from TV characters.

As it turned out, I seemed to take my inspiration from caricatures of large African American women who had finger snapping, head swirling attitude. My hip swaying, 'you go girl, Hmm, mmm', attitude was about as appalling an act of humanity as you could imagine. Much like a bad transvestite that simply looks like a bloke in a dress, with none of the fineries of femininity, I was a truly bad, sad gay.

We were away for the weekend on a cultural/beer cruise and were staying in a hotel. We arrived at the hotel in our group of about eight and I was trying to camp it up as best I could. I had already complimented the girls on how good they looked in various items of clothing and had given arched eyebrow looks of disdain to anyone who said something OTT. My hands were flailing about like a wind turbine crashing in a storm. I looked bloody ridiculous.

As we stood at the hotel lobby waiting to check in a women came up to me. I was still wearing my rugby cap. Having spotted it she approached. "Hi. I didn't see the score last night," she started politely, pointing at the cap. "What was the score in the end?"

This was my big moment. Everyone, having nothing better to

do, was looking at me. I knew I had the stage and it was my time to shine. Exit bad gay, naughty gay, welcome the era of diva magnifico!

"Well let me just say," I started flamboyantly. "You look FAB-U-LOUS." I even got my hand and swirled it down her torso like I was a magician's assistant pointing at a vanishing box. She looked shocked.

After I did it I couldn't help thinking, "What the hell was that?" I remember her standing staring at me like I'd been let out of an asylum. She took a step back. My friends stared at me in disbelief. WTF? I can clearly recall the silence of the hotel lobby as people – of different languages, nationalities and backgrounds – all stopped and stared at me. It's fair to say that the woman who had innocuously asked me a sports score was not expecting that reaction. Everything was still. I felt as if I had literally stopped the world spinning on its axis and the planet's population was staring at me disdainfully.

I was very aware of the ensuing stunned silence. I stood looking at the woman who was staring at me in disbelief. I didn't even like her dress. I looked at the floor in shame. "They won. Came back at the last few minutes to win 32 – 28."

She nervously thanked me and walked off, shaking and tearful, in all probability. I kept examining the weave of the reception carpet afraid to look up and waited until sound returned to the room and the world started moving again.

"What was that?" asked a friend.

"Not sure," I offered limply, blushing as I did.

Surely, SURELY, that was just beginner's nerves. Surely I could master this. It couldn't be that hard, could it? Later that night when we'd enjoyed sufficient culture we were in a bar. A rather jolly but essentially sedate place. It was young, it was fresh and we'd found a booth in the corner where we decided to decamp for the evening. I had toned down diva magnifico since reception, to consider my rookie mistakes. However now we were out and the drink was working, maybe it was time…

Now. The one thing that this book makes strikingly clear is that alcohol has a profound effect on me. It is therefore well documented that a few drinks will make me a tweak more extravagant. As this was my super sized gay weekend I knew that I had to deliver. I also had to make up for, and move on from, that morning's debacle.

I had to be judicious and pick my moment carefully. The place was rather dark and quite large. There was a large circular bar at the centre, a dance-floor to one side and seats around the remaining perimeter. Music played loudly. It was my turn to go to the bar and so that's what I did. As I stood around a relatively crowded bar waiting to get served one of my favourite records came on. The music was loud, the club was dark, I was getting fuzzy with beer, but more importantly, I had spotted a podium.

Oh yes, a podium.

I can't really explain what went through my head. I just saw this as another gloriously golden opportunity to become the blossoming homosexual I had always meant to be. It was time to unleash the gay that had been shackled by the need to behave straight all those years. The triumphant homo that was screaming to be heard was about to pop its head up and say hello… Either that or I was just a dick.

So, clambering onto the podium I elected to give the bar's clientele my own diva performance of that song. Oh yes. 'Shut Up' by the Black Eyed Peas. (The irony). There I stood during the instrumental opening doing my own version of vogueing. This song is a duet. Naturally I couldn't sing both parts, so I elected to take the men's parts (not for the last time). There I stood. Ignored at first, just another drunk.

As the song got going, so did I. I started sashaying, hipping, hopping, gyrating, lip syncing (yes, I did), wagging my finger, shaking my bootay and generally pulsating.

Slowly, like a Mexican wave of shock, one person nudged another and pointed to the hysterically bad gay flapping about on the podium like a drag queen being electrified. The song, for those unaware of it, also contains many long pauses during the singers' conversation. Wow...

That provided me the opportunity to pause, freeze and throw an arched eyebrow at the crowd now assembled around my elevated dance platform. I saw my friends gather, unable to stop laughing, people watched in bemusement, then amusement and then to my dismay – unbridled hilarity. There before a crowd of strangers I had given my dying swan diva number. A grown man gyrating like a teenage girl trying to offend her father.

The song stopped… well in truth, the DJ stopped the song, I think there is a difference. I got down from the raised platform to some wolf whistles and ironic applause. I went to the bar as if nothing had happened and returned with the drinks. Everyone was smirking and saying nothing as I handed the drinks round.

"Oh just fuck off," I said and sat down with a hefty plop.

I knew then that I was destined eternally to be a bad, naughty gay with red spots and blotches. And you know, for once in my life, I was actually quite happy with that.

DARKNESS DESCENDS

It was three years since that bomb and I was living like a monk. Well, maybe not exactly a monk, but compared to my life of old I was practically a saint. Yes there was a trip to the walls every now and then but essentially I was living in a mute sexual state. As my social life was much improved, the need to go and find people to spend time with had diminished. The pressure to be with someone had been addressed. I was going out and enjoying myself. In many senses I was too busy to feel self-pity.

The Internet was the new big thing. People were doing things like sending letters by computer that got there super fast and they could chat to one another no matter where they were – assuming their dial up connection held out long enough. Internet dating was just starting up, but it was thought it was only for people who had exhausted the pool of talent locally and had been forced to search for love further afield. Internet dating was, therefore, only for people who couldn't find meaningful relationships during daylight hours. There was a view that Internet dating enabled losers to meet other losers. Naturally, that's where I was.

The Internet was just coming into popular consciousness and so chat rooms and online personals were becoming increasingly accepted. At that time, however, adverts were still for 'Unhappy married woman seeks man to satisfy her and show her love,' 'Successful businessman seeks lady to spoil, to love and live life with.' In other words, people still wanted sex, sex and more sex.

The gay adverts were just starting to creep out of secret code. Gay chat rooms were emerging. Then gay interest chat rooms. You could see the Internet evolving and diversifying as people thought, 'hey, I want a chat room just for bears or just for older men or skins…' It wasn't long before the Internet was like the best gay bar ever. Throbbing with willing cock and every kind of preference you could imagine. You may get chatting to someone, exchange pics and decide to meet and then find out they lived 300 miles away. At that point they'd suggest cyber and you'd log off, rather than get off. That evolved very quickly into A.S.L. Which enabled the chatters to determine their Age, Sex and Location. After that, 'what you looking for' usually followed it. I often replied 'I'm just after a quote for a replacement boiler.' I felt sure if that made someone laugh I might have a future with them. That ignored the fact that anyone I could have a future with wouldn't start a conversation with A.S.L., but hey ho.

Soon, everyone was talking about chat rooms and meeting up with others. It was like a prehistoric social media. The gay scene was expanding and becoming more open – on and offline. Gay bars started to replace their frosted glass windows with clear glass. It seems farcical to think about it now but up and until the 1990s gay bars were still largely hidden away, chiefly to protect the identity of those inside. One bar still had a hatch in the door, which you spoke through to gain entry. The hatch would close, you'd hear bolts unlock and then you'd be let in. Like most gay bars that hid behind shutters or darkened windows, I always thought that if people could see inside they'd be amazed by how dull it was… The secrecy, the need for unhealthy privacy was changing. There was a general feeling of uplift. We had a new government, a new direction and gay people weren't being hounded out of houses and chased down streets with the same regularity as before. I allowed myself a small upsurge in optimism and tried my hand at online dating.

I was at a point where trying to be someone I wasn't, was at an end. I was going to be myself, warts and all. I ran an advert that summed up, as far as I could manage, a good description of me. I wanted to be honest and fair. I was done with lies. Whoever replied (assuming anyone ever did) then what they saw was what they'd get. I was brutally honest and offered no nasty surprises. This is that <u>very</u> advert....

Hi there.
My name is Jack. I am 5 11, I have blond hair (rapidly disappearing sadly), blue eyes, I'm slim, straight-acting and looking. I keep active through sports and general keep fit.
I don't smoke but I do drink when I go out socialising which I enjoy doing on a regular basis (socialising not drinking... although...)
I am equally at ease going out to clubs and pubs (usually not scene – I don't have a problem with it and occasionally visit, but get bored with its superficiality if I go often – usual story) as I am staying in and watching some TV or out at the cinema, theatre, comedy club etc. etc. – at the end of the day I like all the things you would expect someone to like – socialising, cinema, theatre, eating out, eating in, cooking, TV, music, keep fit etc.
I am very down to earth and don't have any (many) heirs and graces. What you see is very much what you get. I am not one

for superficiality or insincerity, which is why I tend to
wear my heart on my sleeve.
I am easy going and relaxed generally but would now like to
quit worrying about being single and meet someone who is
'normal' and with whom I can share the highs, lows and
generally everyday life with. At the end of the day I am at peace
with myself and mentally sorted – if you know what I mean.
Erm what else? I am caring, considerate and can equally be
thoughtless and selfish. In short I'm human.
So, if you are interested in someone who is essentially
settled, content and ready to take the next step in life, then
please send me a mail and we can take it from there.
Cheers, Jack

I was as popular as a yapping dog with diarrhoea on a long haul flight. No one wanted honesty. They wanted showroom shiny – not a bloke with a mysterious stain on his rugby shirt who admitted to going bald. The silence was deafening. Yet like a teenager waiting for my pen pal to reply, every night I would return from work and check my new fangled email. Would there be a reply? Would someone want to get to know me? In a nutshell – no.

Weeks became months and months slowly melted into years. The pattern stayed the same. The darkness, which had been beaten into retreat by the verve of my new life, was beginning to make an unwelcome return. As my life stood, seemingly still, those around me moved forward. They were getting married and starting families. Professional young people became professional young couples and then professional young families. I began to wonder, once again, whether gay men were simply destined to be eternally single. It seemed like there was no evidence to the contrary. Our bars were less secretive, our politicians started to stick up for us a bit more, we could be more visible and yet where were the all of gay couples?

Everyone, including sexual health consultants, told me that gay couples were never faithful. One doctor told me bluntly that I should never trust a man to be faithful. Black is black, white is white and all men were bastards. There was no room for discussion. I began to think that was the reality.

I hadn't previously thought of myself as being a 'couples person,' because I could never see myself as part of a couple. The reality was dawning – I wanted to be in a relationship. I craved a life so ordinary you could walk past it on the street without noticing that it was there. I needed to live life just like those friends around me. I needed the warmth and security of mundanity. I didn't look for someone to validate me, but I did hope to find someone who would make my feelings feel real. Having been on the outside of society for so long, I just wanted to be with someone that made me feel like I wasn't abnormal. Was that too much to ask?

Man walks into bar and orders a burger and a beer. Sounds unexceptional doesn't it? Gay man walks into bar and orders burger and a beer. Any different? Despite the supposed growing acceptance, the need to label people by their sexuality and make clear what they were, continued at pace. A gay man walking into a bar isn't there for the burger and the beer, he is obviously there for something else. Why else mention he's gay? Why indeed. Yet this labeling was everywhere. It felt like I was never going to have a relationship – but a gay relationship. That, by virtue, was different and beyond normal. Stupid though it was, if I went into a bar I would almost narrate myself. 'Gay man walks into bar…' What was I up to?

If I wanted to be in a relationship, it was never going to be, 'two men go into bar and order burgers and beers,' it was 'gay lovers order food and alcohol' in bar. The emphasis was always on us as being different. You'll never read 'Heterosexual lovers have drinks before dinner' in a paper, but 'homosexual lovers drank together in front of children,' was quite a common sight. We were still being made an exception. Why was sexuality relevant? I felt as if any love I did manage to find would be suffocated under a blanket of innuendo and suspicions. I didn't want love, I apparently wanted 'gay' love. It needed its own label. It could never be unexceptional. It would never be the same or equal. My feelings would always be exceptional – remind us, what float are you?

Everyday I would see couples in shops, restaurants and bars and I would feel a pain in the pit of my stomach. There they were laughing, loving, kissing – just being. It hurt. I would never know that. 'Gay men kiss in shop, CCTV images here…'

It occurred to me that I could die and simply never know what it was like to be in love. Just that thought brought me untold darkness. If that was true, what was the point of going on? How long could I hold out being that funny single uncle at every family function? The 'confirmed bachelor' at every social event that people discussed and dissected but never embraced.

Given all of this, if I ever managed to convince myself that maybe, just maybe, there would be a chance to meet someone, it felt like we'd only be allowed to live half a life. I was back to the fact we couldn't hold hands or book a hotel room together (which was still illegal). It felt like whatever happiness we found would only be half allowed. We would both be exposed to bigots and haters and after all of that – he'd be unfaithful! The future – even at its most optimistic – felt bleak.

I appreciate how pessimistic it seems now, but it was very real then. Everything seemed to suggest that two men couldn't have a meaningful and loving relationship. It was a cunning myth. Was my life to be a lonely existence peppered with soulless one-night stands by people who, as I grew older, would either seek to exploit or ignore me? The stakes grew higher and harder every week. At the time, I felt as if time was literally running out. I could hear a clock ticking. I felt like a kid who has been separated from his parents. He can see them drift away, seemingly unaware that he is lost and stranded in a crowd. I was beginning to feel helpless.

Around then 'gay life' began appearing on the fringes of mainstream life, but what was it like? It was the Queer as Folk explicit, in your face, side of the gay scene. It was the pride parade on TV. The Queer as Folk phenomena that allegedly put gay life into realistic perspective served only to demonise and stereotype gay men further. From what I saw out and about at the time, it did more harm than good. I watched it and I just shook my head in despair. What a wasted opportunity. It was a one-dimensional monosyllabic view of the gay scene.

Even that seemed to be clear about gay men and relationships.

356

There weren't any! Where were those gays who liked baking, tartan rugs, the National Trust and scones? Queer as Folk made relationships look broken. Who was in one? Who wanted one? Those that wanted a relationship couldn't achieve or sustain one. It was a life of 'community,' not family. A life as a collective of singles not couples. It was all about casual sex and anonymity. It depressed the shit out of me.

Around that time there was also a rather menacing hoax that started doing the rounds on the Internet. It had been reported that someone had found a cure for being gay. It was said that people were flying to America to take this magic cocktail of happiness. I was straight onto the net with my super fast dial up speeds of 56kb a second to find out more. When I realised it was a cock tale, I felt exhausted. I was genuinely ready to try anything to change my future. Conversion therapy anyone?

I hadn't come out to my family still. My general policy was – when I have something to tell them (a relationship) – then I will. Until then there was nothing to share. I was the same person as I was before so why did they need to know anything?

In hindsight this probably excluded them from my life more than was constructive. Back then it seemed sensible and normal, but I may have been happier if I had just shared. The millennium was upon us. The biggest date change in, well, in a millennium. The attitude was one of hope and fear. Would the 'Y2K bug' have planes falling from the sky? Would our tomorrows be better? I fluctuated between being positive and fearing the future. It was ten years since I started Uni. It was seven years since that attic room and three years since the bomb. I hadn't really moved further or forward. I felt like I did in those depressing early days. Yes, I had admitted I was gay but it appeared to deliver nothing but a different kind of empty and broken promises. That was my fault for building up coming out so much. (I see that now.) Back then I just felt betrayed. Not sure by what or who, just betrayed. It's fair to say I just felt flat!

I didn't give up though. I kept going, sure that the sun would shine on me one day. Advert after advert, reply after reply, they all came to nothing. Gloom was descending further. This was my new reality. I felt like I was part of a circus sideshow. Friends would laugh at the tall tales from my life as a single man. The stories were funny but the feeling of isolation wasn't. As time went on, the facts seemed to become absolute. It just wasn't possible for me to be gay <u>and</u> happy. I wanted a relationship, but because they weren't possible, I would have to spend my life alone. My greatest fear was dying alone. My life flashing before my eyes knowing I had never known love. That kept me awake at night. I know it sounds morose, but that's where we were as a society and where I was as an individual.

Any notion or romanticism that I could be both gay and happy seemed, once again, to be diminished. I saw nothing to convince me that gay life wasn't anything other than the string of one-night stands or being alone and a bitter old queen – something I could very easily see myself becoming. (Becoming?)

I had been out and about working at gay charities, I'd been in every gay pub there was, in every club, moved across several cities, answered adverts in magazines and papers and gone on blind dates galore. I had met people through work, at parties and just by chance on a street. I had trawled the Internet, which was meant to be filled with pond scum and people grateful for eye contact. I was ten years into my adult journey and three to four years into my search for love. I hadn't had so much as a bite. WHAT WAS THERE LEFT TO DO?

Those few years looking were exacerbated by the years of isolation and confusion that preceded them. I wasn't just another single bloke looking for love, I was a single bloke that had just come to terms with his life. I was trying to forget the damage my emotionally mangled journey had caused me. I was trying to forget the guilt at feeling I was abnormal. I was trying to feel like I was worth a shit. Every rejection wasn't just a knock-back it was affirmation that all those fears and pains were valid. Every sour date or cruel comment was giving breath to bigots and their view of my kind. I was looking for something to make me feel I wasn't evil, just normal.

I just wanted to have quiet weekends and bake bread. Yes I wanted stupid bloody walks on the beach. If we had a fire I'd settle in front of it. If we had a DVD player we'd watch them. If there was a sofa then yes, I wanted to curl up on it. I wanted to be settled, not having to settle. Surely it wasn't that much to ask? By this point my loneliness was causing me physical pain. I actually hurt. The anguish of being alone was eroding my actual quality of life. What was there for people like me? If there wasn't happiness what was there? The gay scene was a young place. The older I got the further away it was. I'd seen older guys abused and ignored and looked at them thinking 'is that my future?' I had heard one guy in a bar say, "See that guy over there, why is he here? Old people are gross." I looked across and saw a guy who was probably mid forties. (Although given my judgment he may have been 80.) Old people were a gross infringement on the gay scene. Weirdos. What did they want? They were life's failures. Was that my life? A life alone, then death alone. Sounds miserable doesn't it? It was.

It was becoming a terminally depressing state. Day after day seemed to be dark. A spiralling, claustrophobic, crushing sense of darkness. It enveloped my head and all of my emotions. It felt like life was holding a pillow over my face. Some days I wondered why I fought back and breathed. I was using up more energy to stay alive than to live. I began contemplating some serious 'solutions'. These days I'm sure people would say I was suffering depression and should have sought help. Back then, it felt like my life was destined to be an endlessly unhappy, loveless existence. I would lie awake and think of ways to end the pain. That tall building, those pills. Everything raced through my mind. I imagined how people would react and take the news and it felt like most people would shrug their shoulders and move on. Yet deep down, I knew that such an event would cause my family untold pain, far greater pain than anything I was currently experiencing.

To be honest it was that, and only that, which stopped me. It was that buffer that prevented me from following through. I am not sure whether I would have gone all the way with those 'solutions' but I felt like I was getting closer with every loveless month. The grim reality of that 'solution' began to look less grim, less severe. Yet, honestly, I didn't feel self-pity. I still held out some flicker of hope. I told myself to keep on going. To keep believing. I went to church. I went to social groups. I went anywhere I thought I could find answers. In the end I kept on living, kept being alive not so much for myself but for my family. I remember thinking that I was only staying alive to prevent them feeling pain. That in itself caused more pain.

Imagine lying flat on the ground and the force of life, like a strong river, a torrent of energy, running over your body. It felt like that. As if this was so strong I was prevented from sitting up. I lay there, weak, unable to lift myself up. I tried and tried, but life forced me back down. It was exhausting. When darkness came I would go out for a walk or the gym – just to raise serotonin levels. More often than not I would just go to sleep – no matter what the time. I prayed that when I woke the dark shadow following me would have evaporated and I could go on a bit further.

Christmas came around and I endured, rather than enjoyed, that. It was the new millennium and I was ready to adopt the positivity everyone seemed to have as we kicked off the new century. As Spring approached I decided it was time for another roll of the dice. In the back of my head I kept telling myself this was the last roll of the dice, although I doubt it would have been.

I told myself that if nothing came of this, it would be time for one of those solutions. In truth, I suspect, I would have got out on to a rooftop and just shit myself. I had read up on suicide and every way seemed grizzly. 'You don't want to go that way,' articles would say – as if compiling a top ten of ways to pop your clogs. Every solution seemed to be painful, traumatic or messy. I suspect I was just using it as a whip to crack myself into action. Every time I felt like giving up I snapped the suicide whip and I would pick up the pace again. It was a rather dark way to stop me giving in. Surrender now and it's that grizzly death…

I wasn't sure what would happen or how I would react if nothing came from this particular dice roll. I kept telling myself I couldn't go on if nothing happened and would then think about ending it all, but as usual it just scared me silly. What worried me, however, was the moment when it failed to scare me silly. That reality seemed a viable and terrifying prospect.

Deep down I still held a small candle of hope that there may be someone – otherwise why was I actually still doing this? If I did genuinely have no hope, then why bother at all? Evidently I had hope. It kept my head above water. Hope and fear in interchangeable quantities propelled me forward.

As before, I saw no point pretending to be someone I wasn't, so I planned to send the same advert as before. I knew that whomever connected with that was right for me. Don't ask me why. I just thought it was the ultimate litmus test. It was, in its own way, uniquely me. Then if I was duly rejected or ignored, although it would be more painful, I knew that was because they didn't want me. Not some picture postcard me. Then, conversely, if anyone did reply it would be because they liked the actual, real me.

I looked through a mountain of personal ads. As the Internet was becoming more available and increasingly popular the ads were plentiful. Having scoured every single one I decided it was time to go for broke. So I sat down with my lime green iBook and I replied to all of them. Every. Single. One.

If you had an advert on Yahoo Personals at that point, you'll have got a reply from me. I didn't care if the advertisers were unhinged, said they loved doing it up a tree wearing blue body paint or had an old sofa they were looking to get rid of. I just sent the same reply to all of them. I simply didn't care. One by one I went down the list, click, reply, click, reply, click, reply, click, reply, click, reply…

In some cases I didn't even read their advert.

I sent my stock reply to all of them, copying and pasting my search for love. That was that. That was all I had left to offer. That was definitely it. I got to the last few of a very long list and began to doubt my own sanity. What the hell was I doing? I sat there motionless. Fed up. I looked at the remaining three adverts. One was from someone who enjoyed doing it outdoors in the woods, one liked knitting and whilst the other one seemed ordinary, I was fairly sure he'd be a freak too. It felt utterly hopeless. A futile gesture in a fool's quest for love. Maybe a 'solution' would be better for everyone. Maybe I wasn't worth bothering with and that's what the universe had been trying to tell me – give up already! I rapidly copied and pasted the last few loonies a reply and slammed my laptop shut. At the very worst, surely the knitter would reply. I'd always be good for Argyle knitwear and Christmas gifts for family thereafter.

It was Easter time, which meant that I was with my family. I decided to wait at least a week before checking to see if I had any replies. All week I kept wondering if anyone would reply, but didn't check once. Every night before sleep, I'd hope the inbox was buzzing. Maybe it was full of replies. I'd even set up a generic email account just for replies – partly to protect my identity and so that I could accommodate the vast amount of replies. There were people who said they replied to all emails no matter what, so I knew I'd have a handful, even if they led nowhere. My week passed and with great trepidation I logged in. To my dismay there were none.

Not one.

Not a single one.

Not even from those that said they would reply to every message.

The. Lying. Bastards.

What about the guy who knitted? I mean, surely he hardly got any action? There was a guy who liked building model toys and cars. For fuck's sake, had it come to this? People who seek the company of wool and toy cars over another adult were rejecting me. In that moment I sank lower than even I thought possible. There is something bone crunchingly depressing about being rejected by a stranger who promises to reply to you, even if you are a mutant, but then doesn't. What on earth does that say about you?

My inbox may have been empty, but my emotional inbox was inundated with soul-sapping pain. It was devastating. How many times can one soul bounce back?

I returned to work after the Easter break wondering why I should bother carrying on with life. It had been nearly twenty years too far. How many more decades would it take? I sat staring out of my office window. It was high up a large office block and had access to the roof. When you stepped out up there, the wind would push you back. Looking down made me sick. I decided, as only a pragmatist would do, that before any rash decisions were made I would finish my current project at work. Accordingly, life went on as normal for just a few more days. After that, it was time to look at those solutions with more determined eyes. Then, out of the blue, there was a reply from one of the adverts…

I stared at the envelope icon as if I was seeing things. Was this a brave soul that was happy to date a neurotic balding man with low self-esteem? It was that knitter wasn't it?

I just stared. What was wrong with him? Fleetingly, I ran through a variety of things that could discount the guy immediately. Maybe he was the one who wanted to buy a cat. Surely he wasn't the naturist who said any first date would be in the nude? Finally, after an age of staring, I opened it and read it. It wasn't. It was a guy from the last three adverts on the list – just below the naturist and the knitter.

Knowing it wasn't from anyone who spent their leisure time with yarn, I read the reply eagerly, sucking up each word as if it were loaded with diamonds. This was a strange and new position. Did I reply straight away? Did I wait? Did I try and make it look like I was blasé or eager? But how eager? Would eager look too eager? Would too eager look desperate? Would blasé look too blasé?

I also learned something vitally important right there and then as I quivered over the contents. My mood rocketed. I felt a sense of hope and happiness that I hadn't felt for years. Surely then… even if this guy was a loony, that feeling of hope meant I wanted to believe, that I wanted to live. Maybe I wasn't ready to throw in the towel just yet?

In the end I decided that the time was right for even more

honesty. I wasn't going to play any bloody games. I replied saying that I didn't know if I was looking too eager but I was sick of the games and the nonsense of the scene. I was utterly honest and open and about what I wanted. What did I actually have to lose? Amongst a fairly desperate plea for him to reply, I included this…

I am certainly not someone who is insincere or false, it's not in my blood. I am a true northerner in the sense that I will speak as I find. It has taken me years to learn diplomacy but I'm getting there! Comes in handy at work when I want to tell people their stuff is crap. I am also programmed to receive equal honesty back…it's not just a one-way street.

I must admit I am so fed up of one-night flings it gets depressing. I am ready for a relationship and something that is based on more than a physical attraction – that's rarely much good when you want to go to the cinema or go out for a meal is it? Forgive me if that sounds whatever, but I have had enough of trying to be someone I am not or pretend so as not to put people off. I want a compatible relationship that's based on mutual trust, honesty, compassion and respect for independence. I also don't go in for open relationships.

Then…

My umbrella exploded today. I put it up as it started to rain (which seems logical given the fact that's what they were invented for) and all these bits of metal shot out. The canopy flew across the road, I thought a small child was going to get injured with the flying shrapnel and a bus queue of people started laughing at me. That's the kind of thing that happens to me on a regular basis.

To my utter amazement, he replied. Over the space of a few emails and the odd photo exchanged (I thought he was astonishingly good looking and amazingly sexy) we decided to speak on the phone.

The thing that stunned me – he kept replying. He'd seen a pic of me yet he was still replying. All of my cards were on the table. My honest, ugly, hair receding cards and he was still replying. Was he normal? I didn't want to do myself an unnecessary disservice but a looker I was not. So, miracle one, he replied. Miracle two, he kept replying. Miracle three he didn't live that far away. Was this happening? Having travelled so many miles on the road of disappointment I refused to get my hopes up… then after a minute or two, began wondering 'was this the one…?'

Our chats had to take place late at night because he used to finish work very late. I would stay up and we would chat about his work and my work. It was all rather boring and stilted, as conversation between two strangers often is. Yet despite that, it was also relaxed. In the end, I suggested we meet. We had to take this to the next level. Although technically a blind date, we'd already laid more ground than any date I'd had before. I suggested we meet at noon that sunny weekend. I had planned to watch the football later that evening at 8pm. I figured that was plenty of time to meet, get duly rejected, come home and eat before the match.

We agreed to meet in the city I was living in. It wasn't that far from where he lived and, well, I lived there. We were to meet outside of the library in the city. We both had each other's photos and so would, by and large, have a good idea of what the other looked like. From experience of meeting pen pals at train stations, it was always easy to spot someone looking for you. Usually they were the only other people walking around staring expectantly at strangers like a tit.

I got there early and finding the bench opposite the library empty, I sat down and waited. A few deep breaths. A few casual glances at the town hall clock. Some more deep breaths and I began to wonder what was to come. Was this going to be another doomed blind date? Would he, as one had done, demand that we eat halal meat or we had no future? Would he, as one had done, invite me home to show me his extensive Star Trek figurine collection? Who knew? I was prepared for any eventuality.

As I sat in the summer sun it struck me that this could very possibly be it. This could be my last chance at happiness. Or the one I'd been looking for. Salvation or damnation – no pressure!

I had dated. I had been rejected. I had been ignored… degraded… attacked… belittled… abused… lied to… The list went on. I had little or nothing positive to associate with my experience so far. I tried not to feel fatalistic and told myself this wasn't my only shot at happiness, yet deep down I wondered if it were. Suddenly I was torn from my thoughts as a hand rested on my shoulder. I tensed and turned around.

"Alright!" Boomed a voice.

I turned and then sighed heavily. It was my floor mate from the first house share.

"What you doing here then?" He said brightly. He was always very jolly.

I looked at him sternly. "I'm on a date," I snarled testily. He looked around and then back at me. "Well he's not here yet!" I said hurriedly.

"Oh right, sorry!" he said. "Well look. When it doesn't work out me and the missus are over there having a coffee. Just pop over."

Such was my reputation for luck.

"Thank you," I managed, my nerves taking over.

"Shall I order you a coffee then?" He asked genuinely.

"Goodbye," I spat at him and sat back down.

As I sat down again, frowning, the chill of fear evaporated and I felt the warmth of the sun. I watched my friend walk off towards the coffee shop and shook my head in dismay. What did he mean 'when it doesn't work out?' 'WHEN?' I allowed the sun to warm me. I closed my eyes and tried to just be.

"Hello" said a voice, suddenly.

In shock, unexpected, as if I had forgotten why I was there, I shot up. The sun blinded me and I could see nothing but the outline of a shape of a man in what looked like an ill judged shirt. Were they mirrored sunglasses? They'd have to go.

I stood up and raised my hand to my head.

"Hello," I replied to the shape. The man came into view. Sunglasses off. He stood there nervously smiling back at me. Yes – that was the guy from the photo.

The road that we were standing on was long and narrow. It was lined with classic English timber buildings. Before I could say anything else I felt myself being flung back like I had had sat on a bomb. I could see the buildings fly past. I was spinning, totally out of control. I could feel the air, the sounds of time and the rushing wall of noise. I felt like I was flying around, tumbling in mid air, crashing and being forced backwards. It was as if I was in a washing machine, I was all over the place, out of control, the sound, the sights, the smells, everything was overpowering. I tried to take control, tried to stand, to stop – but couldn't. Every one of my senses was smashing into me all at once. I was catapulted several hundred feet backwards as if shocked by the world's most powerful cattle prod. Not another bomb, please God, not now…

After what felt like an eternity, I came to. I was able to gather my senses and regain my faculties. When I restored my composure, I was astonished to see that I was still standing in the same place, by the bench. The guy was still standing in front of me. Had I been hit by a thunderbolt?

The pain, the worry, the anguish, the hurt, the tears, the hate, the emptiness, the fear – everything, it evaporated in that second. I could feel it lift. Blown away by a force so powerful I couldn't comprehend or imagine it.

Two strangers. One city. One chance. I was transfixed. We both stood staring at one another, blinking away the sun's unwanted intrusion. What was THAT? There was timelessness to this. Had we been standing there all of our lives or just a few minutes? It was hard to say.

"Shall we?" I managed – pointing down the street. We set off in silence to a bar for lunch and a beer. Gay men walk into a bar for a beer…

As we walked I glanced over at a shop window and saw both us walking side by side. It didn't feel weird, odd, nasty, awkward or anything. It felt normal. Was *this* possible? Could *it* be possible? Could I be happy? I could – couldn't I? *Couldn't I?* I was staring at the window so much I nearly walked into a lamppost. I was transfixed by the vision I was watching. There was something else happening, far more curious and intriguing than my sense of normality. As I saw our reflections walk through those streets I didn't feel like I was walking with someone else. It didn't feel like I was walking next to another person at all. This was not a stranger striding beside me. It felt as though I was just looking at one entity. As if I was whole. We were one. It felt as if the chasm in my life had been filled, there and then. A gaping wound had seamlessly, and miraculously, been healed. For once, I was felt complete. I had never, ever felt that before. I felt peace and a calm that I believed was out of reach to me (and people like me). I did not experience fear or nerves, just calm. That was not what I'd expected. Was HE the one?

Our date lasted from 12pm until 11pm. Yes, eleven hours. We talked about so many dull things it is amazing we decided to see each other again. I talked about ghosts, he talked science. I talked about loneliness and he talked about moving away. I talked about my hopes and he talked about not moving away.

Towards the end of our marathon date we agreed to meet up again in a few days – this time where he lived. He dropped me off at the end of my street on his way home. We stood at the end of my road and we said our goodbyes.

No kisses. No handshakes, just smiles. I stood and watched as he drove off. I stood there at 11pm, the evening still pleasant but with a slight chill, watching him disappear into the night. 'That'll be handy,' I thought, 'a car to bring the shopping home.' I was sick of walking from the shop with groceries.

Little did I know, as I waved him away, that I was about to embark on that next stage of my journey… Little did I know then that it wouldn't be long before I was having my argument about tomatoes in the supermarket car park… Little did I know how much my life was about to change... Little did I know how happy I could be… Little did I know, as his car turned the corner and out of sight, that on our 15th anniversary together I would be writing this final page in this story.

My old life, along with all of its eviscerating pain, was over.

A new stage in my life was beginning, and in many ways, it was more tumultuous than the last…

I have read through this book again (about a zillion times). I can see things I've toned down (most of the sex – both bad and good) and some things I've left out (for fear of hurting people).

My name isn't Jack by the way. I suspect you know that already. I am not ashamed of who I am and this story I have. I just need to think of those around me. Those who might read this and think that they have failed me. That's a luxury hindsight offers and a pain I have no intention of inflicting. Then there are those people who may be plain horrified at what I went through or what I got up to! Sorry guys, it's all true though, all of it…

I don't know what I hoped to achieve by telling my story. It wasn't because I wanted some cathartic experience. I am amazed at how bad I felt for such long periods of time. I remember that hopelessness, the feeling that life would never get better – or could do. I can still remember that raw pain. Yet I am amazed that I felt that bad for that long. I presume I was a product of the time. Life wasn't as gay friendly as it is now. I've some builders in doing work today and they are chatting about me being gay, like it was nothing important. We then go on to discuss football. That wouldn't have happened when I went through all of this. So maybe it's all sorted? I just hope that by looking back at my life it may help others to look forward.

With the power of hindsight, I wish I had been a bit bolder. I wish I had believed in myself, had more confidence. Then again, maybe I wouldn't be here now or have what I have. Perhaps I needed to endure that journey to be the person I am now. That said, maybe I would have been a lot happier, a lot sooner. Maybe I would have had a better life. Maybe the pain I felt was a down payment on the happiness and stability I have now. Maybe things would be different. Maybe, maybe, maybe… Who knows? I just wish I had spared myself all those years of anguish and many years of pain. I wish I could have been more honest.

I don't know whether this kind of book is needed anymore. I don't know whether anyone will read it. With so many advances in LGBT equality it may serve only as a historic reference, rather than something of relevance.

Having recently watched a programme on the LGBT community in Russia and everything they are suffering I know that my story seems tame compared to their struggle. They are going through what we went through – only much worse.

I hope that, if nothing else, you have enjoyed reading it. I hope you liked the bits about weird sex and stupid dates. They made me chuckle a bit remembering them. I got into the mood to write this book by listening to music from the corresponding years of my life. If nothing else, I've thoroughly enjoyed three decades of top pop music. That's been a highlight…

I said at the beginning that I hoped this book would help someone, anyone, just one person and that's true. Obviously I would love it to sell zillions and touch lots of people. If only so I could tell people I had touched many thousands of men in my life… I hope it made you think and/or made you smile. I hope it helps, gives you faith in yourself or just keeps you entertained on the beach or as you commute. Maybe you are already full of self-confidence and belief!! Maybe you'll be amazed at my low self-esteem. Whatever – I hope you enjoyed it.

Like I say, it's true and it all happened to me. If by writing this I can help someone, straight, gay, bi, confused, happy, sad, out, in – whatever – to be a little bit happier, then I will be a happy bunny rabbit. There's plenty more to say. The next chapter is just as dramatic. I just hope I have a reason to write about that too.

Believe in yourself. Ignore the haters. Be who you want to be. Be who you know you have to be. It's never as bad as you imagine. Be fabulous – just not bad fabulous!

I allowed someone to read this book. They said that my 'low self-esteem dripped from every page.' I am not sure if that is true, but if it is, should I be surprised? My formative years (and a bit beyond) were filled with the message that who I am and 'what' I am is evil, dangerous and wrong. When you are enveloped in such suffocating negativity that penetrates every pore, it is difficult to break free from that belief. Is it any wonder mental health issues affect gay men so badly?

I don't believe in people who say they 'deserve' things. I think that's a very western consumerist attitude. 'Oh you deserve a holiday – you deserve that TV…' Bollocks. I do believe, however, that we all deserve to be happy. I think we deserve to find love (or have the chance to) and no person, organisation, Government, religion or ideology should stop that. Be yourself and if that offends others – so be it. You'll be the stronger and happier for it.

Love yourself and love whomever you want. That's the most powerful thing you can do and haters can do very little to fight it… So there you have it. That was the early life of a perfectly average homosexual.

Thank you for reading x.

Made in the USA
Monee, IL
07 July 2026

56549090R00225